10.15.16

Lydia,

To all things: creative.
healing, loving.

Warmest,

Jama

ADVANCE PRAISE FOR IMAGINE THAT!

"If you want to age with passion and joy and be in the best mental health possible, it is absolutely essential that you reinvent yourself. This is the book to help you do it! James Mapes's *IMAGINE THAT! Igniting Your Brain for Creativity and Peak Performance* is provocative, challenging, stimulating, and exciting. His ideas in this book are not only effective—they are invaluable!"

—Ken Dychtwald, PhD, *Bodymind and Age Power: How the 21st Century Will Be Ruled by the New Old*

"If you want to make the most of your possibilities and life, an experienced guide can be of great help. *IMAGINE THAT! Igniting Your Brain for Creativity and Peak Performance* offers that guidance to those in need and helps you to live a healthier and more loving life. There is much value in your words."

—Bernie Siegel, MD, Author, *Prescriptions for Living* and *365 Prescriptions for the Soul*

"I admire 'guts.' It takes guts to write a book this personal. And this is good. The 'real stuff' is the 'hard stuff' to deal with. James Mapes has not written a 'page turner.' He has written a 'life turner.' Savor it. Please. *IMAGINE THAT! Igniting Your Brain for Creativity and Peak Performance* has made a difference to me at an important moment in my life's passage."

—Tom Peters, Author, *In Search of Excellence*, *The Pursuit of WOW!*, and *The Little Big Things: 163 Ways to Pursue EXCELLENCE*

"If you want to be a winner in life and achieve your dreams, you've got to have a game plan. Mapes gives it to you—period! James Mapes's *IMAGINE THAT! Igniting Your Brain for Creativity and Peak Performance* will not only help you reignite your purpose, it's going to help you be the best you can be."

—Lou Holtz, Legendary Football Coach

"James Mapes is the rare coach who can both impart knowledge *and* turn that knowledge into insight and action. *IMAGINE THAT! Igniting Your Brain for Creativity and Peak Performance* is a wise and powerful book that can help anyone use the world's oldest values to unlock life's newest opportunities."

—Daniel H. Pink, Author, *A Whole New Mind, Drive: The Surprising Truth about What Motivates Us,* and *To Sell Is Human*

"Your ability to focus your imagination, manage your thinking, love, and be loved determines your success and happiness more than any other factor. *IMAGINE THAT! Igniting Your Brain for Creativity and Peak Performance* opens your mind and heart in a beautiful, intelligent and inspiring way."

—Brian Tracy, Author, *No Excuses: The Power of Self-Discipline* and *Million Dollar Habits*

"Leadership is all about learning to focus your imagination. So if you want to be better leaders, read *IMAGINE THAT! Igniting Your Brain for Creativity and Peak Performance* and apply its great advice."

-Ken Blanchard, Co-Author, *Leadership, The One Minute Manager,* and *The Secret*

"To be successful on or off the field you've got to be clear about what you want, passionate about what you do and have the support of the people who care about you. James Mapes's *IMAGINE THAT! Igniting Your Brain for Creativity and Peak Performance* will fire up your enthusiasm and help you have the spirit of a winner—in every area of your life. This is the real deal!"

—Joe Theismann, ESPN NFL Analyst and Washington Redskins Star Quarterback

"Real wisdom will leap off these pages and draw you into a deep journey of self-knowledge and empowerment. The keys to love and happiness await you in this book!"

—Tom Morris, Best-Selling Author, *True Success, If Aristotle Ran General Motors,* and *The Art of Achievement*

"James Mapes has written a most important book on letting go, love, and forgiveness. *IMAGINE THAT! Igniting Your Brain for Creativity and Peak Performance* is inspiring and practical at the same time and is filled with nuggets of wisdom."

—Gerald G. Jampolsky, MD, Psychiatrist, and Author, *Love Is Letting Go of Fear*

"James Mapes has found his calling as an inspiring teacher whose great gift is to help us to relinquish fear—fear of love, fear of success, fear of being ourselves. With *IMAGINE THAT! Igniting Your Brain for Creativity and Peak Performance*, he takes us on the journey he has made himself—the journey to freedom."

—Erica Jong, Author, *Inventing Memory, Fear of Flying*, and *Sappho's Leap*

"*IMAGINE THAT! Igniting Your Brain for Creativity and Peak Performance* is not only a powerful and practical guide to creating loving relationships, it is an inspirational and valuable book which shows us how to let go of fear and create a loving future—now. This book will be a gift of love to everyone who reads it."

—Neale Donald Walsch, Author, *Conversations with God*

"I'm most familiar with risk. It comes in many guises and I have some experience with most of them. Risk makes us feel exposed and vulnerable, causing us to retreat into our survival mode. We are terribly vulnerable when we surrender to and confess our love. James's unique approach with *IMAGINE THAT! Igniting Your Brain for Creativity and Peak Performance* tells us how to transform our survival response into finding a loving, safe self."

—Walter Cunningham, Apollo 7 Astronaut

"After reading James Mapes' *IMAGINE THAT! Igniting Your Brain for Creativity and Peak Performance*, I have taken his advice on practicing Love-Centered Communication and it works! What a gift this book was to myself. It is a must-have for everyone!"

—Ann Rhoades, President & Founder, People Ink

"The master of the mind, James Mapes, gives you a road map mastering your mind. Here is the secret! *IMAGINE THAT! Igniting Your Brain for Creativity and Peak Performance* is written in stereo! As one track is performing lessons about your mind, the track in the background is enacting morals for a harmonious life. The mix is a powerful experience that will leave you enlightened and inspired. Buy the book and get ready for an exciting ride."

—Chip R. Bell, Best-Selling Author, *Sprinkles*
and *The 9½ Principles of Innovative Service*

"You sure can write."

—Tom Wolfe, Author, *The Right Stuff* and *A Man in Full*

"James Mapes reminds us that recognizing and pushing through fear is at the core of living a joyful life. He not only gives practical advice on creating loving relationships, he also provides an inspirational road map for creating a loving future. I highly recommend this book."

—Susan Jeffers, PhD, Author, *Feel the Fear and Do It Anyway* and *End the Struggle and Dance with Life*

"I have read *IMAGINE THAT! Igniting Your Brain for Creativity and Peak Performance* by James Mapes with a critical eye, because the title fascinated me and I didn't want to be seduced by it. I wasn't. The manuscript is full of wisdom and excellent practical advice. It challenges the reader to look at himself beyond the expected boundaries. I couldn't put the book away."

—Leon Tec, MD, Child Psychiatrist, Author, *Fear of Success* and *Targets*

"The mystery Mapes explores is the greatest one of all: love. He writes about it with candor, honesty, and remarkable insight. The result is a truly magnificent book."

—Evan Hunter (a.k.a. Ed McBain), Author, *87th Precinct* series and *The Birds*

IMAGINE THAT!

JAMES MAPES

IMAGINE

Igniting Your Brain *for* Creativity *and* Peak Performance

THAT!

GREENLEAF
BOOK GROUP PRESS

Published by Greenleaf Book Group Press
Austin, Texas
www.gbgpress.com

Distributed by Greenleaf Book Group

For ordering information or special discounts for bulk purchases, please contact Greenleaf Book Group at PO Box 91869, Austin, TX 78709, 512.891.6100.

Design and composition by Greenleaf Book Group
Cover design by Greenleaf Book Group
Cover image: ©Shutterstock/Vector pro

Cataloging-in-Publication data is available.

Print ISBN: 978-1-62634-282-8

eBook ISBN: 978-1-62634-283-5

Part of the Tree Neutral® program, which offsets the number of trees consumed in the production and printing of this book by taking proactive steps, such as planting trees in direct proportion to the number of trees used: www.treeneutral.com

TreeNeutral®

Printed in the United States of America on acid-free paper

16 17 18 19 20 21   10 9 8 7 6 5 4 3 2 1

First Edition

This book is dedicated with love and gratitude,
after the longest courtship in history,
to my wife, Susan,
who is the essence of love.

CONTENTS

PREFACE

This work has been more than fourteen years in the making. When I finally finished what I considered an acceptable draft, at almost the exact moment I typed the final sentence of the final chapter, I had an odd experience. A question suddenly formed in my mind that I had never asked myself: "Why have I invested so much time in writing this book?" The answer that came to me was straightforward—I wanted to share the knowledge and experience I've gained in my thirty-plus years as a researcher, speaker, and personal coach.

Throughout my life I have thrived on challenge. And whether it has been learning the craft of stage and film acting, creating a summer repertory theater, directing theatrical plays, becoming a clinical hypnotist, working with athletes to enhance sports ability, developing and performing a hypnosis stage show, conducting workshops on the power of the mind, speaking on creativity and leadership, or becoming proficient at hot air ballooning, scuba diving, and jumping out of a plane, I have always enjoyed the process. Writing this book has been just such a challenge, in this case on literally every level. It forced me to reexamine every nook and cranny of my life—from my relationships with friends and family to my marriage, from my hopes and dreams to my expectations and accomplishments. It made me question my assumptions about how and why we believe what we believe, how habits are formed, and how we can influence our subconscious. It even led me to rethink the way I think. It also prompted me to read every recent book, article, and research paper I could locate on the subject of the mind, as well as reach out to experts in the field who might enable me to understand it better.

It wasn't easy, and there were many times that I felt so frustrated about ever finishing the book that I put the manuscript away in a drawer and tried to forget it. But time and again I went back to it and, with renewed creativity and enthusiasm, refocused on my goal and kept on going. Now I am very happy that I did, because I learned many valuable lessons in the process. I learned how and why I made the life choices I did, both positive and negative, and why they led to the results they did. I also learned that even though my successes were joyful and fulfilling, it was the mistakes, failures, and rejections that compelled me to dig in, learn, and grow. Perhaps most important, I learned that all the techniques I employed to help manage the irascible, unpredictable, and whimsical mind, and all the exercises I presented to help others gain perceptional control of their lives and harness their imagination—all of these had their roots in something larger than me, something beyond psychology, something indefinable and mysterious, something that I can only describe as spiritual, sacred, or transcendent—perhaps simply a deep sense of being alive and interconnected with the world.

• • •

That something stood me in good stead when, in 2009, having just returned to my home in Connecticut from Scotland, where I had been acting in a most challenging role in a feature film entitled *The Wicker Tree*, I suddenly felt so uncharacteristically low emotionally that I went to see my physician. After giving me a quick examination, he sent me to see a cardiologist. Later that day, following an echocardiogram, the cardiologist informed me that I had an aortic aneurism and that there might not be much time remaining before it ruptured. My wife, Susan, and I immediately sought out an excellent surgeon, and on August 25, 2009, I had open-heart surgery to replace my aortic valve.

And it was that indefinable something that, in spite of my ever-growing fear, enabled me to make a decision that helped me keep my emotional equilibrium throughout the ordeal: I would use this life-threatening experience to learn valuable universal life lessons and share them with others. Less than six months later, I was back in the gym lifting weights. Four and a half years later these experiences lead me to develop a CD program called *Patient Pre-Op/Post-Op Healing Therapy™*, which was designed to help presurgery patients mute fear, reduce pain, instill confidence, and heal faster. And now it has led to the publication of this book, through which I can pass the lessons I've learned on to you.

• • •

Every challenge I've met, accomplishment I've attained, dream I've achieved, fear I've surmounted, and physical and psychological wound I've had that's been healed could never have happened without the tremendous love and support of a number of very special individuals. Some of them have influenced me by their works: Leo Buscaglia, Wayne Dyer, Deepak Chopra, Gerald Jampolsky, Anthony Robbins, Daniel Pink, Jonathan Haidt, and Norman Vincent Peale. Others have taught me by taking me under their wing and sharing their insights: the great hypnotist and therapist Harry Arons, psychiatrist Milton Erickson, neurologist Donald Granger Sr., humanistic psychologist Jean Houston, actor Anthony Hopkins, writer Evan Hunter, and the co-creators of Neuro-Linguistic Programming, linguist John Grinder and psychologist Richard Bandler.

There are also my others teachers—the clients with whom I have worked over the years and the many people who have participated in my workshops. They have taught me that although we may not know why we feel isolated, separate, or alone, love can heal our deepest hurts, betrayals, and disappointments. Through them I have come to understand that even in the direst of circumstances we can learn to let go of fear by learning to forgive.

Finally, there are those who have been of such great help in enabling me to translate my sometimes chaotic thoughts and ideas into words and into video clips so that others can understand and benefit from them here, in this book. These include my wife, Susan Granger, who at the beginning of this thirteen-year journey waded through six hundred pages and cut them down to three hundred; editor Beth Lieberman, who shepherded this project for several years; Louise Keim and Peter McCrea, who read many drafts and gave me excellent advice; my assistant, Linda Wechter, who has worked so hard with such grace that a mere thank you seems rather insignificant; my brother, Dave Mapes, who patiently listened to me read two edits of this book from start to finish; my dad, Earl Stephen Mapes, and Ted Stanley, who gave me financial support to complete this project; my videographer, Peter Clayton, who has hung in there for nine months editing and reediting the video clips; and, finally, my editor, Rob Kaplan, who has done miracles with my words. To each and every one of them I offer my heartfelt thanks.

—*James Mapes, 2016*

INTRODUCTION

LIVE AN EXCEPTIONAL LIFE

"All men should strive to learn before they die what
they are running from, and to, and why."[1]
—JAMES THURBER, "THE SHORE AND THE SEA"

Welcome to what is going to be an incredible adventure of the mind. You are about to learn how to fire up your imagination, manage your thinking, and create and live what I refer to as an "exceptional life." What do I mean by an exceptional life? Does it mean always being happy and having a good time? Does it guarantee having perfect relationships or making a lot of money? Does it mean devoting yourself to helping others? In fact, living an exceptional life is purely subjective and based entirely on each person's own unique set of values, beliefs, dreams, and expectations. That is, an exceptional life is exactly what each of us thinks it is.

There are, however, certain traits that are shared by all those who live exceptional lives, traits that are rock-solid universal, many of which have been around since the beginning of humankind. In the following pages I have done my best to make them understandable, accessible, and user friendly in a way that will help you embrace and fold them into the fabric of your life. Important as they are, these traits are only the broad strokes of self-creation, and it is your job to add fine lines, color, and texture. These traits include:

- *Having Purpose.* Purpose fires the imagination, inspires us, and ignites a passion for life. It gives us a reason to move forward and to embrace life and all its wonders. A purpose can be almost anything that draws, propels, or inspires an individual to action in the pursuit of a goal. It might be raising a family, volunteering, writing, learning a language, or coming up with a solution to a problem either alone or with others. Purpose engages you in life.

- *Being Curious.* Walt Disney once said, "We keep moving forward, opening new doors, and doing new things, because we're curious and curiosity keeps leading us down new paths." Curiosity is an important aspect of living an exceptional life because it enables us to see new possibilities by making our minds more active and observant. It manifests itself in daily life by reading, asking questions, and challenging assumptions, among other activities.

- *Saying "Yes" to Opportunities.* This may sound so obvious that it's not even worth mentioning. But the reality is that recognizing and even creating opportunities is one thing, but embracing them is something entirely different. Those who live exceptional lives say "yes" to their dreams. They get up off the comfortable couch of the status quo and go for it. They commit. They become serious. And once they say "yes," they create their own luck, and doors that were shut suddenly open.

- *Committing to Lifelong Learning.* Regardless of what form this commitment takes—whether it is attending classes, surfing the web, reading magazines and books, following the news, or having meaningful conversations with like-minded individuals, it is an essential trait. Gathering information and using that information to examine and challenge our own beliefs and perceptions, to gain insight, and then to apply what we have learned enables us to live in a positive, proactive way.

- *Focusing on What You Can Control and Letting Go of What You Cannot Control.* Many individuals spend a great deal of time focusing, obsessing, and worrying about things over which they have no control, which not only drains their energy but creates enormous negative stress. Those who live exceptional lives are able to identify what they can control and focus their mental energies on exercising that control. The result is a sense of progress, a feeling of being in control, and the satisfaction of accomplishment that, in turn, motivates them in their future endeavors.

- *Being a Partner in Your Own Wellness.* Those who possess this trait seek out and do what needs to be done mentally, spiritually, emotionally, and socially to help them make choices that contribute to the quality of their own lives and the lives of others. This includes surrounding themselves with nurturing life-enhancers, eliminating life-diminishers, expressing gratitude, making a difference in others' lives, and doing what they have to in order to keep their bodies healthy and able to perform efficiently.

- *Making Short-Term Sacrifices for Long-Term Payoffs.* When faced with making decisions, those who choose to look at the big picture are able to develop a vision of the future that becomes not only a motivating force but also a compass for pointing them in the right direction. We are always choosing, sacrificing one possibility for another. We cannot get something without giving up something first. But it is essential that we look ahead in making decisions if we hope to attain what we have determined we want in life.

- *Committing to Self-Knowledge.* "Know thyself," the ubiquitous phrase attributed to the Athenian philosopher Socrates, can be easily applied as a present day mantra for self-growth. Socrates believed that self-knowledge was vitally important to finding peace and happiness and discovering your potential, and it is as true today as it was in 350 BC. Self-exploration means asking yourself the right questions and providing answers that enable you to better understand who you are and who you can be. In turn, it leads to new insights and, therefore, new beliefs, actions, and behaviors that can enhance the quality of your life and the lives of others.

- *Taking Personal Responsibility and Being Accountable for Creating Your Life.* This may sound like common sense, but there are an astonishing number of people who depend on external forces to rule their world and then blame someone or something else for their circumstances. When we take responsibility for ourselves we can move to action, choose to craft a vision, map out a path, and make a plan to acquire the skills, knowledge, experiences, support, and resources we need to do what we love. It enables us to focus on our strengths, face our challenges, overcome obstacles, and attain the exceptional lives we want.

• *Acknowledging Grievances, Letting Them Go, and Forgiving.* Whether the grievances we hold against others—and we all do so—are major or minor ones, the difference this ability can make in our lives is literally incalculable. Gandhi once said: "The weak can never forgive. Forgiveness is the attribute of the strong." The beauty and elegance of forgiveness become visible in the one who forgives; when a person faces pain head-on, forgives, and lets go, he or she becomes emotionally stronger. Forgiveness is not, however, only about letting go of our anger at—or disappointment with—others; it is also about forgiving ourselves. Forgiveness is truly the highest form of love.

• *Applying Your Imagination and Influencing Your Subconscious Mind.* This trait, whether it is natural or learned—and it can be learned—nderscores all the other traits. Having it is essential to leading an exceptional life because it enables us to manage our thinking and to identify and mute the kind of fear that is essentially a figment of our imagination. In the process, we can create the choices that lead to positive results and the kind of life each of us wants to live.

• • •

If all of this sounds as though you are going to have to put in some work to achieve an exceptional life, you're right. I'm not going to sugarcoat this. Learning to manage your mind requires effort as well as a whole lot of commitment. It is also, however, both exciting and exhilarating. When you make that effort, you will challenge your assumptions about what you believe to be true. You will experience the tremendous excitement of discovery. You will uncover the mindsets, beliefs, and fears that stand in your way, and blast through them. You will have the opportunity to take new actions, create new behaviors, and become more mindful.

It is important to remember, though, that to a great extent you already have what you need to lead an exceptional life. The purpose of this book is to help you fine-tune what you already know, to help you learn how to get—and stay—out of your own way, and to apply your imagination. In order to help you achieve all this, I will essentially become a "coach of the mind" for you; that is, I will help you gain perspective, seek out and identify the areas of your life in which you can improve, clarify your strengths, and help you grow. After all, sometimes we all need another individual to ask questions we are unable to ask ourselves. The reality is that "the eye cannot behold itself."

I will do this first by providing you with a basic understanding of how the mind actually works, and then by providing you with the tools that will allow you to manage your thinking in ways you might never have thought possible—perhaps never even thought about. By taking you through a series of steps I will show you how you can manage your thinking, shatter limiting myths, become an "Artist of Possibility," meet your needs, create a stretch goal, set the stage for loving communication, communicate, transform fear into love, learn how to know when you are loved, let go, and, finally, practice forgiveness, the ultimate "letting go." In short, I will show you how, by harnessing the power of your imagination, you will be able to attain an exceptional life.

· · ·

Before we get started, though, it is important to clarify the difference between imagination and creativity. Although they are intimately connected, and achieving an exceptional life requires us to make use of both, they are not the same. The dictionary defines the word "imagine" as meaning "to form a mental image of something not present or never before wholly perceived in reality." In practice, that can mean anything from imagining phantasmagorical scenes that bear no resemblance to reality, to projecting into the future and imagining numerous alternative paths to achieving a goal. The imagination is open-ended and unlimited, and anyone can imagine anything within the realm of his or her own mental capacities. It is, in fact, our greatest gift. However, unless the imagination is harnessed, it is like a wild child out of control.

The word "create," by comparison, is defined as meaning "to make or bring into existence something new." I view creativity as the rearrangement of the old into the new or, as creativity guru Sir Ken Robinson has said, "Creativity is the process of having original ideas that have value . . . Imagination is the root of creativity. It is the ability to bring to mind things that aren't present to our senses. . . . Creativity is putting your imagination to work. It is applied imagination. . . . Creativity is possible in all areas of human life. . . . [O]ur creative powers can be cultivated and refined." [2]

In other words, creativity is a procedure. First we must imagine something, let's call it a vision of possibility. In order to move from the imagination to a creative outcome, we must take the vision (outcome we want) and effectively and clearly communicate it. For a writer, the vision may be the completed book; for a sculptor, a statue; or as a team leader, the vision must be communicated in a way that enrolls and motivates others to become part of the creation. Until what is imagined is turned into reality, it simply remains trapped in the world of fantasy. Only when what is imagined is transformed into something tangible—such as a product, service, song, artwork, book, or building—is it truly a creation. So we can think of creativity as "applied imagination," a term that is now used in counseling, therapy, healing, and peak performance coaching. It means putting the wild child of your imagination to work in a purposeful and strategic way to make something new and, hopefully, unique. Imagination allows us to generate ideas, conceive of something that has never existed before, think in different ways, and solve problems. And that is exactly what this book will enable you to do.

• • •

Just to give you a better idea of what I am talking about, I'd like you to look at the following drawing. What do you see?

"Circus in the Clown"
(based on an illustration of the artist Larry Kettelkamp)
© G. Sarcone, giannisarcone.com. All rights reserved. [3]

Do you see a clown? Is that the only figure you see? Are you sure? Would you like to see more? Then turn the book clockwise ninety degrees and look again. Now what do you see? If you look closely you will be able to see horses jumping, a dog balancing a ball, a unicyclist juggling, and elephants marching in the background. With one small change, one slight shift, you can see much more than you did before. You can see the whole circus! Would you have seen the full potential of what the picture held if I hadn't suggested turning the clown's head sideways?

What is more important, though, is what you had to do in order to expand your vision and see new possibilities. You had to be willing to play along, and choose to do what I suggested, even if what I asked you to do appeared to be simple. You had to be curious and believe in the possibility that there would be some kind of payoff. You also had to make the choice to do something different. You paid attention, chose to be engaged, observed, and changed your perspective. The point is that, as with the sketch of the clown, you can look at everything in life more than one way—you can change the meaning of anything in an instant by changing your perspective. And that's what this book will enable you to do.

Can a book really do that? Well, it depends on the book. As you probably know, there are many good books available that are excellent at presenting sound theory but leave the reader on his or her own to implement those theories. This book, however, is designed to be experiential; that is, it goes beyond the printed word. The exercises, strategies, interactions, and information presented in the following pages are equivalent to numerous coaching sessions. They are simple and straightforward, although not necessarily easy. They are also thought provoking and sometimes even fun. But above all, they involve participation and interaction, which will, in turn, yield valuable insights, pump up your motivation, and support you in your effort to achieve an exceptional life.

This participation takes several forms, the first of which are the numerous exercises you will find throughout the book. These exercises have been time-tested and proven to be extraordinarily beneficial in helping both my private clients and workshop participants to grow mentally, spiritually, emotionally, and socially. Doing them is also extremely important because they are designed to provide you with new insights, new beliefs, and new and empowering behaviors.

The second form of participation is a series of video clips that I have created to enable you to not only read my words but also to see and hear me discuss the subjects presented in the book or coach you through a particular exercise. As you read through the book you will accordingly come across Link Alert notices that will show you how to put the link in your web browser, go to a website, enter a password, and see me as if I were right there with you. Try it now with the first link, the "Imagine That! Introduction." Enter the URL **https://vimeo.com/mapes/intro** in your web browser, enter the password "**intro**" and there I will be!

The third form of participation is a journal I suggest you keep to record your thoughts, insights, discoveries, and feelings. I realize that your waking life is probably booked solid every minute of the day. I know that you are either raising a family, involved in business, and/or checking your smartphone every few minutes. I get it. Even so, it will be tremendously advantageous for you to take the time to keep such a record. The primary reason for this is, to be blunt, our memories just can't be trusted. Case studies, some of which I will cite, clearly show that many of our memories are largely distorted and, in terms of what really happened, often invented. Our minds do not, in fact, record moment-to-moment memories like a video camera. What's stored away in our memory banks are really just snapshots of life, and our beautiful, elegant, and creative imagination fills in the rest. Keeping a journal enables you not only to create a clear record of exactly what's going on, but also to track your growth as you go through the process of developing an exceptional life.

When my wife really, really wants me to do something, she turns to me with a pleading look in her eyes and says, "I beg of you." That's the kind of emotionality with which I make the following request. I beg of you to access the videos, keep a journal, and do all the exercises presented in this book. If you want to learn and grow, it is mandatory.

I've structured all the videos and exercises in a specific order to help you identify and appreciate not only your beliefs but also how your mind works. They are designed to help you understand your perceptions and how, through those perceptions, you create your experience, your reality. Yes, that's what I said—you create your reality. So hang in there! By the time you have finished reading this book you will not only understand that statement, you will embrace it!

· · ·

I passionately believe that living an exceptional life is beyond all the wealth and belongings you have accumulated and probably all of the wealth that has ever been accumulated by anyone, anywhere. If you embrace this book with that understanding, that mindset, I can absolutely promise you it will deliver what you are seeking. You will come away from this interactive journey knowing that a simple concept is more valuable and more powerful than anything you have ever imagined.

If you will allow me to become your personal coach, here is my promise. I will teach you how to manage your mind. I will use all my skills, knowledge, experience, and expertise to support and guide you to create positive change. I will provide you with the mental tools to get over life's bumps. And I guarantee that you will move to a new level of personal awareness, excitement, joy, love, and peace. How can I offer this guarantee? I wish there was a way to say this without sounding self-aggrandizing, because that is not my intention. But the fact is that for over three decades, everyone I've coached, everyone who has committed to positive change, everyone who has learned and applied the skills I taught them, has achieved personal, powerful, positive results; and you will too.

1

A BRIEF HISTORY OF THE MIND

"Brains exist because the distribution of resources necessary for
survival and the hazards that threaten survival vary in space and time."
—JOHN M. ALLMAN, *EVOLVING BRAINS*

The purpose of this book is to enable you, through a series of exercises, to create and live an exceptional life. In order for you to do that, though, it is absolutely imperative that you have a clear understanding of how your mind works. So I'm going to start by presenting the basic "mechanics" of your mind. I will also explore why the decisions we make and the beliefs we form as very young children color our lives as adults, why it is necessary to uncover these beliefs, and how, if necessary, we can restructure them.

In my first session with a new client, I always take the time to define the terms and concepts I will be using, because a clear understanding of this information ensures that the exercises I will ask him or her to do make sense. Creating and living an exceptional life requires each individual to begin assembling a personal "tool kit for the mind." The foundation of this tool kit is a working knowledge of what is commonly referred to as the "conscious" mind and the "subconscious" mind.

Being of Two Minds

As odd as this may sound, your "mind," as opposed to your "brain," is, figuratively speaking, divided into two parts. These parts—the "conscious" and the "unconscious" mind—are invisible and dramatically different, yet they must work in harmony if an individual is to live an exceptional life. On the simplest possible level, the "conscious" mind is your awareness, your self-talk, the voice in your head that is always chattering away. It is the seat of your imagination, the visionary part of your brain. One of its greatest talents is to make up and tell stories. However, while the conscious mind can be positive, rational, and visionary, it can also be extremely pessimistic, judgmental, and overanalytical. It maintains the illusion that willpower can overcome any obstacle, and when it does not attain what it wants, it is quick to justify the reason for failing. In addition, it has a tendency to worry and fret, get mired down in overanalyzing, and be easily overwhelmed by too much choice.

The "subconscious" mind (the common, everyday term often used to replace the term "unconscious") is incredibly powerful and has its own unique attributes. In a sense the subconscious is the machinery hidden behind the curtain that controls the conscious mind. Hidden away and deeply etched in the subconscious of our brain's circuitry are the successful programs that have kept us alive for hundreds of thousands of generations. At the core of the subconscious lies the need to survive. It is designed to keep us safe by playing it safe, sticking to the familiar, and, if threatened, instantly launching into a fight-or-flight mode.

One of the most extraordinary characteristics of the subconscious mind is that it cannot tell the difference between a real experience and one imagined by the conscious mind. It also contains our imprinted memories, and responds very strongly to imagined, emotionally charged images and pictures, both positive and negative. This is because the subconscious has no real sense of time. As a result, an event that was experienced many years ago can be perceived as though it occurred yesterday. As I will explain later, the combination of these characteristics makes visualization (imaging) the ideal tool to influence the subconscious.

Thus we really are of "two minds" and these two minds are often in conflict. What we think we desire (our conscious mind) can be drastically different from what we want at a much deeper and invisible level (the subconscious mind). This conflict of the two minds can be seen in action when willpower alone fails to help us permanently take off undesired weight, stop smoking, cease procrastinating, or attempt to break any unwanted, negative habit. Learning to help your two minds work in harmony to achieve peace of mind is one of the keys to achieving an exceptional life.

The Power of the Subconscious

There have been dozens of self-help books that tout the power of the subconscious, but it has only been in recent years that scientists are starting to take notice. By the applied use of Magnetic Resonance Imaging (MRI) to the brain, scientists are just beginning to realize the impact that the subconscious has on our conscious decision making.

An eye-opening article on this subject by Benedict Carey entitled "Who's Minding the Mind?" appeared in *The New York Times* in 2007. Suggesting how unique and powerful the subconscious mind really is, Carey wrote, " . . . the new studies reveal a subconscious brain that is far more active, purposeful and independent than previously known. Goals, whether to eat, mate or devour an iced latte, are like neural software programs that can only be run one at a time, and the unconscious is perfectly capable of running the program it chooses."[1] This observation is intriguing because it implies how little control we actually have over our conscious decision making. Carey further notes that "We have company, an invisible partner who has strong reactions about the world that don't always agree with our own, but whose instincts, these studies clearly show, are at least as likely to be helpful, and attentive to others, as they are to be disruptive. . . . [T]he results suggest a "bottom-up" decision-making process . . . "

As part of my research I also contacted Dr. Richard Granger, professor of psychological and brain sciences at Dartmouth College, and co-author with Gary Lynch of *Big Brain: The Origins and Future of Human Intelligence*.[2] When I asked him how much control the subconscious has over our conscious decision-making process, he said, "The most recent brain research strongly indicates that the unconscious mind controls ninety percent of our choices and the conscious mind controls ten percent." These scientific insights suggest that it is to our great advantage to learn how to assist the two parts of our mind to work together in a collaborative manner and develop the tools necessary to empower our conscious mind to influence the subconscious mind. Although forging a partnership between our "minds" is challenging, we can do a great deal toward that ideal once we discover the secret of creating harmony between our two "minds."

The Conscious Rider and the Subconscious Elephant

Link Alert: Enter the URL **https://vimeo.com/mapes/1** in your web browser and then the password "**mindhistory**" to see and hear me speak about the Elephant and the Rider. This is also explained below.

Over many years of speaking on the power of the mind I searched for the ideal metaphor to describe the conscious and subconscious. For a short period I used Plato's imagery in *Phaedrus*, in which Socrates refers to our conscious, rational self as a charioteer who is holding on to the reins of two horses, one disciplined and the other unruly, which together represent our subconscious. The weakness in Plato's metaphor is that he assumed the conscious mind, the charioteer, had far more control over the subconscious than it actually does. Nevertheless, it was quite an insight, particularly considering that brain science did not even exist yet!

Then, for some years I described the subconscious mind as "computer-like" and the conscious mind as the "programmer." That all changed, though, when I received a call from a close colleague. It was with great enthusiasm that he suggested I read the new book by Chip and Dan Heath entitled *Switch*. "You must read this," he exclaimed. "This book supports everything you believe and will expand your ideas on how you teach." He was right.

In *Switch*, the Heath brothers present a clear and concise picture of how to manage change. But it was their vivid and easily understood metaphor for the conscious and subconscious minds (the Rider and the Elephant) that prompted me to reexamine my approach to describing the workings of the human mind. What was even more impressive was that they gratefully acknowledged borrowing this delightful metaphor from University of Virginia psychologist Jonathan Haidt's impressive book, *The Happiness Hypothesis: Finding Modern Truth in Ancient Wisdom.* "Haidt explains," the Heaths wrote, "that our emotional side is an Elephant and our rational side is its Rider. Perched atop the Elephant, the Rider holds the reins and seems to be the leader. But the Rider's control is precarious because the Rider is so small compared to the Elephant. Anytime the six-ton Elephant and the Rider disagree about which direction to go, the Rider is going to lose. He's completely overmatched."[3]

This description resonated deeply within me, at least partly because, while visiting India several years ago, I had the opportunity to ride an elephant, and it was one extremely edgy experience. Although I had received some instruction in signaling to the elephant the direction in which I wanted it to move, despite my best efforts, that elephant did just what it wanted to do, and I had only as much control as it allowed me to have. I felt very small and insignificant. As a result, when I subsequently read Haidt's book, I found myself viewing the principles I teach through a different lens, and began to refer to the subconscious and the conscious as the "Elephant" and the "Rider."

• • •

In order to help you develop your own insight into how our two minds work, I have listed below what I consider to be the ten most important characteristics of the conscious Rider and of the subconscious Elephant. Remember that the Rider is the rational side, which needs focus, and the Elephant is the emotional side, which needs motivation and direction. Remember, also, that both have strengths and weaknesses. The greater understanding you have of their characteristics, the more you will be able to help them stay out of each other's way and work in harmony.

THE CONSCIOUS RIDER . . .

- is the creative visionary who can imagine alternative paths of choice, and is proficient at crafting mental movies of possible futures.
- is a master storyteller, even if many of the stories are complete fabrications.
- can proactively direct the imagination to influence the Elephant.
- is our rational, reflective side, what is often referred to as our "inner voice," "mind chatter," "inner dialogue," or "self-talk."
- thinks it is in charge but is actually always at the whim of the Elephant, and because it has limited reserves of energy, can easily become exhausted from trying to override the Elephant's power.
- can see both problems and opportunities, but since it has a natural tendency to see mostly the negative, it often focuses on solving problems rather than searching out opportunities.
- is overanalytical, easily paralyzed in the face of uncertainty, and often overwhelmed when presented with too many choices.
- is a master of rationalization and justification, and can almost instantaneously make up logical reasons when overridden by the Elephant's ingrained habits.
- is able to delay immediate gratification because it is willing to make short-term sacrifices for long-term payoffs.
- can only see its reflection or know itself with the help of other Riders or by using tools for introspection.

THE SUBCONSCIOUS ELEPHANT . . .

- is the heavy lifter, taking care of the autonomic nervous system (heart rate, respiration rate, digestion, etc.), and freeing up the Rider to do what it does best—think, contemplate, create stories, and visualize.

- is the core of our emotional self, and therefore reacts very strongly to emotions and feelings, especially those of fear and love.

- does not think, contemplate, or reflect in the traditional sense but, rather, reacts with absolutes, constantly and automatically deciding between right or wrong, good or bad, left or right, flight or fight, etc.

- cannot tell the difference between a real experience and one imagined by the Rider.

- is extremely suggestible.

- is basically in charge of our choices and actions, but can be influenced by the Rider when presented with emotionally charged, vivid, crystal-clear, and easily understood directions in the form of pictures and images.

- is fearful, skittish, and programmed with the basic default setting for survival.

- does not like to take risks, think out of the box, or follow "the road less traveled," so when the future is uncertain it always follows a familiar path.

- is fundamentally lazy, always wants the quick payoff of instant gratification, and is accordingly unwilling to make long-term sacrifices for short-term gains.

- responds to suggestions given by the Rider that are clear, precise, realistic, and logical, and is more comfortable moving on a different path when taking small steps.

It might help you to think of the Rider as a new chief operating officer (COO) of a large and complex company, and the Elephant as the entrenched, unspoken, and underlying rules that guide the organization.

The new COO steps into a culture whose rules have been part of the company for so long that they have become the norm, the status quo, a set of invisible paradigms. They just are. What can the COO do?

The COO can certainly make every attempt to learn about those rules, but most likely will only get a glimpse. He or she would most likely learn a lot more by studying what has made the company successful, as well as what belief systems within the company have created barriers to success. Ultimately, the job of the COO is to both define a vision and develop short- and long-term goals that will move the company forward to turn that vision into a reality. So while the Rider, the COO, can only influence rather than control the Elephant, the company, it can develop a vision for the company and teach the skills that are necessary to support its success.

Our Three Brains

We all carry around our own unique programming or conditioning. Most of it comes free of charge, locked away in our genes, and the rest is a reflection of what we have learned. But we didn't start out that way. As is the case with every part of our bodies, our brains developed into what they are today over a period of thousands of years by a process of natural selection. That is, of the countless random changes that occurred over time, only those that proved to further our survival were retained.

In the early 1950s, neurologist Dr. Paul MacLean created one of the most well-known and efficient models for understanding the evolution of the human brain. In his theory, three distinct brains developed—one in front of the other—to form what we now label as the human brain, all of them cohabitating in the human skull. Interestingly enough, it turns out that the brain has a structure very much like my family's cabin in the Northwoods of Wisconsin. The cabin started off as a house trailer. Many years later a second section was added, which included a living room. Years after that another bedroom was built onto the existing structure. Each addition incorporated and enhanced the one that came before it to form a well-functioning and roomy cabin. You can, then, view the development of the human brain like the progression of my family's cabin, except of course on a much, much longer time frame.

BRAIN ONE: THE REPTILIAN BRAIN

According to MacLean's theory, we can thank our reptilian brain (Brain One), the most ancient and primitive part of the brain—developed around 250 million years ago—for all our basic survival mechanisms. This so-called Brain One not only controls the required body functions for sustaining life, such as body temperature and breathing, but all our instinctive and automatic responses. It is primitive as well as compulsive.

As part of our packet of survival skills, our reptilian brain gave us the ability to quickly spot anything that was a threat to us. It is like a Secret Service agent constantly watching our backs, scanning for potential threats. This is good news and bad news. The good news is that due to this encoded, protective skill, our species still exists. The bad news is that this survival skill now gives us the penchant to see the bad before we see the good. As Jonathan Haidt notes in *The Happiness Hypothesis*, "Psychologists find that the human mind reacts to bad things more quickly, strongly, and persistently than to equivalent good things. We can't just will ourselves to see everything as good because our minds are wired to find and react to threats, violations, and setbacks."[4]

BRAIN TWO: THE MAMMALIAN BRAIN

Subsequent to the development of the reptilian brain came our mammalian or *limbic* brain (Brain Two). It's like the first addition to my family's cabin, and was added on around 150 million years ago. I say "around" because the exact timeline of our brain development is fairly vague. Brain Two is wrapped about Brain One and forms what is referred to as the "limbic system," which accounts for our animal instincts and emotions.

It was in Brain Two that enormous changes took place. The autonomic nervous system developed to unconsciously control body functions such as digestion, body temperature, fluid balance, and blood pressure.

The hypothalamus took over as the controller of our basic drives and emotions, and the hippocampus evolved, specializing in making explicit, conscious memories. Here, new experiences, both positive and negative, are filed away in what I view as our "storehouse of experience and memory."

It is also in Brain Two that the amygdala took on the role of recognizing danger, of emotional learning, and of responding according to past fear-based experience. It seems that feelings such as attachment, anger, and fear have emerged with associated behavioral response patterns of care, fight, or flight. Brain Two, the limbic brain, is the seat of our rapid-fire value judgments. These often occur on an unconscious level and exert a strong influence on our behavior. Together, Brain One and Brain Two form the subconscious, or what I refer to as the Elephant.

BRAIN THREE: THE NEW BRAIN

Lastly, the neocortex—Brain Three—began its extraordinary expansion in primates two or three million years ago, with language following somewhere between two million and forty thousand years ago. Like the third addition to the Mapes family cabin, this is the most recent step in the brain's evolution, or simply what I call the Rider. It is this massive chunk of gray matter, which amounts to about 85 percent of our brain mass, and enables us to behave like human beings. Basically, this large structure consists mostly of two hemispheres, mirror images of each other, which are connected by a huge bundle of nerve fibers called the corpus callosum. The corpus callosum allows the two hemispheres to communicate with each other. Think Ethernet cable.

It is due to the addition of Brain Three that we're able to communicate, reason, and see alternative paths for the future. Brain Three gave us the ability for abstract thinking, planning, and perception. The Rider can now think about the consequences of the Elephant's actions and, hopefully, put the brakes on inappropriate behavior. Like the three sections that make up the entire living space in our family cabin, Brain One and Brain Two (the reptilian and limbic brains, or the Elephant) cannot be separated from the neocortex (Brain Three, or the Rider). As you can see from this description of the brain, the Elephant makes up our *automatic* responses and the Rider our *controlled* responses. The Elephant, our more primitive brain, is ultimately the real power and can handle many tasks at once. The Rider, on the other hand, can only consciously think of one thing at a time.

Developing a Personal Survival Strategy

Our three brains, then, represented by the Rider (Brain Three) and the Elephant (Brains One and Two), enable us to be reasonable and emotional, logical and powerful, analytical and instinctive, progressive and primitive, and controlled and automatic. While there is potential for internal conflict between the Rider and the Elephant, it is also possible for them to work together in harmony. Because the Elephant's basic programming is fear-based, the Rider must learn to help the Elephant let go of its primitive fears, stay calm, and work from a center of safety and love. But in order to begin this process, it is necessary to understand how we develop a personal survival strategy.

A personal survival strategy is essentially a combination of your genetic, preprogrammed need for survival and what I refer to as your learned survival strategy. The basic need for survival is what has kept and keeps our species alive and thriving despite war, famine, and disease. It has guided us to avoid the dangers of starving or being eaten by predators; it has programmed us to procreate and keep our species in existence. It is also the filter through which we, as children, discover, test, refine, and burn into unconscious memory our learned survival strategy. However, while survival comes built in to our subconscious mind, our learned survival strategy is a reflection of our experience and conditioning, and it has both a light and a dark side.

The light side of this learned strategy is exhibited when we express empathy, compassion, love, and forgiveness. If we had loving and compassionate models as young children (parents, relatives, and teachers), we naturally express love and compassion as adults. If our early examples taught us to be honest, play fairly, and respect the dignity of others as children, we are much likelier to have solid relationships and a strong social network as we move through life.

The dark side, on the other hand, can, without awareness and self-examination, influence us with limiting beliefs, anger, revenge, guilt, fear, and anxiety, all of which can stifle both our emotional and spiritual growth. It can also make it impossible for us to see the very things that many of us spend our lives searching for—abundance, acceptance, freedom, peace, fulfillment, and love. If we are not aware, alert, and diligent, our learned survival strategy may trick us into looking at life through the lens of fear and manipulate us to shoot ourselves in our own cosmic foot.

It's important to note here that I refer to this dark side as the "ego," or what many call "the ego mind." Since you may already be familiar with Freud's structural model for the human psyche, you may think of the ego as the more organized and realistic part of the mind. I am, however, going to ask you to look at it from a different perspective. In fact, in the universe of spiritual and mental growth, the ego mind is seldom your friend. Although this point of view may be out of sync with the classical Freudian definition of ego, I think it is appropriate.

LIFE FACT: SURVIVAL IS AT THE CORE OF YOUR BASIC BELIEF SYSTEM, AND THE SURVIVAL STRATEGIES YOU DEVELOP ARE THE RESULT OF YOUR CHILDHOOD CONDITIONING.

Ultimately, our ability to get the Rider and the Elephant to work together depends at least to some extent on the learned survival strategies we develop as we grow up. Other than the genetic circuitry we are born with, our unconscious is a blank slate when we start off our journey into the world. To an infant there is no "I"—no separation from others. We just want what we want—to be fed, safe, loved, and, most important, to survive. These are the things that are hard-wired into our brains. However, at a very early point in development our minds switch over to a more software-like operating system and our basic learned programming begins.

If you watch children carefully you can't help but notice their need to gain attention, feel powerful, and find their place in the world. Children do what needs to be done. They seek to explore, and they calculate, absorb, and reflect back the actions and responses from the adult world, especially those of their caregivers. Eventually they develop strategies that work or, in some cases, do not work. These strategies are directly linked to what is known as Attachment Theory, the belief that children's behavior is driven by two basic goals—safety and exploration, and that the relationships they develop with their primary caregivers are the key determinants of their social and emotional development.

Devised in the mid-twentieth century by British psychiatrist John Bowlby, the theory is based on the idea of imprinting, that is, learning that occurs at a particular age or stage of life. Positive imprinting is a result of ideal, loving relationships, those that help the child develop the skills and emotional intelligence needed for life as an adult. Negative imprinting, on the other hand, is a result of less-than-ideal relationships, those that spark fear and insecurity. As Sharon Begley explains in *Train Your Mind, Change Your Brain*, " . . . some children come to feel that the person who takes care of them is a reliable source of safety and comfort; other children find that this person is either an unpredictable harbor who is sometimes there to comfort them and sometimes missing in action, or is outright rejecting."[5]

In the 1960s and 1970s, developmental psychologist Mary Ainsworth, building on the basic idea, introduced the concept of the "secure base," and developed a theory of attachment styles in infants—secure, avoidant, and resistant. These three styles, which reflect consistent parental behavior toward the child, were based on her observations both in scripted settings and in the children's homes. The children who showed secure attachment were most likely to have mothers who were loving, warm, and available when the child needed comfort. These children reflected their security by being open, curious, and playful. The children who developed an avoidant attachment style were those whose mothers were unresponsive or detached. These children had learned not to count on their mothers.

And the children with resistant attachment styles had mothers whose behavior was unpredictable and inconsistent. These children were often guarded and learned not to expect much affection and comfort.

Like most beliefs, then, our attachment styles are not solidly imprinted by one single event but rather by a series of events over time. These events form a "perceptual lens" through which the child views the world or, as Jonathan Haidt writes, "No one event is particularly important, but over time the child builds up what Bowlby called an 'internal working model' of himself, his mother, and their relationship."[6] While our future relationships may affect our attachment style, more often than not our early programmed attachment style is carried with us into adult relationships. And our attachment style most certainly influences the development of our personal survival strategy.

We all develop an attachment style. As children, we become mirrors, listening and reflecting back what we observe, hear, and experience. It is by trial and error that we discover the survival strategy that we believe works best for us as both children and adults. Successful or not, we all do the very best we can at the time to be noticed, feel special, and be taken care of. Depending on the attachment style, some children's survival strategies are scripted around being good and doing the right thing, while others imprint the learned behavior of bullying, aggression, or lying. Some children accomplish their ends by isolating themselves and being quiet, withdrawn, or contemplative. Still others achieve their needs by developing an outgoing social style. There are also some who build their strategy on being a victim.

As we experiment with our strategy for survival, we unconsciously pay very close attention. Depending on the feedback, we adjust and make course corrections. Out of these choices we develop our beliefs, our strategies, and our "life scripts" of what works best to get what we want, even if what we choose may not always be in our best interests. These unique scripts become the "software" of our mind and are tucked away in our subconscious, our Elephant, to become who we are as adults. As Sharon Begley writes, "Those early experiences as well as experiences throughout life that reinforce them leave a deep imprint on the personality, attitudes and behavior of a child as well as the adult he becomes."

What kind of an adult does the child become? Although nothing is set in stone, and our attachment style is in play throughout our lives, the attachment style developed as a very young child does point the way to specific adult attitudes and behaviors. It will affect how we respond to stress, the kinds of relationships we form, our self-esteem, and how we communicate and interact with others. It is therefore important that we have at least a rudimentary understanding of attachment styles. In the years since Dr. Ainsworth first devised her theory regarding them, much additional research has been conducted; and they are now generally accepted as falling into four categories: secure, anxious-preoccupied, fearful-avoidant, and dismissive-avoidant.

As previously mentioned, very young children who develop a secure attachment style become more outgoing and creative. They become adults who feel deserving of love and therefore create relationships built on trust, forgiveness, love, and gratitude. These individuals have a positive attitude and view problems not as obstacles but as things to be managed.

The children who have parents, relatives, or guardians who are unreliable or not readily available for emotional support develop into adults who often perceive normal obstacles as being insurmountable and lack the confidence to take risks. Having an anxious-preoccupied personality, they will go to embarrassing lengths to be noticed, gain attention, and seek approval. They are clingy, insecure, overly dependent on their partners, and easily triggered to jealousy. These people live in constant fear of being abandoned and rejected.

Individuals who fall into the category of fear-avoidant are caught between the fear of being too close to others and of being too distant. They are highly emotional, wanting to move toward others to have their needs met but fearing that others will hurt them. And even when they do get close, they bolt. Therefore they live in a state of constant anxiety.

Finally, children who develop a dismissive-avoidant attachment style become adults who will not let themselves get close to people, will avoid intimacy, and appear to be compulsively self-reliant. They avoid confronting their weaknesses for fear of becoming dependent on someone else and refuse to examine their emotions. They reject anyone's bid for love.

My purpose in identifying these attachment styles is both to make you aware of how complex and unique we all are and to give you a glimmer of hope. That is, although we may exhibit these styles, they are not hard-wired into our brain—they are learned programming based in fear. And all learned programming can be rewired by learning to shift fear to love.

Learning to Develop a Loving Self

Finally, there is one extremely important fact about the Elephant that I would like you to take away from this brief history of the mind: While the hard-wired, primitive survival self is part of you, the software of your belief systems is actually programmable. This is a key to all mental growth. Your brain, regardless of age, is flexible, malleable, and change-able. The Elephant can change and grow, at any and all ages. It just needs the Rider's help.

LIFE THOUGHT: WHEN WE ARE IN FEAR, OUR PERCEPTIONS NARROW AND LOVE DISAPPEARS.

The information stored in our genes and our early-learned behavior has an enormous impact over the choices we make on our meandering path to adulthood. But adulthood also opens up a whole new set of pos-sibilities. As adults, we can learn to expand our awareness and grow both emotionally and spiritually. We have the potential to transform a fear-driven survival self into a loving self.

Where the childlike survival self demands controlling behavior and competition to "have enough," the loving self lives in the state of awareness, abundance, creativity, love, possibility, contribution, and spirituality. Where the survival self can win only at the expense of someone else losing, the loving self makes its choices to assure a win-win outcome for everyone. Where the survival self is in a constant state of fear and stress, the loving self lives in peace, grace, enthusiasm, curiosity, harmony, and joy.

Unfortunately, some of those who develop an anxious or avoidant attachment style never achieve their true potential because, on some level, they get stuck in a childlike state. Simply put, they carry the useless baggage of limited, early-learned beliefs and behaviors. As adults, they continue to operate on the basis of old, outdated, and often destructive sets of rules, and carry erroneous, fear-based beliefs into the home and the workplace. They deflect connection, and refuse to forgive. These childlike adults will win at all costs and are easily triggered to anger when their beliefs are challenged.

But it doesn't have to be so. Reading this book, and doing the exercises it contains, will enable you to recognize and break any cycle of fear that lies deep within the Elephant. Like a fun-house mirror, fear distorts perception. But despite the destructive nature of fear, you have the ability within yourself to reject its pull. You have the power to transform fear into love. To be honest, it's a lot of work. It means signing on to a lifetime evolutionary process of raising your awareness, opening up perceptions, identifying and breaking fear's hold, learning to let go, developing new habits, forgiving, and making the choices that enrich the quality of your life and the lives of others. But it's worth it.

Your challenge is to learn what needs to be learned and do what needs to be done so that you can manage your mind and tame the ego. It's to recognize and let go of the fear-based belief systems you've picked up in your early years without losing the curiosity, spontaneity, and delight of your inner child. It's to learn how to tap into your safe-self, your spiritual self, your loving self. And all this is possible once you learn how to create harmony between the Elephant and the Rider. Imagine that!

THINKPOINTS

- We are actually of two minds—the conscious and the subconscious mind.
- Each of these two minds has its own distinct characteristics, and they do not always work in harmony.
- The conscious mind is like a Rider on the back of the massive, subconscious Elephant.
- The human brain is essentially three brains in one, each controlling different aspects of our thinking and behavior.
- The working of these three brains results in each of us developing a personal survival strategy.
- The relationships we develop in early childhood, according to the Attachment Theory, determine the type of relationships we form in adulthood.
- The brain, regardless of age, is programmable, malleable, and changeable.

MANAGE YOUR THINKING

"Sow a thought, reap an act;
Sow an act, reap a habit;
Sow a habit, reap a character;
Sow a character, reap a destiny."

—ANONYMOUS

Link Alert: Enter the URL **https://vimeo.com/mapes/2-1** in your web browser and then the password "**thinking**" to see and hear me speak about how to manage your thinking. This is also discussed below.

When my doctor told me, "You need heart surgery *immediately*," I thought it was the end. Of course, he was trying to communicate that a successful operation would save my life, but all I could envision was my heart stopping and the horrifying darkness of death. I was scared out of my wits.

I fled to Wisconsin's Northwoods, a place I had been going to all my life, a place that represented calmness and peace for me. There I could be free to deal with the enormity of the task ahead. At our cabin on the lake I would sit for hours in a boat or on the dock. I let myself breathe deeply, see the darkness, feel my fear. Then, I envisioned the operation and began to reframe my view.

In the new view, my heart had a brand-spanking-new valve. It was working. I was alive. All I had to do next was regain my strength, and allow the support of my loved ones to help me through it all. I ran through this scenario in my mind's eye dozens and dozens of times between my time at the lake and my surgery a week later, and it made all the difference. By looking at my situation from a different perspective, by managing my thinking, I was able to replace fear with hope, doubt with confidence, and worry with positive expectation. I created a mindset for healing and wellness.

Changing Your Perspective Can Help You Reframe Your Thinking

We gather meaning from the way we see things. If any part of our frame changes, then the meaning also changes. It can happen by accident or by a deliberate process. Imagine, for example, that you hear the blasting sound of sirens—fire engines, ambulances, and police cars—in the distance. Your heart races as you imagine some horrible accident. Later, you are watching the local news and see that there was a parade down Main Street. You now realize that the fire engines, ambulances, and police cars were part of that parade and that the sound was actually part of a celebration. This is obviously an instance in which your frame changes inadvertently, but it's important to remember that we also have the ability to shift our point of view intentionally and, as a result, see things in a different light.

• • •

Take a large breath and recall a specific time you were on a vacation, and imagine you are back in that moment. Is it rainy or sunny, windy or calm, hot or cold? What color is the sky? Are you alone or with someone else? You can take any situation from your past and restructure a memory like this. And it will seem real to you, even though it's actually taking place in your imagination. This is an example of visualization. We visualize all the time and we usually don't realize it. And those pictures and images, those mental movies in our imaginations, have a huge impact on how we feel.

Reframing how we think affects how we picture or hold images in our mind, which in turn determines what we feel. Images and pictures that we visualize as big, bright, close, and vivid have greater emotional impact than images that are small, dull, and far away. I learned this some years ago when my company created a documentary about past life regression through hypnosis called *Through the Portal*, which we sold to a major television network. In order to produce the film, we had to make a number of creative and logistical choices, all based on the vision of what we wanted the end result to be. The simple arena-style set was designed to fill a large, nondescript studio space. We used four cameras to capture the actions of ten people going into past life regressions. In order to achieve the effect we wanted and capture the high emotional intensity of the volunteer, the director instructed the camera operators to go extremely close to the faces of the people being regressed. We also had the set lit in such a way that it was very bright and crisp, because emotionality that is shadowy would be creepy. And it worked wonderfully! The images evoked exactly the kind of emotion we wanted.

Think of reframing as making a movie—re-creating, changing, or tinkering with the elements that make a mental picture or image. That is where the power of the imagination comes in. And it can be used in many different ways—everything from changing a bad habit or negative self-image to negotiating more effectively, and from giving better presentations to eliminating a fear of flying, as well as countless other ways.

YOUR TURN

Now, I would like you to do an exercise in reframing at its most basic level.

1 Vividly recall a person from the past who has hurt your feelings or made you angry. Imagine that person's face two feet in front of you. Notice the discomfort or unhappiness that person generates in you.

2 Imagine moving the image of the person's face fifteen feet away from you.

3 Make the image of the face smaller by shrinking it in your imagination to the size of a doll's head.

4 Make the image of the face black and white.

5 Make the image transparent so you can see through it.

6 Make the image fade away and disappear.

Notice how much better you feel? You just changed the way you feel by changing how you frame the memory, and by doing so you changed the impact that person or situation will have on you in the future. You have just used your imagination to make something better rather than letting your imagination get the better of you. Do this reframing exercise one or two more times using other people or situations that keep replaying in your memory and have caused you emotional upset. You really can influence the Elephant!

Link Alert: Enter the URL **https://vimeo.com/mapes/2-2** in your web browser and then the password "**reframing**" to see and hear an example of what this reframing exercise might look like. Or you can simply carry out the instructions that follow.

YOUR TURN AGAIN

Now I would like you to do another kind of exercise, this time one that, rather than changing a negative memory, creates a positive emotion.

1 Imagine—make up—a mental movie of something happening that would make you feel happy, fulfilled, excited, or joyous "as if" it were happening now. Imagine you are viewing this movie on a big screen.

2 Now imagine that you are walking or floating directly into the "you" in the movie. See it through your eyes, smell it, hear it, feel it. It is happening to you now, in the moment. You are the picture. Go for the details.

3 As though you were turning up the volume on your iPod, radio, television, or computer, imagine that you are making the movie bigger, brighter, louder, and more vivid—full of sound and detail.

How does this exercise make you feel? Don't you experience an elevation of your spirit through having created this imagined mental movie, charged with positive emotions?

 LIFE FACT: THE WAY YOU THINK AFFECTS YOU ON A PHYSICAL LEVEL.

Under the auspices of the Cleveland Clinic Foundation, a group of research scientists participated in a study on the power of visualization. The results were published in an article in *Neuropsychologia* by Vinoth K. Ranganathan, Vlodek Siemionow, Jing Z. Liu, Vinod Sahgal, and Guang H. Yue titled "From Mental Power to Muscle Power—Gaining Strength by Using the Mind."[1]

Thirty healthy volunteers participated in the study, the purpose of which was to determine if mental training alone could induce strength gains in the little finger abductor as well as the elbow flexor (bicep) muscles—all used during general daily activity. In addition, researchers wanted to quantify the cortical signal that determines the voluntary contractions of the two muscle groups.

The volunteers were divided into four groups. The first group was trained to perform "mental contractions" of the little finger, and the second to perform "mental contractions" of the biceps. Both of these groups were asked to visualize as strongly as possible moving the muscle being tested, to make the imaginary movement as real as possible. The third group was not trained but simply served as a control group, and the final group performed "physical" training only of the little finger muscle.

After training for twelve weeks, fifteen minutes per day, five days a week, Group One (mental contractions) had increased their finger abduction strength by 35 percent; Group Two (mental contractions) increased their bicep strength by 13.5 percent; Group Three (no activity) had no change; and the physical training group, Group Four, increased their little finger abduction strength by 53 percent. The conclusion reached was that the mental training—visualization—enhanced the cortical output signal, which drove the muscles to a higher activation level and increased strength.

If this sounds unbelievable, consider that the measurement of the brain activity during the visualization sessions suggests that the gains in strength were due to improvements in the brain's ability to signal muscle activity. The benefits of visualization on our physical self are clear and the possibilities fascinating. While there is no substitute for actual strength training exercise, visualization is a great adjunct. It may seem that strengthening a finger and bicep muscle by simple mind power is no big deal, but it is. The Rider's imagination impacts the Elephant's strength.

You Can Use Visualization to Manage Your Thinking

Visualization is the skill of creating pictures, images, and emotionally based mental movies with your imagination. Visualization is a skill that will become one of your favorite mental tools. It will help you to innovate, to motivate yourself, to control stress, as well as to let go and forgive. There is no better way to help you understand how applying your imagination (visualizing) impacts your body than to do the "pendulum" exercise.

Link Alert: Enter the URL **https://vimeo.com/mapes/2pendulum** in your web browser and then the password **"pendulum"** to see and hear me speak about the power of the pendulum. Or you can simply carry out the instructions that follow.

YOUR TURN

1   The first thing you have to do is make a pendulum. Start by cutting a piece of string approximately 10 inches long. You can use twine, thread, or kite string. Attach a weight—a ring, a washer, a key, or any other small object—to one end.

2   Using the circle in the figure below, or duplicating it by hand on a piece of paper, hold the top of the string between your thumb and index finger, and let the weight hang down approximately one inch above the center of the circle. Keep your elbow elevated off the surface of the table.

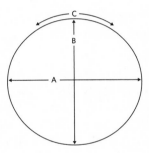

3   Holding the pendulum, focus your attention on the horizontal line. Feel the weighted string, and imagine—visualize—it swinging back and forth, left and right, like the pendulum of a grandfather clock. Focus. If other thoughts creep in, simply let them go and refocus your attention. It may take as much as a minute, but the pendulum will actually start moving left and right as if you were shaking your head "no." And if you imagine and visualize the movement becoming stronger, the weight will move accordingly. Why does this happen? At its most simplistic, whenever you have a thought, neurons fire, communicating with one another. Electrical impulses and chemical signals carrying messages are sent at lightning speed across different parts of the brain and between the brain and the rest of the nervous system. The result, in this case, is movement in the direction you're thinking. Action follows thought.

4 Imagine or visualize the pendulum stopping. It will. Now change the direction of your thinking. Focus, concentrate, and imagine the weight moving along the vertical line, away from and toward you, as if you were nodding your head "yes." Visualize the swinging movement becoming bigger and feel it becoming stronger. Once it's moving, switch your thinking again, and visualize the pendulum moving in a clockwise circle. Imagine the circle becoming bigger and bigger. Once the circular movement begins, reverse the direction. Imagine it making a counter-clockwise circle. (The swinging motion of the pendulum will stop before the direction reverses.)

How was that experience? Try it with your children and your friends. I guarantee they will also be amazed.

Your Inner Dialogue Affects How You Think

The fear-based voice of the ego can have an enormous effect on your thinking. It can, for example, shield you from facing the truth and learning from failure by justifying your choices. "It really wasn't that important," it might say. "I didn't want it anyway." "It would never have worked out." It is also quick to blame anything or anyone for your present circumstance. If you listen carefully, you will hear it reflected in your inner dialogue. "It's her fault." "It's his fault." "It's my fault." "It's my boss's fault." You can also recognize that voice when your Rider's self-talk rationalizes or makes excuses for the way you perceive life to be: "If only I could lose the weight, people would accept me." "If she [or he] would change, I'd be happy." "If only I had enough of everything, I would be satisfied."

The bottom line is that your self-talk is often interesting, but it is not always your best friend. In order to live an exceptional life you have to learn to recognize and manage the self-talk that is fear-based, unrealistic, restrictive, or overly judgmental. The first step in doing that is being aware. Observe your self-talk. Then lower the volume, neutralize negative thinking, and *reframe*. In order for you to appreciate the effectiveness of this tool, I would like you to do the following exercise.

YOUR TURN

1 Briefly summon up and vividly recall something that makes you feel uncomfortable. You can accomplish this by thinking about some task that you now feel under pressure to complete but have avoided, or about a situation you've just become aware of in which you feel you have little control. Perhaps it's the high price of gasoline, global warming, the deficit, or a personal problem, financial issue, or other troubling thought that's creating negative stress.

2 Once you have this stress-inducing situation clearly and vividly in your mind's eye, listen to your self-talk. You will hear the volume of your inner dialogue and I suspect it will be loud.

3 Now pretend that you can regulate the volume of your self-talk as you would regulate the volume of your radio, television, or iPod. First, become aware of your unsettling thoughts. Then imagine you are holding a remote control in your hand, and lower the volume. As the volume decreases in your imagination, you will also notice something quite interesting—the emotional impact of negative thoughts and emotions will also diminish to a whisper.

4 Finally, imagine turning the volume off.

Congratulations. You have just neutralized negative mind-chatter. Now, you can learn to *live in the result*—that is, substitute positive affirmations for negative beliefs. This will give you the ability to take positive action where you never could

• • •

The effectiveness of positive self-talk has been studied extensively, especially in the field of athletic performance. At the 2014 Winter Olympics in Sochi, the Olympian athletes on the United States team used visualization, also called imagery, to give themselves the best possible chances of winning. Aerialist Emily Cook worked with a psychologist to create "imagery scripts." As reported in *The New York Times*, she described the process as follows:

> "I would say into the recorder: 'I'm standing on the top of the hill. I can feel the wind on the back of my neck. I can hear the crowd,'" Cook said. "Kind of going through all those different senses and then actually going through what I wanted to do for the perfect jump. I turn down the in-run. I stand up. I engage my core. I look at the top of the jump.
>
> "I was going through every little step of how I wanted that jump to turn out."

Cook then played the recording back as she relaxed, eyes closed, feeling her muscles firing in response. She said that . . . she had used imagery to break the cycle of negativity. Whenever fear surfaced, she would picture herself pricking a big red balloon with a pin.

"That sound and that immediate switch would kind of snap me out of it," she said, adding, "The last couple years, I've definitely gotten to a point where when I'm on the hill, it's very quick for me to switch from a negative thought to a positive one."[2]

Here's another example of how self-talk affects your thinking. I recently had the opportunity to help Robert, a semiprofessional golfer, take his game to the next level of excellence. Our first session was in my office, where we played a game. I crumpled up half a dozen pieces of paper into balls. Handing them to him, one by one, I instructed him to throw them into a wastebasket I had placed about twenty feet away across the room. On the first attempt, he stood and tossed the paper balls without any mental preparation, and managed to get only two of the six in.

Before his next attempt I asked him to sit, close his eyes, and take a couple of deep breaths, and then I took him through a deep relaxation exercise. Only then did I instruct him to visualize easily throwing all the paper balls into the wastebasket. I asked him to pay attention to the details of his actions. In his imagination, he felt his arm going back, experienced his hand opening and releasing the ball, and observed the trajectory of the paper as it went into the wastebasket. I had him anchor his mental success movie by feeling the pride and satisfaction of succeeding. I then instructed him to repeat imagining his success movie five times.

I then directed him to open his eyes, stand, take a big breath, and duplicate what he had done in his imagination, that is, live in the "result" of his already being successful. He got all six paper balls in—twice! Robert had created his success first in his mind and then duplicated it in the world. He was delighted and amazed.

We then stepped it up a level and headed out to the course, in this instance, PGA West in California's beautiful Palm Desert. Just before we walked onto the first tee, I attached a digital recorder and a small microphone to Robert's belt and shirt. As he was playing, Robert was to say everything out loud that he would normally think to himself.

His first hole was mediocre, and he told himself as much. The second began with more promise. As he stood over the tee, he said into the microphone, "I'm focused. I can see the ball sailing down the fairway." Then he took a couple of deep breaths and swung. It was a really impressive tee shot! Unfortunately he sliced his next shot, and I could hear him mutter under his breath, "Well, that was just stupid." On the third hole, he drove it straight and long from the tee, but later on overshot the green. "Damnit, I always do this. I hate myself," he said. By the fourth hole he was so tense that he cursed at himself continuously, then got angry at me. On the fifth hole, he turned off the recorder. Thankfully we were playing only nine holes.

The game over, we headed for the clubhouse. We sat down in a private spot and I replayed the recording. Robert's usually confident demeanor turned to sheepishness as he heard himself curse and berate his performance. He listened for about five minutes before asking me to shut off the recorder. I let him settle in silence for a few seconds and then asked, "Do you have children?"

"Yes, three—nine, twelve, and fourteen," he replied.

"What do you think would happen to their self-esteem, motivation, and performance if you spoke to them like you spoke to yourself?"

Looking totally chagrined, he replied, "It would destroy their self-esteem and crush their confidence."

"What makes you think that your self-talk doesn't affect you the same way?" I asked.

He got it. Was the process easy or comfortable for Robert? No. It took willingness, persistence, work, and a little self-forgiveness, but from there on in, Robert was able to use visualization and nurturing self-talk to give himself the edge he sought.

. . .

As you can see, it is extremely important that you become aware of the quality of *your* self-talk and recognize its tremendous power. As a self-suggesting, self-programming, and self-reinforcing mechanism, your inner dialogue both reflects and reinforces your beliefs, which, in turn, feed back to your performance. How do you know if you are plagued with fear-based self-talk? Look at your life—your present reality—honestly. Observe and question your thinking, challenge your assumptions, and be willing to look at your truth.

The fact is that negative inner dialogue not only has a major impact on your attitude, it can affect your health as well. An article by the Mayo Clinic staff entitled "Positive Thinking: Stop Negative Self-Talk to Reduce Stress," published on the clinic's website on March 4, 2014,[3] says that a positive attitude and positive self-talk can affect the quality of your life in several ways. Included among these are increasing your life span, lowering rates of depression, increasing your resistance to the common cold, reducing the risk of death from cardiovascular disease, enabling you to cope better during periods of hardship, and generally increasing your psychological and physical well-being. (The article also offers some helpful hints on how to reduce your stress by being aware of your self-talk, reframing negative to positive self-talk, and surrounding yourself with positive people.)

When you become aware of, and familiar with, the frequency of your Rider's worry and negative self-talk, you have the ability to turn down the volume, put the brakes on negative thinking, and reframe to positive, healing thoughts. The next exercise is accordingly designed to help you build awareness of your inner dialogue. In it, you are going to experiment with scripting your thinking, recognizing negative thoughts, and reframing them into positive ones. The exercise stretches over a three-day period, but the actual work isn't all that demanding. It will require only about an hour of your time altogether, and a slightly larger commitment than the previous exercises. Since this is a three-day, three-part process that involves writing, keep your journal or computer at the ready.

YOUR TURN

DAY ONE

Day One is your warm-up day. I would like you to begin this exercise in the afternoon or early evening. When you are ready, stop what you're doing and open your journal or turn on your computer. You decide the exact time.

Take five minutes to do the following: Review any portion or portions of your day that were even slightly unpleasant or stressful. Briefly record your judgments, observations, or comments concerning the specific event. Whatever comes to your mind, write it down. When you are finished, close your journal. That's it for Day One.

DAY TWO

Immediately upon arising, after you brush your teeth and before coffee, tea, juice, or breakfast, open your journal and write the following sentence: "Today I will be mindful of my self-talk." It's a simple sentence, but you should not underestimate its power. By writing it down, you are giving yourself a suggestion that will act as a trigger, a reminder to be mindful throughout the day.

Stop and record your mental commentaries five times during the day: late morning, midafternoon, late afternoon, early evening, and just before bed. Write for one to five minutes. Write quickly, letting your stream of consciousness flow.

By the time you complete this second day, you will have dialogue covering many areas of your life. Your observations may include everything from the way you present yourself to other people to how others present themselves to you. You will most likely have written both criticism and praise of your job, your family, the traffic, your body, the food you've been consuming, and maybe even the exercise itself. Your mental dialogue will reflect your frustrations, worries about the future, guilt from the past or enjoyment of the present. Then close your journal and go to bed. That's it for Day Two.

DAY THREE

This final portion of the exercise will require approximately ten to thirty minutes. I want you to read over everything you have written over the past two days in a very special way. That is, pretend that what you have written was actually recorded by another person—a complete stranger or someone with whom you have only a passing acquaintance. Then using what you have written as your research material, write one short paragraph describing that person.

After you have finished writing their description, ask yourself, "Would I want to be his or her best friend? Would this person enhance my life? Is this individual living from fear or love?" If he or she reflects only love, you don't need to go any farther. However, if the description hints of any negativity, go back to your journal entries and rewrite the negative self-talk, turning it into positive, loving, gentle, self-supportive, and compassionate dialogue.

This should be very easy. Suppose, for example, that my negative inner dialogue went like this: "I really think that person is a jerk for getting angry in the airport ticket line and I would like to have put a piece of tape over his mouth." You might choose to rewrite it like this. "I feel compassion for that person. I've been there myself. I know that he is tired, frustrated, and wants to be home with his family. I wish him well."

It might also help you to review the negative self-talk that you have recorded in your journal and pick a specific event, worry, or concern that has been nagging you. Then, imagine that you have just told this worry to your best friend. Acting from your friend's point of view, what would you say that would be supportive and encouraging? Keep in mind: A friend is gentle, kind, focuses on the positive, and supports you to live an exceptional life!

After doing this exercise, you will notice your self-talk. By challenging your inner dialogue, you can blow apart the myths and self-deception that keep you stuck in old behavior. And in doing so, you gain control to make new, loving, positive, and supportive choices, in the moment, and every moment.

Saying "Isn't That Interesting?" Can Change Your Life

"As food is to the body, self-talk is to the mind.
Don't let any junk thoughts repeat in your head."[4]
—MADDY MALHOTRA, *HOW TO BUILD SELF-ESTEEM
AND BE CONFIDENT: OVERCOME FEARS, BREAK HABITS, BE SUCCESSFUL AND HAPPY*

Wouldn't it be tremendously helpful if I could give you a magic bullet to easily neutralize and instantly reframe negative, stress-inducing, and self-destructive self-talk into something positive and empowering? In order to help you accomplish that seemingly impossible feat, I would have to somehow make you aware of negative self-talk in the moment. Then I would encourage you to put on your mental brakes, freeze the thought, examine it impartially, let it go, and replace it with something better. Can it be done? Yes it can. It requires only that you learn a very simple mental tool. Let's approach it in a far-out way.

Imagine that, like Mr. Spock in the *Star Trek* television show and films, I could do a temporary "Vulcan Mind Meld" with you. (One of Spock's other-worldly talents was the ability to read minds by forming a psychic bond.) Once we were mentally linked, I could read your thoughts in real time (an idea I suspect may be a horrifying concept for both of us). Nevertheless, when your thinking turned to the dark side, whenever you had a fear-based thought, judged yourself or others harshly, or fell into the trap of worrying about what you can't change, I could immediately interrupt your thinking. Since I could read your mind, I would be able to alert you by thumping you over the head with a newspaper and yelling, "Stop! This is faulty thinking! Look at how it's making both of us feel! Now freeze that negative thought, look at it, and say, 'Isn't that interesting?'"

Actually, I don't have to do that because you can learn to recognize your own negative thoughts, freeze them, and reframe to more empowering thinking. And here's even better news: As you practice and become comfortable with this reframing skill, your overall thinking process will become more positive and empowering.

Yes, that's all you'd say: "Isn't that interesting?" And believe it or not, those three words can and will substantially improve the quality of your life. How? First and foremost, they would give you distance, or disassociate you, from your negative thought. In doing so, they would help you neutralize negative thinking and release the hold that your ego has on you in the moment. That's why using these words is one of my all-time favorite strategies. Don't be deceived by its simplicity. It is both powerful and effective. Second, by saying "Isn't that interesting?" you come to the present and become an observer of your thinking. When you become an observer of your thinking the ego loses its hold and, like a mythical vampire that cannot stand light, runs away. When you free yourself from the hold of negativity, you instantly have the ability to reframe, shift, or change your thinking to a mental script that is more positive and empowering.

Of course, I can't—nor, frankly, do I want to—do a Vulcan Mind Meld with you. I can, however, teach you to help the Rider manage its unhelpful, judgmental, negative mind chatter without me being privy to your thinking. It's easy, effective, and you can use it in every situation in your life—from improving your tennis game to letting go of guilt to enhancing your communication. All it takes is a little practice and you will gain control of your thinking and learn to influence the Elephant. Isn't that interesting?

You Can Learn to Control Your Responses

Our subconscious Elephant reacts so quickly to perceived threats that sometimes it seems like we just can't control our responses. Clients have told me that they find it a challenge to hold back when they feel anger or frustration, and that they often regret responding that way. The reality is that you can learn to hit your mental "pause" button. This gives the logical-thinking Rider time to catch up to the emotionally responsive Elephant, and allows life to catch up with you. It does take practice but, like any skill, you can learn to do it. You hit your pause button by becoming aware when you are experiencing a powerful emotion, stopping, and taking one deep breath. It works.

Here's a good way to start. Open your journal and write the following statement: "Whenever I judge myself or others harshly, when I am feeling guilty or attempt to make others feel guilty, when I am worrying or inventing fear-based scenarios of what might happen in the future, or when I feel fear-based emotions, I will notice my thoughts, stop, observe them, and say to myself, 'Isn't that interesting?' I will then reframe my thinking and choose empowering self-talk that reflects what a loving, caring, and compassionate friend would say to me." Then, every morning for the next month, read it before you start your day.

You can also try this. Pretend you have realized that you tend to bully people when you are under pressure, tired, or stressed, but as hard as you've tried, you have been unable to break the habit. With this new tool, since you are aware of when you are about to act aggressively, you can immediately put on your mental breaks, observe your negative thoughts, and say to yourself, "Isn't that interesting?" Now you can make a better choice and reframe your thinking. You have learned to change your behavior by changing your thinking.

Here's another scenario: Imagine someone has gotten angry or aggressive toward you, and you responded by pulling back rather than being assertive. Looking back on these events, you berate yourself as appearing timid and weak. Now, though, you don't have to do that. When someone gets aggressive, you can catch yourself when you are about to retreat, stop, and say, "Isn't that interesting?" You immediately release yourself from the hold of fear-based thinking, gain distance, reframe, and choose more empowering behavior. And when you consistently do this, you give yourself new self-confidence.

Not only is this a popular technique with my coaching clients, I often use it myself. Here are a couple of personal examples: A Connecticut blizzard was roaring. I ventured out to get gas for the snowblower and pick up a few things from the market so my wife and I could hunker down for the next couple of days. Someone who was speaking on a cell phone almost hit me in the parking lot. I felt a rush of anger. I immediately took a deep breath, stopped, noticed my harsh self-talk, and said to myself, "Isn't that interesting?" My response was almost comical. I chuckled. That didn't mean that I didn't still feel the person was a jerk. But it did mean that my anger and hostility dissipated, I didn't say or do something stupid, and I instantly lowered my stress level. Later the same day I was on the phone trying to order a Christmas present. I kept getting cut off. I felt my frustration turning to anger. I caught myself, noticed my thinking, took a deep breath, and said, "Isn't that interesting?" Once again, I felt the anger dissipate and my patience and perspective returning.

You can make this judgment-releasing, awareness-building, and ego-eliminating phrase part of your tool kit for awareness. Read your paragraph every morning for one month and put the phrase "Isn't that interesting?" into practice throughout the day. The key to successfully using this phrase is to internalize it, and that will happen within thirty days.

You Can Choose the Way You Think

"We choose all our actions and thoughts, almost all our feelings, and much of our physiology. . . . Choice Theory teaches that we are much more in control of our lives than we realize. Taking more effective control means making better choices as you relate to your children and everyone else."[5]

—WILLIAM GLASSER, *CHOICE THEORY*

Have you ever secretly wanted to be a star, even if just for a moment? Now is your chance. I would like you to imagine yourself the leading actor in our following drama. I'm asking you to walk in another's shoes, just like an actor. In your imagination, I want you to see and hear what the character sees and hears. Keep in mind, though, that this character is you! Here is the script. I've written it from your point of view.

After reading an article in the travel section of my local newspaper, I decide to spend a beautiful Sunday afternoon taking a mini-vacation. The description of an old-fashioned country fair in a neighboring state sounds ideal. Although I usually spend most of my time in the big city, I now feel I want to expand my horizons. I rent a car, grab a map, and enthusiastically head out into unfamiliar territory. However, in my excitement I neglect to get precise directions. I'm not particularly concerned because I have a general sense of where I'm going, and this is, after all, an adventure!

Even though I want to drive slowly and enjoy the scenery, everyone seems to be in a rush. Feeling a bit pressured I pick up my pace. Eventually I arrive at a very confusing, crowded five-way intersection where I am visually accosted by an overwhelming number of large, colorful billboards and signs. I search in vain for the signs that identify the names of the streets. I freeze with indecision and feel my brain is about to explode as people honk and impatiently yell at me. Panicked, I attempt to find the correct way to turn, then haphazardly make an impetuous decision based on nothing but a gut feeling. I choose what seems like an endless, unpopulated road only to discover that I am traveling in the opposite direction of where I want to be. My once bright and sunny mood shifts to one of black and stormy clouds.

As I reverse direction, I curse the people who failed to mark the route clearly, the other drivers who made me feel pressured, and myself for not getting directions. I arrive at the fair late, only to discover that the craft booths and attractions are about to close.

My irritation grows as I fight the traffic returning to the city.

I yell at pedestrians crossing the street, blast my horn when a car ahead of me doesn't move quickly enough, and rage at the universe. Turning my rental car in to the agency, I snap at the attendant when she informs me that there will be an extra charge for being an hour late and not filling the gas tank. Slamming the door behind me as I burst into my apartment, I conclude my crummy day by yelling at the cat. I feel every bit the justified victim. The world has, after all, conspired against me.

Do you think your negative experience was caused by the choices you made, or did the circumstances dictate your frustration and anger? Now I want you to read a slightly different version of the story. In this version I have substituted the name "John" for "I" to help you disassociate yourself from the character. And this time I want you to experience the script as if you were an audience member watching a movie up on the big screen.

After reading an article in the travel section of a local newspaper, John decides to spend a beautiful Sunday afternoon taking a mini-vacation. The description of an old-fashioned country fair in a neighboring state sounds ideal. Although he usually spends most of his time in the big city, John now feels it's time to expand his horizons. He rents a car, grabs a map, and enthusiastically heads out into unfamiliar territory. However, in his excitement he neglects to get precise directions. John is not particularly concerned because he has a general sense of where he is going, and, this is, after all, an adventure!

Even though John wants to drive slowly and enjoy the scenery, everyone seems to be in a rush. Feeling a bit pressured, he picks up his pace. Eventually, he arrives at a very confusing, crowded five-way intersection where he is visually accosted by an overwhelming number of large, colorful billboards and signs. He searches in vain for the signs that identify the names of the streets. He freezes with indecision, and feels his brain is about to explode as people honk and impatiently yell at him. Panicked, he attempts to find the correct way to turn, then haphazardly makes an impetuous decision based on nothing but a gut feeling. He chooses what seems like an endless, unpopulated road only to discover that he is traveling in the opposite direction of where he wants to be. His once bright and sunny mood shifts to one of black and stormy clouds.

As John reverses direction, he curses the people who failed to mark the route clearly, the other drivers who made him feel pressured, and himself for not getting directions. He arrives at the fair late, only to discover that the craft booths and attractions are about to close.

His irritation grows as he fights the traffic returning to the city. He yells at pedestrians crossing the street, blasts his horn when a car ahead of him doesn't move quickly enough, and rages at the universe. Turning his rental car in to the agency, John snaps at the attendant when she informs him that there will be an extra charge for being an hour late and not filling the gas tank. Slamming the door behind him as he bursts into his apartment, John concludes his crummy day by yelling at the cat. He feels every bit the justified victim. The world has conspired against him.

Do you think it is possible that John created his experience, his reality, by the choices he made? Was there any significant difference when you looked at the scenario from John's point of view as opposed to your own? Do you see other choices John might have made if his attitude had been different and he had been calm and centered with a foundation of inner peace? While it is sometimes hard to achieve, making inner peace a priority presents many options to achieve that state, ranging from daily meditation, to relaxation exercises, to deep breathing. As my brother, Dave Mapes, used to tell his children and students, "You can make any choice you want to make, as long as you are willing to pay the price."

Unfortunately, the eye really cannot behold itself. Therefore, it is much easier to see the consequences of the choices that other Riders make than it is to realize the consequences of our own choices. It is also far more comfortable recognizing that others have a great number of choices to which they are blind than it is to accept that we, too, have a variety of choices in how we think, respond, and take action.

 LIFE FACT: YOU ARE ALWAYS AT CHOICE.

The process of taking one's vision from an idea to reality is another example of how we constantly make choices in order to achieve a goal. For example, I find great satisfaction in creating short video presentations, both as training tools and for publicity purposes, and one day a few years ago I woke up inspired to launch a project that would require videotaping a new speaking program. Not only would it require time and a substantial financial investment on my part, but also given the time frame, it had to be shot, edited, and delivered to my speaking bureau within two months. Unfortunately, as so often happens, it took much longer than I had imagined, and was fraught with frustration.

Even so, once the videotaping was complete, I sat down in the editing room inspired to move forward, only to discover that the video crew had neglected to turn on one of the three cameras, so the shots I needed to fulfill my vision were not there! Despite my dismay, and with serious misgivings, I decided to move forward. After two months, and many, many hours in the editing room, I delivered the tape to my agents and awaited their reaction. I didn't hear anything for two days. Then I called. It was not good news. They thought the subject matter was interesting but they unanimously agreed that the video didn't sell it. Needless to say, I was a bit discouraged. On top of that, I knew deep down that I should have trusted my instincts when they told me not to move forward after I'd seen the initial footage. I knew I had to start over, but my creative juices were tapped out. I needed to gain perspective so, reluctantly, I decided to back off for at least a week.

Within a few days, though, a new idea suddenly popped up in my conscious mind, and I decided to start over with a completely new program. Instead of going back to my original plan, I chose to frame the program around participants breaking a board with their hands. I figured that by presenting it this way the audience would be able to identify a problem or barrier in their personal or organizational life and, using the board breaking as a metaphor, blast through those barriers! Doing it like this, I reasoned, would enable participants to define their personal vision of the future, develop a success strategy, learn to visualize, and move to action. So hiring another crew, we taped the seventy-five-minute presentation using four cameras. The taping went extremely well, and then we went back to the editing room.

At first the project seemed overwhelming as I had to edit the finished tape down to a solid forty-five minutes so my agents could choose short video clips to put on their website. Working with my editor, I began by methodically selecting segments from the seventy-five-minute tapes of each of the four cameras. Every day I looked at the choices I had made the day before and analyzed how they fit into the bigger picture, and as I did the project began to take form. Moving forward, though, required some extremely challenging choices. In order to be true to my overall vision and make sure the video fit within the allotted time frame, I had to let go of some of my favorite moments. Each day brought new challenges and different choices. My editor and I plowed through the seemingly endless editing and reediting, trying to take the jumble of small moments and make them into something exciting and powerful. Finally the tape was complete. I confidently submitted the finished twenty-minute video to my agents, ahead of schedule this time, and prepared myself to wait for their feedback. Twelve hours later the phone rang. They loved it!

Do you have any idea the number of choices I made during that period, even just about my career? I chose to develop a program, and to invest my own money and time in it. In spite of knowing I did not have the right video shots, I chose to move forward. When I had a confirmation that the project had failed, I chose to let myself feel disappointment, and then search for the lesson within the failure. Eventually, I chose to let it go. I then chose to take another risk with a new video. I chose how much time to spend in the editing room. I chose what sections would remain in the final product and what pieces to ignore. I chose to encourage input from my editor. I chose the sequence of video clips that formed the final product. Finally, I chose to celebrate its success, big time! It wasn't easy, but as the great speaker and author Jim Rohn says, "You have the ability to totally transform every area in your life, and it all begins with your very own power of choice."

The idea that you are always at choice is not some whimsical, made-up, self-help, touchy-feely theory that I'm attempting to persuade you to embrace. This goes far beyond experiencing the momentary, artificial, intoxicating high of inspiring speeches, positive-thinking books, and meaningful quotes. I want you to own this as a life fact for the following reasons:

- If you are willing to accept that you create your experience out of the choices you make, and that you are accountable for those choices, you open up a pathway to making the correct choices that will give you a life of limitless possibility.

- When you remember that you are always "at choice," you refuse to let the Rider be controlled by the Elephant's genetic, predisposed, fear-based conditioned responses.

- By refusing to play the "blame game" you will stop giving your choice away to others.

- You will be able to recognize when you fall into the trap of "victimization" and immediately take back your power of choice.

- When you accept that you are always at choice, you will be able to see alternative pathways to creating an exceptional life.

You Must Take Responsibility for Your Choices

At the beginning of my Choices workshop, I always ask the audience members, "How many of you would rather be on a beautiful tropical island than sitting in this room?" Virtually all the hands go up. "I don't believe you," I say. "Otherwise, you would be there, not here. You are choosing to sit in this room now rather than vacationing on the beautiful tropical island. Who disagrees with me?"

Hands go up, defensive and justifying statements are made, and eventually someone observes, "You are right. I could be on an island if I set my mind to it. But I chose to be here because I thought it would help me." That observation is the one that opens up a discussion of how ownership of our choices, both good and bad, leads to change. Change begins by taking responsibility. By the end of the workshop the majority of the participants get it. This epiphany does not make everyone happy, because it's often easier to believe we are under the control of others—victims of our programming, our genetics, our upbringing, the environment, or even fate—than it is to accept that we are responsible for our choices. But as Susan Granger, movie critic and journalist, says, "You have to have the personal integrity to stick to your important choices and grant yourself the grace to change your mind."

Think about the multitude of choices that you make every day, the experience you create through these choices, and the consequences of each one:

- You choose to go to the doctor or to ignore personal health warning signs.
- You choose to have sex or to be celibate.
- You choose to say "hello" or to ignore someone.
- You choose what foods to eat or not to eat.
- You choose to be active or sedentary.
- You choose to put alcohol or drugs into your body or not to.
- You choose what to say or not to say.
- You choose to blame others for your circumstances or to take responsibility.
- You choose to stay in a self-destructive relationship or to look for a loving relationship.
- You choose to learn, stretch, and grow, or to stagnate.
- You choose to let other people get whatever advantage they can by allowing them to impose their rules for relationships on you.

- You choose to worship or not to worship.

- You choose when to take risks and when to play it safe.

- You choose to be thankful or not to be thankful.

- You choose reckless behavior without regard to your personal safety or the safety of others, or you consider the consequences of your choices as they relate to yourself and others.

- You choose to change or not change your behavior.

- You choose the way you speak and relate to yourself either positively or negatively.

- You choose to lie or to tell the truth.

- You choose when to isolate yourself and when to socialize.

- You choose which people to have in your life and which to avoid.

- You choose to trust yourself or not trust yourself.

- You choose to discover and help others meet their needs or not to do this.

- You choose to trust others or not.

- You choose to be of service or not.

- You choose love or you choose fear.

- You choose how you judge others.

- You choose how you react to all past and present situations.

- You choose to forgive or not.

While you may intellectually understand the concept of self-creation through choice, it's sometimes a challenge to internalize it at the core of your being. If you really do accept that you create your experience, you will learn to recognize and let go of rationalization and justification, and you will know that every choice you make has consequences and that you are accountable for your choices and your experiences. Once you own this as a life fact, you will also let go of blaming yourself, your family, your friends, the fates, society, or even God for what you have or don't have in life. Once you own your choices there will be a shift in your thinking. Not only do you become free of the ego, you become what I call a true Artist of Possibility, and you discover that love does matter.

Finally, self-knowledge opens up choice, and choice opens up the possibility of influencing the Elephant. Understand that I am not suggesting that you are wrong for judging, rationalizing, or blaming. These coping tools are all part of the Elephant's survival mechanism and are at the core of your survival self. As a child, you didn't have the maturity and growth to always make your own choices. Therefore, you are not responsible for what may or may not have happened to you in the past. But you are responsible for how you relate to those events now, and you must take responsibility for it. All this awareness does take a little effort, and courage; but if you make that effort, and bring that courage to your everyday life, you will be able to achieve the exceptional life you want and deserve.

THINKPOINTS

- You can learn to shift your perspective by learning how to reframe your thinking.
- How you think about things—how you imagine them—affects you on a physical level.
- Awareness is hard work but the payoff is always greater than the sacrifice.
- Visualizing your goal affects you on a subconscious level and helps you move in the right direction to attain it.
- Your inner dialogue, the "voice in your head," affects how you think.
- By challenging the assumptions of your inner dialogue, you can move beyond the control of your old conditioning.
- You can manage your negative, fear-based thinking by catching yourself, stopping, and saying to yourself, "Isn't that interesting?"
- You are always "at choice" as to how you choose to react to any situation.
- You are accountable for your choices and your experiences.

3

SHATTER LIMITING MYTHS

"I therefore claim to show, not how men think in myths, but how myths operate in men's minds without their being aware of the fact."[1]
—CLAUDE LEVI-STRAUSS, *THE RAW AND THE COOKED: MYTHOLOGIQUES*, VOLUME 1

Within your imagination you can be anyone you want, go anywhere you want, and do anything you desire. That's the power of imagination at work, and the fantasies you create in your mind are real, at least in the moment of imagining. But myths—usually thought of as made-up stories that explain some belief, practice, or natural phenomenon—are fantasies as well, and they cannot be separated from imagination.

Think of a movie, television show, or book that totally absorbed you. If it was a thriller, didn't your pulse pick up? If it was extremely sad, didn't you feel like crying? If it was a comedy, didn't you laugh? You were affected because your subconscious Elephant interpreted the illusion of the movie, television show, or book as reality. But if you continue holding on to and replaying these stories and fantasies, like a reinforced hypnotic suggestion, they can become real, an ingrained part of your belief system, part of your Elephant.

The good news, and the bad news, is that this synthesis of reality and fantasy has already happened within your mind. It is the nature of being human. You and I and more than seven billion other human beings have unconsciously accepted certain illusions as facts that have become our own personal myths. This is true, at least in part, because, as visionary George Orwell said, "Myths which are believed in tend to become true." Like it or not, myths are part of your history and give meaning to every area of your life. They compose who you are and what you believe, and dramatically influence your decisions and behavior. The question is whether the myths you believe are helpful or hurtful. The answer depends on what myths you hold to be true.

There is no reason for you to identify or question those myths that provide you with hope, joy, and balance. I do, however, want you to recognize and blow apart the kind of destructive myths that cloud your perceptual filter and act as a barrier to keep you from living an exceptional life. It is the deceptive power of myth that may blind you to love and open up the door to fear. Here, the ego is at work. I call this deceiver the "Trickster," which the *Merriam-Webster Dictionary* defines as "a dishonest person who defrauds others by trickery," "a person skilled in the use of tricks and illusion," and "a cunning or deceptive character appearing in various forms in the folklore of many cultures."

When the Trickster is at the top of its game, the very myths we hold to be true lead us to set up impossible expectations that result in wasted energy and frustration. Myths like these can beguile us into believing that we can achieve happiness and gain fulfillment and success by simply using willpower, even though willpower is a finite resource. They can lead us to assume that one must always think positively in order to meet with success, even though, as you will discover, negative thinking can actually be used as a source for achieving our goals. Myths may influence our choices and behavior by swaying us into believing that our words and actions have little impact on others, or that feelings always determine our actions, although, in fact, we can learn from feelings without acting on them. At their most destructive, myths can lead us to believe that love is limited and must be rationed, should only be given under certain conditions, or should be used as a tool to manipulate or control others.

These myths stem from numerous sources—cultural norms, education, superstition, family, friends, peers, mentors, and teachers. Throughout our lives myths are absorbed by the Elephant until they become our beliefs and are accepted as the truth. This is not necessarily bad—we need myths to give our lives meaning, texture, depth, and color. But there are some myths, like those I've just mentioned, that do not serve our best interests. In this chapter we are going to shatter seven of the most common and potentially destructive myths. You will learn how to increase your awareness and understand both the destructive nature of the ego and the healing power of love. I will also present strategies that will guide you to use negative thinking to increase your odds for successful goal completion, apply your willpower where it can be most beneficial, and use your feelings as a tool to identify limiting beliefs.

Myth Number One: Positive Thinking Works for Everyone

I am passionate about positive thinking. Dr. Norman Vincent Peale, Zig Ziglar, Reverend Robert Schuller, David Schwartz, Claude Bristol, and Napoleon Hill were my earliest sources of inspiration. With their positive messages they have helped innumerable people, who in turn have inspired millions of others. They view the world through the filter of love and possibility. Positive thinking, however, does not always work for everyone, particularly for invested, rigid, and locked-in negative thinkers. For these committed negative thinkers, positive thinking, especially if communicated as a suggestion that the negative thinker needs to change, might easily be interpreted as criticism. This could result in the negative thinker becoming angry, defensive, or even feeling guilty. No one likes to have their belief system threatened. As you will see, however, negative thinking can be used to create a positive outcome by making appropriate preparations.

Are you a positive thinker? If the answer is "yes," then my guess would be that sometime in your life you have attempted to thrust your positive thinking on a negative thinker. What was the result? The negative thinker probably pulled away emotionally, and you were left feeling impatient or frustrated. Why? Because negative thinkers often feel—and are—just as right and justified in their negative thinking as positive thinkers are in their positive thinking. As a result, the more you attempt to change negative thinkers with positive communication and cute, positive sayings, the more entrenched they will become. By espousing positive thinking to negative thinkers you are not only subtly, or not so subtly, threatening their comfort zone but their dignity as well.

The fact is that even those negative thinkers who want to solve their problems are likely to be disappointed as long as they view the world through a filter of negativity. Until a negative thinker's paradigm shifts, positive thinking is not an option, at least for them. Of course even positive thinkers can temporarily get stuck in the ooze of negativity. The difference is that they have equipped the Rider with the mental tools to recognize when the Elephant gets stuck, and to reframe their thinking. They can experience their fears and worries, recognize them for what they are, and let them go. Can a negative thinker become a positive thinker? It's possible. But it may not even be necessary. In fact, there is another way to look at negative thinking.

 LIFE THOUGHT: NEGATIVE THINKING CAN BE POSITIVE.

If you are a positive thinker it is easy to label those who mostly see the glass as half empty rather than half full as pessimists. But is it always bad to see the glass as half empty? Are these negative thinkers poor and miserable lost souls? Not necessarily. Julie K. Norem, PhD, professor of psychology at Wellesley College, writes in her book, *The Positive Power of Negative Thinking: Using Defensive Pessimism to Harness Anxiety and Perform at Your Peak*, "Many pessimists are highly successful and even happy. Their secret: They have made their feelings the basis of an effective strategy–defensive pessimism."[2]

Using defensive pessimism is essentially anticipating a negative outcome and then proactively taking positive steps to avoid that outcome.

Think about a football team anticipating a number of their opponents' offensive plays and then making plans for responding to them. Or astronauts who run countless negative scenarios so they will have instinctive positive reactions if a situation should turn dire.

Without such a strategy, negative thinking can lead to a life of limited outcomes, distress, and negativity. Unless you learn to recognize and turn fear-based negative thinking to your advantage, you might make choices that lead to your own personal disaster scenario. In order to help you avoid falling into this trap, we will explore in depth the manipulative power of fear and the nature of self-fulfilling prophecies. By developing the skill to recognize when you are in fear and to reframe your thinking, you are able to make empowering choices. We will examine fear in greater detail in a later chapter, but here is a brief look at what I consider the major fears the average person experiences, as well as the negative, fear-based behaviors that could result.

- *Fear of rejection* can create rejection by making you avoid people and isolate yourself, or reject others before they can reject you. It can also create rejection by making you attempt to dominate, control, or manipulate others, thereby pushing them away.

- *Fear of failure* and *fear of change* can create failure by leading you to refuse to take risks, avoid challenging jobs, pass up opportunities, and step out of your comfort zone.

- *Fear of success* can create failure by making you do the things that will create a barrier to achieving success. Classic symptoms include procrastination resulting in missed deadlines, poor communication, and getting into arguments with peers or friends

- *Fear of commitment* can create failure by keeping you from committing to anything or anyone, or by making you overcommit and unable to say "No."

- *Fear of poverty* can make you—or make you feel—poor by leading you to spend more than you earn or by hoarding what you have.

LIFE THOUGHT: PESSIMISM WITHOUT A PLAN OFTEN LEADS TO FEAR-BASED CHOICES AND SELF-DEFEATING, SELF-SABOTAGING BEHAVIORS.

In my workshops and personal coaching sessions I often help clients by enabling them to clearly identify their fear, and then use their pessimistic and negative view of the future to create an action plan for success. While this does not always guarantee a positive outcome, it does set people up with an edge for success by helping them increase their self-confidence, take ownership, create a strategy, and move forward with positive steps.

One instance in which I did this was with a client named Josh, who was a senior vice president of sales for a large software company. Because he was afraid of failing, making a fool of himself, and being rejected, every time he was asked to address his team he assigned the task to someone else. This behavior not only made him appear arrogant and distant, it also caused him to feel guilty and isolated. All he could see in his future mental movie was more of the same, so he came to me for help. He needed to develop a strategy to use his fear, his negative thinking, as a template for creating a positive outcome.

What I did to help him was essentially teach him a basic six-step strategy to overcome his fear and achieve his goal. First, he had to clearly identify a specific and realistic goal and then write it down. In Josh's case the goal was to address his team with confidence, clearly express his vision for the team, and make sure each member was on track to fulfill that vision. Second, he had to visualize himself successfully achieving the goal—in other words, live in the ideal end result. For Josh this meant having a clear mental movie of himself giving a presentation with total self-confidence and having his team respond positively. Third, he had to put his thinking in reverse, back up, and identify what needed to change or be learned in order to achieve the goal. Josh needed to learn the skills to present with self-confidence. Fourth, he had to determine specific, short-term, and doable action steps that would not overwhelm the Elephant. For Josh this meant taking an acting class, and then writing and rehearsing his script until it positively influenced his Elephant. Fifth, he had to set a deadline, and sixth, he had to take action.

Josh threw himself into the assignment with great enthusiasm, and when he was ready to make a presentation to his team I was there to see it. Naturally, at first he was a little nervous; but as he engaged his audience he relaxed and did a magnificent job. His success on that occasion, and his continuing success, flowed directly from his using fear and negative thinking as a guide to do what he had to do to create a positive outcome. He used his Rider to positively influence his Elephant.

In another situation, I worked with a client, Barbara, who asked me to help her get rid of negative thinking. I explained to her that, instead, I could assist her in using her negative thinking as a strategy for success. She was skeptical but agreed to come for a private session. When we met she told me that she was so afraid of rejection that she had on several occasions chosen not to show up for scheduled job interviews. I asked her to imagine the outcome and tell me how she saw her future unfolding. When she tried, however, she visualized walking into the interview feeling nervous, speaking in a desperate manner, and, of course, ultimately making a fool of herself—and getting rejected.

To counter this, I had her make a list of every negative future, fear-based mental movie she could imagine, and then pinpoint exactly what she visualized herself doing or saying that would cause her not to be hired. Then I had her play a game with me. Pretending I was being interviewed for a job and she was the interviewer, I made up a script based on her fears. As I acted out her role as interviewee, Barbara, now acting as an observer, gained a new perspective, and was then able to see the steps she needed to take and what she could do, or learn to do, to prepare herself for success. She imagined every possible question the interviewer might ask and wrote down her most positive response. She visualized her ideal outcome or success picture in great detail, including what she was wearing, her makeup, her hairstyle, and how she carried herself. By creating a "success movie" depicting the outcome, she used her critical Rider to make the Elephant comfortable and confident.

Working with Josh and Barbara I was able to show them how to use their negativity as a map to avoid what they feared most, and how to take a proactive position in that effort. They both adopted the strategy of using their negative thinking as the basis for defensive pessimism, and, I'm glad to say, were successful in spite of some lingering whispers of negativity.

What, then, are the steps you can take to use negative thinking for positive outcomes?

1 Recognize your negative thinking and identify the fear behind the thought.

2 Challenge the negative thought. Ask yourself, "How realistic is this?"

3 Write down the worst-case scenario.

4 View your negative thinking as a signpost to take you to a positive outcome. Use the imagined negative outcome to develop a strategy for positive preparation by determining what you can learn from it and what you can control to prevent it.

Myth Number Two: Willpower Conquers All

"It's not that some people have willpower and some don't.
It's that some people are ready to change and others are not."
—JAMES GORDON, M.D.

The myth that willpower conquers all perpetuates the flawed belief that it alone is enough to overcome obstacles and create positive long-term change. This myth has been responsible for much mental anguish, guilt, and shame. It implies that we are weak-willed if we are unable to permanently eliminate a negative habit, break through depression, overcome fear, achieve a goal, or sustain a relationship. It also suggests that we would rather be unhealthy than healthy in mind, body, and spirit. Shattering this myth allows you to leverage your willpower to achieve positive outcomes.

The reality is that willpower never works at full throttle over the long term. The reason for this is that the Rider, which is where your will-power comes from, has limited reserves of energy. If the Rider can tug hard enough on the reins, it might get the Elephant to change direction, at least temporarily. But eventually the Rider is going to get exhausted and the Elephant is going to do what it wants to do, unless the Rider employs its own unique skills to influence the Elephant—that is, learns to self-supervise.

Of course, during your early childhood years, your parents, relatives, or guardians acted as your supervisors. They had total control of your activities. They made decisions for you because you were not ready to go out and survive on your own. As you grew and matured, you were more exposed to the environment and other people, had more experiences, failed, and learned; and, with pressure from various other factors, you developed your own personality. Hopefully, you also developed the ability to supervise yourself, because once you have learned to do so, you gain control over both the personal and professional aspects of your life.

Although self-supervision is only achievable through willpower, it is not just about resisting the ice cream in the freezer, having just one cocktail, or cutting down on the number of cigarettes you smoke. Self-supervision is also about learning a new skill, having a difficult conversation with your partner or child, taking care of someone, and resisting the temptation to shut off the alarm and sleep in. However, all of these activities, as well as many similar ones, burn up your reserves of mental energy.

This doesn't mean that willpower is useless. In fact, its power is immense. Throughout the ages it has helped people overcome seemingly insurmountable barriers. What it does mean is that using willpower is a drain on the Rider's mental creative battery, and that eventually the battery must be recharged. Not surprisingly, the more challenging a goal, the bigger the change; the bigger the change, the larger the growth—and the more intensely the energy drains. When the mental battery is depleted, self-control is lessened and the ability to focus, persist, and think creatively is dramatically diminished.

Like the imagination, though, willpower can be a useful tool in your artist's tool kit, if you use it wisely. In fact, when willpower, perseverance, letting go, and forgiveness are linked up with belief and the force of the imagination, there are very few outcomes that are not possible. In later chapters you will learn the skills necessary to leverage your power of will by developing a vivid, emotional, clear, and realistic vision of the future.

Myth Number Three: We Are All Separate from Each Other

> "Tenderness emerges from the fact that the two persons, longing, as all individuals do, to overcome the separateness and isolation to which we are all heir because we are individuals, can participate in a relationship that, for the moment, is not of two isolated selves but a union."[3]
>
> —ROLLO MAY, *LOVE AND WILL*

The myth of separateness is one of the darkest of illusions. Not only does it deny the healing power of love, it enhances the destructive nature of fear. Those who operate under this myth believe that their words and actions do not make a difference. They are blind to their personal power to impact others and often manipulate, blame, and hurt, and then feel victimized by the very reality they have participated in creating.

 LIFE THOUGHT: YOU CANNOT *NOT* AFFECT OTHERS.

Helen Keller said, "When shall we learn that we are all related one to the other, that we are all members of the same body?" If we are all connected, all of the same body, you cannot *not* affect others. Your attitude, the way you present yourself to the world, the way you advise, criticize, laugh, anger, or smile has a profound effect on other people. Whether you isolate yourself or are social and outgoing, you affect others. Whether you litter and pollute or choose to clean up your messes, lie and deceive or have the integrity to keep your word and serve as a positive role model, you influence and affect others. Like it or not, you always make a difference. You have had, do have, and will have a wide circle of influence.

Many years ago a performer friend of mine was complaining that every time he came home from a tour his wife would be in a bad mood. It had gotten so uncomfortable that he told me he no longer wanted to come home because he expected her to be in a dark mood. I gave him a simple suggestion. "Why don't you close your eyes and imagine her being in a good mood when you return?" He retorted, "But that's impossible. She's always in a bad mood." Even so, I was able to persuade him to spend a little time visualizing walking in the door and being greeted with love by his wife.

Needless to say he found it challenging. And yet, the first time he did his visualization exercise it seemed to work. "A coincidence," he told me. The second trip home she seemed to be even warmer. "Confusing," he reported. The third time he asked to meet with me. "I feel like such a jerk," he said. "Why?" I quizzed. "Well, I finally sat down and expressed my feelings and asked what was going on with her. 'It's simple,' she responded. 'You always came home in such a bad mood that I felt defensive before you even arrived. Then you seemed to change. You came in with a smile and asked me how I was. And each time you came home you seemed warmer to me.'"

Like my friend, if we realize how much we impact others we could work at being conscious of our attitude and more aware of what we say and do. The fact is that we are often a partner in the outcomes we experience. As you move through this book, you will discover that when you view the world with pure love, you feel connected. You will know, without a doubt, that you make a difference and that what you do or don't do, say or don't say, has an enormous impact on your relationships, your community, and ultimately on the world.

Myth Number Four: A Healthy Ego Is an Advantage

"Two people have been living in you all of your life. One is the ego, garrulous, demanding, hysterical, calculating; the other is the hidden spiritual being, whose still voice of wisdom you have only rarely heard or attended to."[4]

—SOGYAL RINPOCHE, *TIBETAN BOOK OF LIVING AND DYING*

There are many definitions, descriptions and interpretations of the ego. For example, Freud, in his psychoanalytic structural model of the psyche, states that the ego is responsible for mediating between the unrealistic id (the seat of instincts and primary body processes) and the superego (the seat of our social conscience). Dr. Wayne Dyer once told me that the ego is just an idea we have of who we are, the material possessions we own, what other people think of us and our achievements. In his video blog, Deepak Chopra says that the ego is our self-image, not our true self. It is the social mask we put on, and that it lives in fear and needs constant approval. Therefore, the ego is manifested as judgments and fantasies. As defined in the Urban Dictionary, the ego is the part of our personality that separates us from the rest of the world. And in modern vernacular, it's often used to mean one's level of self-esteem and self-confidence.

I think of the ego as a Trickster—powerful, never satisfied, greedy and full of deceits. Defined this way, the ego can be seen as the source of all negativity in our lives. It espouses the illusion of separateness and blinds us to spirituality. It is the voice of fear and the enemy of love. It convinces us that putting our interests first is the only way to gain love, and will do whatever is necessary to sway us into believing that love is conditional. It is the essence of scarcity and reflects the fear that we can never have enough. It is our mind's identification with social labels, customs, and beliefs, which include our nationality, name, material possessions, thoughts, body, social position, religion, desires, likes, dislikes, and fears. In other words, the ego is the Elephant's primary fear directive, always shouting, "Survive at any and all cost!"

This survival mentality is yet another reflection of the primitive, reptilian mind. It is preoccupied with self-interest and self-protection. The ego demands we put our needs first and will help justify any behavior, even if it means steamrolling over others to get what we want. The ego views life through the lens of scarcity, wants instant gratification, and refuses to allow us to be grateful for what we have or to apologize for the damage we have done to others. Like Mandrake the Magician, the ego clouds the mind into believing that getting is more important than giving, that competition is more effective than cooperation, and that being right is better than being happy. It does not like disagreement and loathes criticism. It will anger, lie, cheat, deceive, control, envy, or be jealous. It can never be satisfied.

Perhaps the most dangerous thing about the ego is that it keeps us trapped in the past by not allowing us to forgive others and ourselves. As Dr. Gerald Jampolsky and Diane Cirincione write in *Love Is the Answer: Creating Positive Relationships*, "The ego looks at relationships in a very negative way. It sees them as dangerous and as potential enemies. It would have us concentrate on differences, rather than similarities, and tells us to look upon these differences as potential sources of deep hurt in our lives. It will have us believe that without fear, we would not know how to protect ourselves and, therefore, would not know how to be safe and secure." In later chapters you will learn to identify the destructive nature of the ego, and be provided with the tools you need to turn fear into action.

Myth Number Five: Feelings Determine Actions

"We need to get rid of the unrealistic and outdated notion that feelings determine what we do. They do not. When we are freed from that myth, we discover that unpleasant feelings are not simply troublesome, they are informative."[5]

—DAVID K. REYNOLDS, *A HANDBOOK FOR CONSTRUCTIVE LIVING*

At this very moment, how do you feel? I'm not asking if you feel happy, sad, angry, hurt, depressed, or ecstatic. I'm asking, "*How* do you feel?" Does asking you this question make you uncomfortable or is it easy to answer?

Are you honest with yourself or do you deny and suppress your feelings? Do you learn from your feelings or do you ignore them? Do you use your feelings or do your feelings use you? When you feel angry, depressed, or fearful, do you act out and yell at others, dumping your negativity on anyone who listens and dragging them down with you, or do you take responsibility for how you feel?

Most people never think about, examine, or learn from their feelings, nor do they realize that what and how they think actually creates the very feelings they don't want to examine. And, because they have never examined the nature of feelings, they mistakenly and often destructively let those feelings determine their behavior. Here is a quick exercise that will test the waters of your imagination.

YOUR TURN

Complete these four sentences as quickly as possible. Go with your first thought and trust your intuition in completing them.

I feel most frustrated when _____.

I feel angriest when _____.

I feel most loved when _____.

I feel happiest when _____.

Record each of the four completed sentences in your journal or on your computer.

You may find yourself judging what you wrote as "right" or "wrong" or want to redo your answers. If so, pull yourself back from doing so. Let it go. It's just information to help you understand why you think and act the way you do. As simple as this exercise may appear on the surface, though, your answers to each of these questions will not only show you how fast your emotions can shift, but also will provide you with insight into who you are and how you see the world, because, in fact, you see the world not as it is but as you are!

Accepting your feelings without acting on them is vitally important for your emotional growth and mental freedom. Feelings not only assist you in knowing yourself, but they also give you the opportunity to be authentic and connect deeply with others. Negative feelings are often signposts for you to learn about and resolve old issues. As Aristotle wrote, "Anybody can become angry, that is easy; but to be angry with the right person, and to the right degree, and at the right time, and for the right purpose, and in the right way, that is not within everybody's power and is not easy."

YOUR TURN

Let's play another game. Choose something on which to focus for two minutes. It can be any object (picture, light, candle, glass, flower, vase, etc.). When you focus, the only thought you are to have is the object. If other thoughts intrude, notice them, let them go, and refocus. If it is convenient, set an alarm or kitchen timer for two minutes and when you're ready, start focusing . . .

Now, were you able to exclude all thoughts from your mind for the full two minutes? Be honest. If so, you are in a very, very small minority. Most likely you caught yourself wondering to what end you were doing the exercise or thinking that you had something better to do. Maybe you were contemplating eating, working out, shopping, writing a report, worrying about your child, or any of our limitless life concerns. What does this lack of concentration mean? Why doesn't your mind stay focused? Perhaps, at this moment, you don't have as much control over your thoughts as you may have assumed. Here's an awareness flash: You have even less control over your feelings, and you aren't required to. But you are responsible for your actions because you do control them.

While your emotions may flow from the Elephant, the Rider does have control over the images and pictures it creates, as well as over your self-talk, all of which can in turn trigger feelings. So the Rider's ability to think, analyze, and reason can have great influence on your feelings. Nevertheless, as American patriot Samuel Adams said, "Mankind is governed more by their feelings than by reason." And the more you are willing to acknowledge, confront, and learn from your feelings, the faster you will grow on all levels. The more in touch you are with your feelings, the more authentic you will become and the better you will be at having loving relationships. Feelings give us the opportunity to look at *our* truth. It is by knowing ourselves that we can heal the past. Learn to be aware of and accept your feelings. Then use them as a source of information for your growth.

One of my clients—I will call him Everett—was teased, tormented, and physically abused by his peers as a young man. He wouldn't cry because he was afraid of being called weak. He shoved his feelings of pain and fear away until he too began to use his fists, becoming the very bully he was afraid of in his youth. As an adult, he carried his fear into the business world, but instead of using his fists he used words. He mocked, criticized, made fun of, and bullied others. He ignored the warning signs of his emotions until his world began to fall apart.

Over the course of a year Everett's quarterly peer reviews had gotten progressively worse. In the past his boss had ignored the criticisms, because Everett and his team had far exceeded their yearly sales goals. But his final peer reviews were so negative that the CEO brought him in for a talk, and told him that if he didn't lighten up and change his attitude, he would be let go. He would have three months to shape up. That was his wake-up call, and he heard it. Fortunately for Everett, he had the courage to break through his discomfort and look inward. Our work together helped him examine his feelings, confront his past, let go of his anger, manage his thinking, and forgive both himself and others. His big lesson was the realization that he no longer had to let his feelings determine his actions.

If this example resonates with you, or you know someone like Everett, keep in mind that the biggest barrier to healing the past is fear. You might unconsciously believe that looking back at early painful memories would be just too overwhelming or embarrassing. Or you might think that acknowledging, accepting, and examining negative feelings makes you weak. Let me assure you that you are far stronger than you realize.

What can you start doing today to grow emotionally? You can stop ignoring those unsettling feelings that make you feel uncomfortable and, possibly, afraid. Embrace them. Notice them. Examine them. That's all you have to do. Negative feelings are often signposts to what you need to work on. Then again, they may just be fleeting intrusions.

Once you are aware of these uncomfortable feelings, what are you supposed to do? Many feel an immediate desire to express them to someone. That may not be the best choice. Expressing your feelings very seldom gets rid of or diminishes them. In fact, by expressing negative feelings at an inappropriate time to the wrong person, you can work yourself into an emotional frenzy. Let me put it another way: Expressing your negativity to others can be life-diminishing, hurtful, or just plain boring. Unless you are with a coach, therapist, or someone who is absolutely willing to listen, don't do it! Your fear-based feelings do not have to determine your actions—ever. In and of themselves, feelings are never the problem. They are a natural part of being human. Learn from them. Use them. Refuse to let them use you.

There is a reason I've spent time helping you understand the need to pay attention to your feelings. As you read this book, complete your exercises, and challenge your thinking, you will most likely churn up a few uncomfortable emotions. That's good. If, though, your feelings are negative, you should resist the urge to act on them. Hit your mental "pause" button. Take a few breaths, count to ten, and, like the wind, they will change direction. As you will see, while you may not have control over your feelings, you needn't despair. You do have control over something far more important—your actions. The following strategy will help you gain control anytime you feel overwhelmed with negative emotions or feel out of control. I urge you to use it!

• • •

Neuroscience tells us that our primitive brain is designed to notice the negative before the positive. From years of personal coaching I have come to see that many people waste 90 percent of their energy in a fruitless attempt to change the unchangeable. It has become clear to me that many who truly desire to transform their lives are often unable or unwilling to acknowledge what cannot be changed. This is not only a waste of time, but it exhausts the Rider and is enormously frustrating. You can avoid this trap by learning to identify what can be changed and let go of the rest—quickly.

This following exercise was inspired by a story I once heard about the great statesman Benjamin Franklin. I don't know if the story is true or not, but I have used the process with great success for more than three decades. It is a perfect tool to help you instantly focus on what you can change and what you can't. Whenever you feel out of control or overwhelmed, use it! This is one of my personal favorites because it helps gain focus quickly. Now, open your journal or turn on your computer and follow the directions.

THE BEN FRANKLIN METHOD

1. As quickly as possible, list everything in every area of your life (mental, spiritual, emotional, physical, and social) that's bothering you now, everything and anything that you are worried about or that you consider a problem, and everything that is causing you stress. Write as quickly as you can. Hold nothing back. Unload your concerns, fears, and troubles. Take as much time as you need.

2. Go through your list and cross out all those things over which you have no control. Get real with yourself and stay aware of your feelings.

3. Review your list and circle everything over which you have some amount of control.

4. For each area over which you do have control, list one action step you can take immediately to remedy the problem.

5. You may not realize it, but by completing these steps you have already taken control by acknowledging what you can't control. Now, think about what you do when you confront the areas of your life over which you have little or no control. Do you get depressed and angry? Do you brood, complain, blame, or dig in and refuse to let go? If you

do, you might consider saving yourself a lot of frustration by taking action, changing what you can change, and letting go of the rest.

6 Now, if you want to go to the next level, reread the action steps you wrote in Step Four and TAKE ACTION NOW!

 LIFE THOUGHT: FREEDOM LIES IN SEEING ALL YOUR OPTIONS.

Because you have very little control over your feelings, you are not responsible for the way you feel. Conversely, because you do have control over your actions, you are both responsible and accountable for your actions and the results of those actions. I hope it's clear to you by now that you do not have to let your actions be dictated by your feelings and, regardless of how you feel, you can always choose what action to take or not take. By challenging this myth, you broaden your options for choice.

Myth Number Six: Love Is Always Conditional

"Love is generally confused with dependence; but in point of fact,
you can have love only in proportion to your capacity for independence."[6]
—ROLLO MAY, *MAN'S SEARCH FOR HIMSELF*

Throughout history love has been the igniting creative spark for hundreds of books, plays, movies, poetry, and art. It has also been the stimulus for both agony and ecstasy; and it has caused wars, mended broken hearts, and healed bodies. How, you might ask, can this one word be the cause of so many things? But is it really? What do you think of when you hear the word "love"? What goes through your mind and body when someone says, "I love you"? What is he or she really saying? What do you mean when you tell someone, "I love you"?

LIFE THOUGHT: PURE LOVE IS ALWAYS UNCONDITIONAL.

As I coach you through this book, I want you to try to view life through the lens of pure love. Pure love is an ideal to strive for, a vision of possibility, a goal to keep you on track for living an exceptional life. I call this pure love because it is the polar opposite of fear, and resonates in a pure sense in harmony with the Elephant. Pure love is love that is given freely with no expectations attached. And it leaves clues. Expressing gratitude, putting others before yourself, volunteering your time, contributing to causes, and performing random acts of kindness are all signs of pure love. When you forgive yourself or others on a moment-to-moment basis, you are also exhibiting pure love. There is a way to determine whether love is pure or not. If you require a response or are hurt when what you give to another is not reciprocated, then what you are giving is conditional love. When love is conditional, it is actually fear and ego in the guise of love.

In his book, *Choosing Joy: Change your Life for the Better*, Gary Null gives us a glimpse of pure love:

> Love is the manifestation of life. Love radiates joy, comfort, kindness and patience. You're drawn to its energy. You know when love is being shared, and when it isn't, by listening to your heart. If someone falsely claims to love you, or tries to prove his love with material possessions, you know it's not real because you do not feel it. You may have lost your ability to love if you are impatient with yourself and others. You will become busy outwardly to compensate for the coldness and lack of love you feel inside.[7]

I vividly recall an experience from my early childhood that had a profound effect on the development of my loving self. I got caught stealing some candy from a local variety store. I was terrified of my parents' reaction and felt deeply ashamed. Before we had a conversation about what I did, my mother looked at me, gave me a hug, and said, "Jim, I want you to know that no matter what you do, you will always have a home and your father and I will always love you." Then I was disciplined. That is unconditional love.

You may be thinking it's all right for parents to give unconditional love and therefore forgiveness to their children, but question whether we should give it to other people. Giving unconditional love may require a shift in your thinking about love, life, and how the burden of unforgiveness can weigh deeply on our spirit. As is noted in 1 Corinthians 13:

> Love is patient and kind; it is not jealous or conceited or proud; love is not ill-mannered or selfish or irritable; love does not keep a record of wrongs. Love is not happy with evil, but is happy with the truth. Love never gives up; and its faith, hope, and patience never fail. In a word there are three things that last forever: faith, hope and love; but the greatest of them all is love.

Pure love is available at every given moment. All you have to do is learn to recognize when you are in a state of unloving, identify the barrier—the fear—let it go, forgive, and return to the state of loving. Does it sound like too big a job? At first, many of my clients feel that it is. I tell them what I now tell you. Forgiving is a skill, and like any skill it can be learned. Learning the skill of forgiveness takes awareness, compassion, practice, patience, and a desire to experience what I call a lightness of spirit. If all this sounds positive, but you feel that forgiving on a consistent basis would be too much effort, I encourage you to reframe your thinking.

Imagine that you and your family have to move into a new home. Everything you have accumulated, every personal possession, must be packed up, loaded, and deposited in another location—all within three hours! How would you feel? Could you do it? Does it seem possible? Is this thought too overwhelming? What if you had six months or even a year to accomplish the task? With one small shift of perception, such a move now seems possible. In the same way, you need to choose the mindset of possibility when you think about transforming fear into love. Letting go simply means that the Rider will help the Elephant remove a lot of useless, cumbersome garbage. You can do this at your own pace as long as you do it consistently. It is work but the payoff is worth it.

When it comes to letting go, consider the metaphor of a computer: If the hard drive of your computer is full and there is no space left, the computer can't take in or even recognize new information. Like a computer, if your mental hard drive is filled up with unacknowledged, fear-based "stuff"—anger, resentments, depression, envy, and jealousy—there will be no space for love.

I would like you to do a very simple exercise. By looking into the mirror of your past, you will recognize those moments when you lost awareness and did not make loving choices. If you learn from the past you will be able to recognize when you respond with fear in the present. It's then that you choose to let go and respond in a loving way.

YOUR TURN

Recall a negative circumstance from the past involving another person or other people. This could be a disagreement with a friend, your child, someone at the checkout counter, a fellow employee, or a neighbor. Search it out in your memory banks and when you have it, replay the scene in your imagination as clearly and specifically as you can.

After you have rerun your mental movie of this past conflict, ask yourself: "Did I attack, defend, blame, speak snidely, criticize, run away, complain, or talk behind someone's back, or did I act and communicate from love, understanding, compassion, and forgiveness?" If you acted from unconditional love in your mental movie, congratulations! But I still want you to recall an event from your past when you didn't act with love. It's there. Find it and replay your mental movie. Allow yourself to be uncomfortable for a few moments. Do it now.

If you vividly reexperienced that conflict, you will realize that at the very moment when your fear-based emotions ran the highest, other people seemed to be unlovable and, possibly, so did you. But you have to remember that other people really are your teachers. That's why it's invaluable for you to use all negative interactions with others as a workshop for learning. Now, run your script again and visualize a peaceful outcome. What new choices did you make to reduce or defuse the conflict? That's the lesson. Take the time to run two or three of your past conflict scripts and determine what other choices you might have made to resolve the issue and heal relationships.

The next time you are feeling unloving or have thoughts of revenge, and there will be a next time, use what you have learned from the past. Once you choose to unburden yourself from being angry, guilty, or holding grudges, you can learn to forgive quickly. When you learn to forgive yourself and others on a moment-to-moment basis, you return to the zone of living in unconditional love. This is a skill you can master, and I will provide you with techniques for letting go and forgiving later on in the book.

Myth Number Seven: You Are Always Aware of What's Going On around You

Are you aware of your awareness? Let's find out. When you complete reading this sentence, I want you to look up and notice your surroundings, your environment. Please do it now.

That wasn't hard, was it? All you had to do was focus your awareness outward.

Now, upon completing the next sentence, I would like you to take ten seconds and focus on your body. Be aware of your eyes blinking, of your breathing, of the weight of your body on the chair or couch. Please do it now.

That should have been easy too, as long as you turned your focus inward to your body. Now, though, I want you to shift your focus again and be aware of the thoughts swirling around in your mind. What thoughts? Whatever you are thinking, saying to yourself, judging, analyzing, fantasizing about, or trying to figure out.

Now stop, take a breath, and once more shift your focus. How do you feel right now? Do you feel angry, sad, happy, hopeful, relieved, burdened, anxious, relaxed, excited, or harried? This time you had to become aware of what many tend to avoid observing—your feelings. But we're not through yet. Finally, I want you to be aware of your awareness.

Years ago a biologist friend of mind made a statement that put the concept of being aware of your awareness in perspective: "When an animal has a pain in its toe, it's aware that it has a pain in its toe. When you have a pain in your toe, you are aware that you're aware of the pain in your toe." This awareness of your awareness is a gift of being human and it is your greatest defense against the ego. It is the built-in function of the Rider, and the spark for change. The question is, do you always use it to your advantage?

How do you become aware of your awareness? You have to fully experience your negativity, fear, and hurt, as well as your joy, excitement, and passion in the moment. To become aware, you must be conscious, present, mindful, awake, alert, and in tune with your surroundings.

LIFE THOUGHT: AWARENESS IS JUST AS IMPORTANT AS INTELLIGENCE.

In a fast-paced technological world where many of us are connected twenty-four/seven, it is a huge challenge to be able to be mindful, to live in the "now" for any length of time, unless you make it a priority to learn the skills necessary to do it. However, doing so is even more important for living an exceptional life than being intelligent, because it is all about the quality and enjoyment of your life experience. While your intelligence may be fairly locked in place—that is, your ability for abstract thought, understanding, emotional knowledge, and problem solving—your awareness, and therefore your appreciation and quality of experience, can be ramped up. Of course, developing your awareness is a challenge, especially when it's so easy to bend to the external pressures of the world, get caught up in performing your daily tasks, or spend your life thinking about what has to be done next.

Developing Your Awareness

One of the most satisfying aspects of my job is to help people expand, grow, and develop their awareness. Once awareness expands, we can identify and shatter the limiting and restrictive myths that create barriers to our mental and spiritual growth. Once we identify and break through limiting beliefs we can make more empowering choices, let go of negative habits, and develop new, empowering behaviors. Therefore, I'm going to devote the remainder of this chapter to giving you a number of strategies and tools to help you develop your awareness and live far more in the present, the now—to spend less time worrying about what will happen in the future and more time controlling what you can control in the present.

I have discovered that the brilliant, critical, skeptical, ever-questioning, easily overwhelmed Rider can come up with a multitude of reasonable excuses that help us avoid confronting ourselves. But if you are committed to emotional and spiritual growth and to creating positive change, you will want to make a commitment to yourself to choose specific small periods of time to slow down and hit the "pause button" in life. It's also important, though, that you understand the "why" behind this idea.

It is when you slow down that you are able to recognize the tug of the Elephant's desire for short-term gratification and let go of the pull of its self-sabotaging fear. It is when you slow down that you can tune into your gratefulness channel. It is when you slow down that you can identify the heavy mental baggage you carry and let it go. One way to do this is to try meditating. I have to admit that when I started meditating in 1972, I felt strange, odd, foolish, and uncomfortable, but it wasn't long before it became a welcomed habit. When you begin using your own relaxation technique, you may feel the same.

So what I'd suggest is that you learn a simple, easy, deep-breathing/relaxation exercise and give it a chance. It will be well worth your while. Going off by yourself for a couple of days would be the best way of learning to do this, but if that's not possible, you can still dedicate short periods of time to quiet your mind through some form of self-relaxation or meditation. Doing a short, five- to ten-minute stress-reduction exercise twice a day will not only increase your awareness, it will give you the mental armor to ward off the negative effects of stress. At the very least, doing a two- to three-minute deep breathing exercise every one-and-a-half to two hours is critical to your creativity, productivity, and clarity of mind.

What follows are three tools and a strategy for developing awareness that may well change your life. (If this is not a good time for you to devote ten minutes to reading the instructions and doing the exercise, I'd suggest that you put the book aside until you are ready and willing to do so.)

Slow Down and Become Aware

The only way to boost your awareness is to make the conscious choice to slow down and learn one of the many relaxation or meditation techniques. I imagine you may be thinking, "I'm just too busy," "I can't find a quiet place," "I can't relax," or "It feels foolish." I understand. But now is the time to put aside a few minutes, pause, take a couple of deep breaths, and slow down. As poet Doug King writes, "Learn to pause . . . or nothing worthwhile will catch up to you."

YOUR TURN

I want you to do this exercise as an experiment for a week. Put your Rider into gear, imagine the next week, and create a commitment schedule. Five minutes, twice a day, for a total of ten minutes a day is all the time required for you to complete it. When you are ready to start, take five minutes, pick a place where you can be undisturbed, and go through the following basic relaxation exercise:

Link Alert: Enter the URL **https://vimeo.com/mapes/3** in your web browser and then the password **"beliefs"** and I will guide you through this relaxation exercise. Or you can simply carry out the instructions that follow.

Close your eyes. Take three deep breaths, slowly inhaling through your nose and exhaling through your mouth. Become aware of your breathing. Become aware of your physical self—the weight of your body against the chair, couch, or bed. Now observe, without judgment, the thoughts that go through your mind, both positive and negative. Simply be aware of them and then let them go. Become aware of the next thought and then let it go. When the next thought comes in, let it go too, and observe the thought behind it, and then let that one go. (When you are doing this exercise it might help you to imagine your thoughts scrolling across a screen, seeing the next thought pass by, and then the next, and the next, etc.) This very basic exercise will help you slow down, develop your awareness, gain perspective, and reduce negative stress. The best thing about it is that you can do it anywhere and at any time, except, of course, when driving or operating heavy machinery.

Creating a Buffer Against the Negative Pull of Fear

Fear makes us do and say stupid things. So the more aware you are when fear has you in its grip, the less likely you are to do or say something stupid. How do you know that you're slipping into survival fear? How can you guard against inappropriately losing your temper? How can you stop yourself from saying or doing something hurtful and cruel? It's a challenge, because intelligence and logic aren't always your best friends. It's only in hindsight that you become aware that you have said or done something you regret. Why didn't you realize it at the time? Because the Elephant went into fear, fear that someone wouldn't comply with a request, fear of possible rejection, fear of being criticized, fear of missing an important call, fear of losing control, and on it goes. So if your intelligence and logic can't help you, what can? Your awareness can.

The "Tool for Truth"

Most people never realize that when you go into a state of fear, the voice of your Rider often deceives you by rationalizing and justifying. However, your body will always tell you the truth. I discovered this quite by accident. As I began doing my own form of daily relaxation exercises I noticed that whenever I was tense, under pressure, or worried about the future, there was a physical sensation of tightness in my chest. By paying attention to my body, I was able to develop the awareness I needed to let go and reframe whatever negative scenarios I was thinking about.

When you go into a state of fear your body also sends a clear message, such as your shoulders tightening, a pain in the stomach, clenched fists, or rapid breathing. Unfortunately, these warning signs are often ignored, dismissed, or have become so familiar that they, in essence, have become invisible. The physical sensation triggered by fear is really a loud voice telling you to "Be Aware!" If you pay attention you can instantly center yourself and gain control. With awareness, you can stop, breathe, shift your focus, reframe and shift your perspective, move through anger, and communicate in a loving way. By learning to be aware of your body's reaction to fear you can manage your mind to buffer fear. This physical sensation is what I call the "Tool for Truth."

In order to use the Rider's visualization ability effectively, you will want to become aware of the tension you feel and the specific location in your body where you feel it. When you are experiencing fear the physical response will always appear in the same area of your body. In my own case, for example, I have learned that whenever I feel fear, there is a tightening sensation in the pit of my stomach. And it never varies. It is my personal early-warning signal, and it gives me the opportunity to be aware of my fear. This provides me with a window to take a breath, do a reality check, and make sure I am not about to act out of fear. It has saved me many times from doing or saying things I might later regret. Now here's a way for you to determine your own personal early-warning signal.

YOUR TURN

First, I want you to close your eyes and vividly recall in detail something that happened in your past that caused you to feel fear, or something you can imagine happening in the future that is frightening. Use all your senses. As you recall the situation that prompted your fear or you create a fear scenario for the future, pay attention to your body.

When you have your fear-based mental movie firmly in mind, answer the following questions: Where, specifically, do you feel your fear? Is there tightness in your stomach, your shoulders, your throat, hands, back, or chest? Is your face flushed? Are you perspiring? These physical sensations are your unique early-warning system. That is your mental alarm going off to remind you to pay attention. Once you are truly in touch with your physical reaction to fear, you can pull back and gain perspective, disassociate yourself from the illusion that fear-based thinking creates, and use your objectivity to gain perspective and reframe. It's like sitting in your favorite chair and watching yourself on a television show. You will learn to separate what is really happening from what your imagination is making up. As paradoxical as it may seem, you become an observer of yourself by being present.

The next time you are in a state of high anxiety, feel overwhelmed, or are aware that you are experiencing an obvious fear-based emotion (anger, resentment, rejection, jealousy, or envy), breathe deeply and slowly count to ten. It will make an immediate difference in the way you feel and therefore the way you think. The Tool for Truth is the ideal mental tool to use when confronted with delayed flights, rude people, and other general frustrations.

Be Aware that Anger Is Almost Always a Cry for Help

Understanding the nature of anger and keeping your perspective is pivotal to maintaining loving relationships. To do this, I want you to consider choosing the mindset that another person's anger comes from fear and is almost always a cry for help. I know that your gut instinct is to meet anger with anger, but you can make a more empowering choice if you remember that anger is the Elephant going into its automatic attack/ protect or flight mode. If you bear this in mind, you give yourself the second or two you need to reframe your thinking, tap into your compassion, let go, and forgive.

I saw a good example of this with my clients Robert and Mia. Robert came home exhausted every day. His workday, including commuting time, was more than twelve hours long. When he arrived home, he just wanted to have a drink, relax, and be left alone for a while. In the meantime, Mia was juggling a part-time job, two children, and a sitter. At the end of her day she was also worn out, and when Robert got home she wanted to commiserate with him, to have him listen to her. The result was that she would get angry with Robert for being emotionally withdrawn and he, in turn, would get angry with Mia for not giving him enough space.

In our first session I instructed them both to write down, in the form of dialogue, what they would like to say to each other, without blaming the other person, suggesting he or she was wrong, or condemning the other's behavior. I suggested to Mia, for example, that rather than saying, "This is your fault, you thoughtless jerk," she say, "When you are not willing to take the time to listen to how my day went, I feel you don't care and it makes me angry." I similarly suggested to Robert than instead of saying, "You are thoughtless because you have no understanding of how tired I am and that I need a little alone time," he say, "When you jump at me the moment I walk in the door without recognizing that I just need a few moments to relax, I feel you don't care." Once they were finished writing I had them switch scripts and read them aloud to each other. Very quickly they both understood that the other's anger was a cry for help, and they made a commitment to be more empathetic and compassionate. Their awareness helped them develop a new mindset. We followed up with a session every month, and three months later they had kept their commitment. They had made the effort to listen to each other and do what needed to be done to have both feel valued and loved.

In other words, when you view another person's anger as a cry for help, you can choose a response that is both compassionate and loving.

Suddenly you have a different perspective on the person who cuts you off and gives you a rude gesture out the car window, the checkout person who snaps at you, the coworker who dismisses you, or your partner who gets angry for no apparent reason. When your ego stops ruling you, when you clearly see what others are really trying to communicate when they are expressing anger, you will spend a lot less time on the battleground of your emotions and a lot more time living a life of peace. And the best way to do that is to practice, practice, and then practice some more.

Living in the Moment: A Strategy for Developing Self-Awareness

Let's look at a simple strategy to develop your self-awareness, break out of automatic-pilot behavior, quiet your thoughts, and open the path to creating positive change. You can use this whenever you feel stressed or fearful.

1 *Stop and observe purposefully.* The next time you are experiencing any fear-based negative emotion, are viewing the world as conspiring against you, or feel as though your head is about to explode, stop. Turn off the radio, television, or smartphone. Close the door, or just walk outside. Take a couple of very deep breaths. Count to ten or do a basic relaxation exercise. You can only observe what you are thinking and feeling when you pause and put on your mental brakes. It is only when you stop that you can shift your perspective by becoming aware of both your thoughts and your physical self.

2 *Pay attention.* After you pause and relax, immediately shift your focus and pay attention to your body. Use your Tool for Truth. You will have a specific physical area or areas that jump out at you when you experience fear. Notice that part of your body, take a couple of deep breaths, and keep your attention focused in the present. A major part of your growth process is learning to be truthful with yourself, to be honest with your feelings, and to deal with negative stress, anger, fear, or resistance at the moment it happens. This means that you can

fully experience—but do not necessarily have to act out—your joy and excitement, or your discomfort, surprise, anger, resentment, or sadness.

3 *Listen to your thoughts.* After you have put on your mental brakes, take thirty seconds and listen to your thoughts, your self-talk. You will notice your mind chattering away with blame, should haves, could haves, or some other form of critical judgment. Simply become aware of your mind chatter, your *Voice of Judgment,* or VOJ.

It's not uncommon for someone to be utterly amazed and stunned at discovering how his or her mind streams with the dialogue of judgment, worry, self-doubt, and negative self-talk. In fact, there's gold to be found within your mental dialogue, because it's there that you will discover how hard you are on yourself and others, and how much you worry about things that will never happen or things you can't control. It is also through listening to your inner voice that you will discover how much negative stress you bring on yourself, and how you can let it go. It really is all in your mind. The more familiar you become with your VOJ, the more rapidly you will grow in self-awareness and the more control you will have over yourself. You will discover that some of those voices are echoes from your parents and teachers, old recordings of negative scripts. You may even come to the point where you realize that maybe, just maybe, the Rider is making it all up!

Everything begins with awareness. Learn to use this gift. It is by developing your awareness that you will move through negative feelings with less resistance. It is through awareness that you will recognize and diminish the hold of fear. It is through awareness that you will discover and let go of attachments that keep you stuck, and it is through awareness that you will find inner peace.

MOVING FORWARD

I've given you a great deal of information and a number of exercises and strategies to experiment with. By making them part of your mental tool kit you will be able to shatter the myths that cloud your thinking. However, as I mentioned earlier, it is also very important for you to write down and record your thoughts, insights, and experiences. If you were a scientist, you would experiment, make notes, and then use those notes to avoid repeating the same mistakes. You are working like a scientist now, a scientist of your mind. You are experimenting, getting feedback, experimenting again, keeping what works for you, and tossing the rest, so you will want a record of it, even if only to look back and review your successes. This is all part of creating new behaviors in order to live an exceptional life. It's also a major step toward becoming an Artist of Possibility. Imagine that!

THINKPOINTS

- Myths can prevent you from experiencing joy, happiness, and pure love.
- You cannot *not* affect others.
- Negative thinking can be used as a suggestion for preparation.
- You cannot always control what you feel.
- Your feelings do not have to determine your actions.
- You can always choose the actions you take.
- Pure love is always unconditional.
- Being aware is more important than being intelligent.
- When you are in a state of fear you will have a physical reaction in a specific part of your body.
- Anger is almost always a cry for help.
- You are writing your own script, so choose what you want to make up.
- Taking action will change the way you feel.

4

BECOME AN ARTIST OF POSSIBILITY

"Be brave to live life creatively. The creative is the place where no one else has ever been. . . . You have to leave the city of your comfort and go into the wilderness of your intuition. You can't get there by bus, only by hard work and risk and by not quite knowing what you're doing, what you'll discover will be wonderful. What you'll discover will be yourself."[1]

—ALAN ALDA

You are an artist, an artist unlike anyone who has ever lived. Your palette is the imagination. Your raw materials are your DNA, your beliefs, and what you can see, taste, touch, hear, smell, and sense. What you create is limited only by what you believe is possible and, therefore, what you perceive. As you will discover, your beliefs literally influence how and what you see and hear. As the artist of your own life, you are defined by both the short- and long-term choices you have made and will make. Your history gives direction to your decisions. The power of focus and the imagination provide color, tone, and texture to your experience.

You are the sculptor of your reality. Reality sculptors fall into three categories—Artists of Restriction, Artists of Possibility, and—where most of us are—something in between.

Artists of Restriction like to play it safe; that is, they are victims of their Elephant's need to maintain the status quo and walk the path most traveled. They are often unwilling or unable to step outside their comfort zone, take risks, challenge their assumptions, recognize and break through fear, or imagine multiple possible futures. Their raw materials are based on what is familiar and comfortable—whatever reflects their belief that the future will be like the past. At the extreme, their imaginations are ruled by limiting myths and their creative spirits are stifled by fear.

Artists of Restriction embody low self-esteem, and are, as Lou Tice writes in *Personal Coaching for Results*, " . . . masters of the put-down and like to point out the faults, flaws, and incompetence of everyone around them. They project onto others the things about themselves they don't like, secretly fear or condemn. And, because they don't have to be accountable or deal with them, they choose to believe that those things are outside themselves. . . . We can continue to deny our own blindness if we can see the blindness in others."[2]

Artists of Possibility, on the other hand, see potential rather than limitations. While they sometimes feel fear, they don't allow fear to restrict their choices. They have developed the ability to transform fear into focused power and energy. They turn failure into learning, judgment into curiosity, and, most importantly, fear into love. Artists of Possibility also question the status quo. At the extreme these outliers might be viewed as troublemakers, people who refuse to follow the crowd, or as just "strange." They are searchers who consistently live in a state of learning and surround themselves with like-minded individuals. They respect the dignity of others. They have learned to create harmony between the Rider and the Elephant.

Once again, though, most of us fall somewhere in between, and unknowingly fluctuate back and forth. My intention is to help you move the gauge and reset your emotional default button so you can spend more time in the zone of possibility. In your effort to do so, your personal history can be your greatest teacher; but it can also throw up barriers to success. Your learned patterns of behavior, and the Elephant's reluctance to take risks, may convince you to play it safe and stop you from venturing out into unfamiliar territory. Whether negative or positive, your ingrained habits and experience make up a kind of programming or software for the brain. However, by self-examination, self-evaluation, and awareness, you can break through comfortable, limiting, familiar, and negative patterns of behavior. You can become a full-time Artist of Possibility by choosing to be accountable, committing to examining your paradigm, learning how to clean up your perceptual filter, becoming aware of your blind spots, learning how to make the invisible visible, and growing through discovery. Let's take a look at these six concepts.

Artists Of Possibility Choose to Be Accountable

"Every human being is an architect of his own fortune."
—APPIUS CLAUDIUS CAECUS, 340-273 BC

Your DNA—your genetic programming—is at the core of the Elephant and is the hard drive of your mental computer. It not only influences your personality but also determines certain things over which you have no control—your gender, the color of your eyes, your height, and other physiological traits. There is a great deal of controversy in the field of science as to exactly how much our genes impact on us in all areas of our lives—including our health and, even, the choices we make. Although the debate between nature (genes) and nurture (environment) is ongoing, research suggests that at least 60 percent of who we are is determined or influenced by our genes. An additional 30 percent of our choices are based on our experienced history—our memories. This 90 percent is essentially the Elephant's memory vault. What about the remaining 10 percent? That is where the Rider's power of influence comes in, where he can become an Artist of Choice.

However, even if you are inclined to believe that you have a predestined future, it doesn't mean you have to go there. There is a great deal the Rider can do to influence the path of the Elephant. According to an article titled "Lifestyle Choices Can Change Your Genes" on the University of Wisconsin School of Medicine and Public Health website, www.uwhealth.org, Dr. David Rakel, director of integrative medicine at the school, says, "A concept known as "epigenetics" empowers people to take control of their health by making choices that may override their genetic code . . ."[3]

So what can people do to minimize their risk of cancer, high blood pressure, heart disease, diabetes or other illnesses that may be part of their genetic predisposition? Rakel says changes in diet, exercise, and personal attitude could actually influence the genetic code and reduce the chances for declining health . . . [T]he concept of epigenetics espouses that lifestyle choices can influence genetic expression. "We have a choice to bathe our genes with joy, happiness, exercise, and nutritious foods, or we can bathe them with anger, lack of hope, junk food and sedentary lifestyle," he says. "This area of research holds so much potential and gives us the hope to say 'Even if my genes indicate a history of family illness, I can make positive lifestyle choices that can keep a gene from being expressed as a disease.'"[4]

Rakel cites a 2007 review by Dr. Steven Schroeder of the University of California-San Francisco. Schroeder's study concluded that the largest influence on the risk of death in America is attributed to personal behavior, such as smoking, obesity, and stress. The paper adds that, even if top-notch health care was available to everyone, only a small fraction of lives (10 percent) can be saved with these high-tech interventions. The largest reduction in death, 40 percent, will result from the adoption of healthier habits.

"Human attitude has a tremendous influence on health," says Rakel. "If you are happy, you are more likely to go out jogging or adopt positive lifestyle behaviors because you have hope. You see what's good in the world instead of what's bad. If I'm seeing what's bad in the world, I won't have the hope that encourages positive lifestyle choices."[5]

But your attitude doesn't impact only on your physical health. Recognizing that you always have a choice means understanding that other people, circumstances, or things cannot make you feel angry, depressed, jealous, or envious. On a subconscious level, you choose your interpretation and response to outside events based on your perception of reality at that moment. Your thinking creates your experience, so how and what you think directly impacts that experience. Your imagination and self-talk add meaning by assigning reasons, evidence, opinions, and judgments. And this concept has huge implications for how you experience everything.

For example, several years ago a singer acquaintance of mine, who was biased against doctors and medicine in general, was having an issue with his vocal cords. He could hardly get through a performance without his throat becoming sore and his voice hoarse. It lasted for weeks and made his job agonizing. Believing he could both diagnose and treat himself, he researched his malady on the web and came to the conclusion that he was straining his vocal cords. Although that didn't really make sense to him—he was professionally trained and knew how to breathe and vocalize properly—he began doing a ten-minute relaxation exercise before he went on stage.

But when the hoarseness didn't go away, his critical and worrisome Rider went into action and he began to worry that his physical problem was symptomatic of something deeper. His fear overrode his logic, and he began to think he might be better off in another profession. Still refusing to take responsibility and do what really needed to be done, rather than seeing a specialist he foolishly sought advice from a number of friends and acquaintances. Not surprisingly, instead of feeling better he felt worse. Eventually I sat him down and had a serious talk about breaking through his fear of doctors and prompted him to see a medical specialist. And guess what happened? The physician discovered he had acid reflux. When he went to sleep, the acid from his stomach was coming up into his throat and wreaking havoc on his vocal cords. One pill a day, and forty-eight hours later, the problem disappeared.

Had he clung to being right about his diagnosis he would never have gotten better. In fact, he might have destroyed his singing career. Because he made choices based on fear, he was unable to see clearly, take responsibility, and do what needed to be done to take care of himself. I don't want you to fall into a similar trap. I want you to break through fear, challenge your assumptions about what you believe, and learn to be accountable for your choices. I want you to learn to take responsibility for where you are in your life, mentally, spiritually, physically, emotionally, and socially. Most important, I want you to make the correct diagnosis of whatever challenge you are facing and seek the treatment that will get you unstuck and moving in a positive direction.

 LIFE FACT: YOU ARE ACCOUNTABLE FOR EVERY ASPECT OF YOUR LIFE AT EVERY MOMENT OF YOUR LIFE.

The bottom line is that if you believe you are at the mercy of what happens to you in life—that you are a punching bag, so-to-speak—then you are choosing to be reactive. If you are reactive, you blame, and when you blame, you give your power of choice away to someone or something that you believe is responsible for where you are in life, what you have, and how you feel. But you do not want to be a victim. You want to be an Artist of Possibility. And you can instantly do that by a simple shift of your mind—by hitting your mental "pause" button and reframing. It really is that easy. You make a decision to be accountable, own your choices, and accept that you create your experience. In other words, you choose to be proactive and take ownership of the statement: "I am free to choose how I react to anything that comes my way, and I am accountable for the choices I make."

If, though, you are unsure of whether or not you believe you should be responsible and accountable for your actions, there's a very simple way of finding out. Ask yourself, "Do I believe that other people should be held accountable for their actions and be punished when they break the law?" If your answer is "yes," then you believe people are capable of free choice. Otherwise how could they be held responsible for their actions?

Now reverse the mirror of this logic. If you believe other people have free choice and must be held accountable for their actions, then you must also believe that *you* have free choice and therefore must be held accountable for your actions.

This is a life fact. We may not like it. We may wish it were another way. We may even try to escape it by any number of diverting activities. But it doesn't matter how much we abhor it or how hard we try to deny it; it's still a life fact. We are accountable for our lives. Gratifying or empty, fair or unfair, ecstatic or painful, good or bad, happy or sad—our lives are our own. We do make choices, we do participate in creating the outcomes in our lives, and we are, at every moment of every day, accountable for those results. If we feel victimized and put upon, we are accountable. If we feel loved, loving, and joyous, we are accountable for that as well.

The first time I conduct coaching sessions with clients it is not uncommon for them to deny accountability for their lives by projecting blame on something or someone outside themselves. As their always-judging and ever-justifying Rider kicks into gear, they call upon their intelligence and logic, defend their stance, and shower me with proof of their "rightness." "I'm overweight because my job doesn't allow me time to exercise." "I don't have sex because my wife doesn't enjoy it." "My relationship isn't working because my wife doesn't understand me." "I hate what I do but I have no choice." At the moment they say these things they are convinced it is happening to them, that someone is doing it to them, that it is out of their control, that it is fate, God's plan, or just plain bad luck.

By the second session, though, they begin to discover and acknowledge that, on some level, they have participated in creating their experience. They also learn another important life lesson—there is nothing to feel guilty about because they did the best they could with the knowledge, awareness, and skills they had at the time. This is an important lesson to learn because blaming yourself for your past choices is not the same thing as being responsible, and to become an Artist of Possibility you must understand the distinction between them. Here's an example of what I'm talking about.

Let's say that your neighbor has been doing something for months that really irritates you. Although you have imagined how good it would feel to do him bodily harm, you have managed to restrain your anger. And then one day you blow your cork, pick up a shovel, and in a blind rage smash him over the head. You've lost control. You intended to cause bodily harm without regard for the consequences, and you are definitely to blame for the act. In fact, you have committed a crime. You may or may not accept responsibility, but you are still at fault. Now let's suppose instead that your neighbor is working with you on a project in your garage, and a board you carelessly placed falls from a rack and hits him on the head. You did not purposefully intend to cause trouble, nor did you foolishly disregard the consequences. It was an accident. You are not to blame. But you are still responsible. That's the difference.

An Artist of Possibility owns his or her experience. How you view your freedom to make choices directly impacts your potential for creating an exceptional life. If you believe that you can choose freely despite your genetic heritage, conditioning, social pressure, and habits, then you are a possibility thinker. It is through your psychological freedom that you will create a life of meaning, passion, and love. I can think of no better example of this than this passage from Viktor Frankl's book, *Man's Search for Meaning*, in which he discusses his experience in a German concentration camp during World War II:

> The experiences of camp life show that a man does have a choice of action. There were enough examples, often of a heroic nature, which proved that apathy could be overcome, irritability suppressed. Man can preserve a vestige of spiritual freedom, of independence of mind, even in such terrible conditions of psychic and physical stress. We who live in concentration camps can remember the men who walked through the huts comforting others, giving away their last piece of bread. They may have been few in number, but they offer sufficient proof that everything can be taken away from a man but one thing: the last of the human freedoms—to choose one's attitude in any given set of circumstances, to choose one's way. The way in which a man accepts his fate and all the suffering

it entails, the way in which he takes up his cross, gives him ample opportunity—even in the most difficult circumstances—to add a deeper meaning to his life.[6]

Artists of Possibility Commit to Examining Their Paradigms

A hallmark of the Artist of Possibility is the willingness to honestly examine what is commonly referred to as his or her paradigm. This paradigm is the standard, or model, for what we believe, and acts as the filter through which we see the world. It is made up of our individual successes, failures, rejections, disappointments, traumas, triumphs, education, and environment, and provides us with an unconscious set of boundaries or mental maps through which the Rider makes choices. It also provides us with a set of rules on how to operate within these boundaries, and tells us what is right or wrong, safe or threatening, good or bad, ethical or unethical. These rules (our beliefs) and the actions we take together make up our individual boxes, which is what defines our comfort zone and our boundaries. If you know your paradigm, know your box, and know yourself, you can open up new possibilities.

• • •

At various times in my career I have experimented with hypnosis, and in the process learned that it can teach us some valuable lessons about how we perceive and deal with the world. Beginning in this section, I am going to present you with two hypnosis demonstrations that dramatically illustrate the power of this technique. Both are pivotal to your understanding of suggestion, communication, belief systems, and perception.

If you are already knowledgeable about hypnosis, these examples will in all likelihood seem perfectly natural to you. If not, you may be inclined to view them as parlor tricks, gimmicks, hoaxes, or just plain off the wall.

Although many people think of hypnosis primarily as a form of entertainment, the fact is that in recent years it has come to be recognized as an extremely effective and useful therapeutic tool that, when used ethically, can do a multitude of good. It can help reduce stress, manage weight, stop smoking, enhance creativity, and even improve one's golf game. Through hypnosis, healing can be enhanced, pain controlled, phobias eliminated, and births made easier. Most important for our purposes, understanding the underlying principles of both hypnosis and suggestion can provide you with valuable insight into how belief systems are formed and how they impact the choices of the Rider. It can also assist you in developing a strategy to help the Rider influence the Elephant. I will accordingly ask you to please keep an open mind about this phenomenon.

You don't really need to understand how to hypnotize someone to appreciate how it relates to managing your mind. Nevertheless, as it can help us understand perceptual filters, communication, and belief systems, it might be helpful if you know, on a very simple level, how it works. Basically, the hypnotist or guide leads an individual, the subject, into a state often referred to as a trance. In this relaxed and receptive state the hypnotist is able to give the subject a suggestion that the subconscious mind, the Elephant, accepts as real. By helping shift the subject's perception, the suggestion temporarily provides the hypnotized individual with a different lens or filter through which to view the world.

The operative word here is "suggestion," which is not only the heart and soul of hypnosis but is also a core influence in daily life. We are, after all, constantly bombarded with suggestions, either from the outside world—the media, politicians, doctors, religious leaders, friends, coworkers—or our own self-talk. Suggestion is powerful stuff. Based on a suggestion given by a hypnotist, a person can instantly feel sad, anxious, joyous, loving, afraid, or any of a wide array of emotions. Suggestion can also dramatically shift perceptions and create hallucinations. Through suggestion, a person can be guided to visualize a healing scenario in preparation for surgery or recall specific information from the past.

The two demonstrations I am about to describe—and present on video links—vividly show the power of suggestion. All the first requires you to do is fire up your imagination, and you can either simply read the description or go to the following link to see the demonstration.

Link Alert: Enter the URL **https://vimeo.com/mapes/4-3** in your web browser and then the password "**lemon**" and I will guide you through the exercise. Or you can simply carry out the instructions that follow.

THE LEMON

Imagine you are holding a big yellow lemon in your hand. Examine it carefully. Imagine touching it. As you run your fingers over the surface notice the small bumps. Imagine smelling it. As you lift the lemon to your nose and take a big whiff, notice how tart the scent is.

Now imagine taking a knife and cutting the lemon in half, picking up one half of the lemon, and giving it a small squeeze. Now you are going to taste it. Visualize it clearly in your mind's eye. You slowly lift the lemon to your mouth and take a big juicy bite. An explosion of sourness blasts your taste buds. You feel the juice dribbling down your chin.

Did you have a reaction? If you really put your imagination to work and focused on the mental image, the odds are that you puckered up your lips or salivated just from reading the description.

This is how I begin all my programs. Following the demonstration, I ask the audience to acknowledge if they had a "real" reaction to the lemon. About 95 percent of them usually do. By focusing on my description of the lemon, their imagination sculpted their "reality" and triggered a physiological reaction out of a suggestion, a mere thought! In this case, illusion becomes reality. This demonstration provides insight into the power of communication, suggestion, and the elegance of the creative imagination. Most important, it demonstrates that the mind and the body are connected and how our thinking affects us on a psychological and physiological level.

Here is another demonstration that vividly shows the power of self-imposed barriers, programming, and being "stuck in the box." Again, you can either just read the description of the demonstration or go to the following link.

Link Alert: Enter the URL **https://vimeo.com/mapes/4-1** in your web browser and then the password **"boxclip"** to see and hear the box hypnosis demonstration as I presented it at Alice Tully Hall in New York City.

THE BOX

First, having hypnotized a man, that is, put him into a highly relaxed and suggestible state, I give him the following suggestion: "When you open your eyes, you will be in a box. The box is ten feet square and you are standing in the center. The walls are invisible and impenetrable. You will not know you are in the box until you attempt to walk out, which will be impossible, but you will forget that I gave you this suggestion."

I then have the gentleman open his eyes. Standing approximately fourteen feet away, I ask him to walk over and stand beside me. He comes toward me until he reaches the edge of the imaginary "programmed" boundary and then stops. When I ask him why he cannot walk to me, he is at a loss to give me a reason.

Attempting to motivate him, I take a hundred dollar bill from my wallet and say, "If you walk over to me and take the hundred dollar bill from my hand, you can keep it." He tries harder to break through his invisible barrier but fails. Pulling out a wad of bills, I offer two hundred, five hundred, and eventually nine hundred. His frustration mounts. He doesn't understand. His intention, willpower, motivation, strength, and commitment have no effect whatsoever on his desired outcome, his goal.

What can we learn from this demonstration? One thing it shows us is the power of negative belief. It might help if you think of negative belief as being like a phobia, a fear carried to a paralyzing extreme. Imagine, for example, that you have full-blown arachnophobia, that is, a fear of spiders, which is a belief carried around by the Elephant. Further imagine that I offer you $10,000 to hold a spider in your hand. It doesn't matter how much you want the money, you can't possibly comply with my request. The Rider is frozen by the Elephant's fear. That's the power of negative belief.

You might be curious as to why I instilled a negative, limiting suggestion in the subject's subconscious instead of a positive, empowering one. The reason is that it is much easier to demonstrate a negative than a positive outcome. Think about it. If you were the hypnotist and I asked you to create a positive hypnosis demonstration, what suggestion would you give and what visible result would you want to create? It is worth considering because, in fact, you are giving yourself and others suggestions all the time with both your words and your actions. The power of suggestion, positive or negative, is powerful stuff! That's why this demonstration serves as a perfect metaphor for the strength and tenacity of your beliefs, your comfort zone, and your mental box.

· · ·

If you are close to my age, you were probably taught as a very young person to stay within the lines as you learned to write. You were instilled with boundaries. As you matured, your learned behavior was reinforced by repetition, self-talk, other people, and your day-to-day routines until they became part of you—your comfort zone and your attachment style rolled into one. As an adult, your Rider makes choices that keeps the Elephant safe within that comfort zone, and as long as safe and familiar choices are made, the Elephant doesn't feel threatened or out of control.

This is where thinking outside the box gets tricky. When you choose to make major changes in your life, you are always going to press up against the boundaries of your box, that is, the comfort of your mental security, the status quo of the Elephant. Even if you are forced by outside circumstances to change, you will almost always come face-to-face with fear. That is why, for almost everyone, the natural knee-jerk reaction to any major change is to do whatever is necessary to stay within the safety of your box, even if doing so is limiting or self-sabotaging. Resistance to change is the action individuals and groups take when they perceive that the change is somehow a threat.

Throughout this book I will continually challenge and encourage you to venture outside your zone of safety and push gently against your comfort zone. You don't have to do it every minute of every day. But I do want you to take well thought-out risks, to recognize, explore, and challenge the limitations of your box, to expand your playing field, and to make the invisible visible. That's the point of the exercises presented in this book. However, before you can believe in possibilities you have to be able to see them, and there is a barrier that stands in the way of your doing so, the lens through which you see the world that I call your perceptual filter.

Artists of Possibility Clean Up Their Perceptual Filters

"Vision is the art of seeing what is invisible to others."
—JONATHAN SWIFT (1667-1745)

In addition to examining your paradigm, it is also necessary to clean up your perceptual filter in order to become an Artist of Possibility. Your perceptual filter is essentially the lens through which you view the world, and is colored by your beliefs, clouded by your fears, and influenced by your biases. The following is a simple example of how this works.

Pretend you are one of four hundred attendees at one of my workshops. You hear me say, "Everyone, look around the room and notice every person who is wearing a red article of clothing." Heads swivel. "Now," I say, "please close your eyes." You reluctantly follow my instructions. "Now," I continue, "I want you to raise your hand if you can recall the general direction of anyone wearing a red article of clothing." I look around the room as I see a multitude of hands rising. "Excellent. You can put your hands down, but please keep your eyes closed. Now, I would like you to raise your hands again if you are able to recall the general direction of any-one wearing a blue article of clothing." There is dead silence and no hands go up. Then you begin to chuckle, as do those around you, as it dawns on you that you cannot fulfill my request.

What you have just experienced, if only in your imagination, illustrates how a simple suggestion can both affect our perceptual filter and influence our expectations. In this specific instance, my suggestion that you notice red clothing shifted your perceptual filter, set up an expectation, focused your mind, and essentially made the color blue invisible! In other words, you saw only what your mind was prepared to see.

The simple fact is that because we view the world through the unique filter of our beliefs, we see the world not as it is but as we are. Have you ever judged a situation or person harshly, only to find out that you were just plain wrong? Or made a decision that someone was trustworthy only to discover the opposite was true? If so, might it not suggest that, at the moment of judgment, you had a specific mindset that influenced your decision? Might that also indicate that you were filtering what you were observing through your beliefs, your values, and your past experiences? The reality is that you project your uniqueness outward on the world. That's why you see the world not as it is, but as you are. Or, to put it another way, every hammer sees a nail.

Looking at the world through your personal perceptual filter is very similar to what you observe when you look at a world map. When viewing a map, you do not perceive the real world—you see a representation, an approximation, of the territory. Your beliefs, positive and negative, right or wrong, also influence the way you experience the world. If your perceptual filter is affected by bias, prejudice, superstitions, and fear, doesn't it stand to reason that the world you see is colored by what you believe? The same holds true with a filter colored by compassion, possibility, and love. The question you have to ask yourself, then, is whether you experience the world through the lens of love or fear?

The bottom line is that your unconscious survival programming is part of you—you need it to keep yourself alive and breathing. It alerts you to dangers and guides you to find whatever resources you need to live and procreate. So you don't want to get rid of your survival self, you want to transform it. You don't want to fight it, you want to honor it. You don't want it to use you, you want to use it. You don't want to ignore it, you want to be aware of it and learn about it. And the only way to transform fear into love is to become aware of what is hidden in your blind spots in life and surround yourself with people you trust to help you see what you cannot.

Artists of Possibility Are Aware of Their Blind Spots

"And folks have a tendency to see what they look for, don't they?"[7]
—STEPHEN KING, *UNDER THE DOME*

As everyone who drives knows, there is a blind spot in every car's side view mirror. It can be more than a little disconcerting when, thinking you can see everything you need to see, you start to change lanes and suddenly come close to getting sideswiped. Like the blind spot in those mirrors, we have blind spots in life. That's the way our brains work. This kind of mental blind spot is called a scotoma, and discovering what your own blind spots are is one of the things you must do if you want to become an Artist of Possibility. Understand, though, that doing so not only requires tremendous desire but also both courage and tenacity.

YOUR TURN

Just to give you a better idea of what I'm talking about, read the following sentence and count the number of Fs in it: FINISHED FILES ARE THE RESULT OF YEARS OF SCIENTIFIC STUDY COMBINED WITH YEARS OF EXPERIENCE.

Now, how many Fs did you find? Most people see only three. There are additional Fs, but it takes more than a casual reading to see them.

It takes work. The reason for this is that, because "of" is pronounced "ov," the brain has trouble processing it. Your subconscious mind has it locked in as "ov" while your conscious mind sees it as "of." As a result, it creates a conflict, and when there is a conflict between your subconscious and your conscious minds, the subconscious wipes out the conscious mind and leaves you with a blind spot. In your eyes it changes the F to a V. That's the power of your subconscious mind.

YOUR TURN AGAIN

Here is yet another example of blind spots. Take your time and play with it a little. On the left of the page you will notice the word "ME." On the right you will see "YOU." Here is what I would like you to do. Close your left eye and keep your right eye fixed on the word "ME." Holding the book out at arm's length, slowly move the book toward you until the word "YOU" disappears. (This usually happens when the page is twelve to fifteen inches away.)

ME   YOU

Where did "YOU" go? It disappeared into your blind spot, and here is why. The human eye has a blind spot in its field of vision. This lies on the point of the retina where the optic nerve leads back into the brain. In 1668, the French philosopher and mathematician Edme Mariotte stumbled on something quite by accident. He found that there is a sizable patch on the retina where the photoreceptors are missing. This missing patch surprised Mariotte because the visual field appears continuous, and there is no corresponding hole of vision where the photoreceptors are missing. But is that really the case?

It may sound logical, but then why don't you see a black hole where the word "YOU" is missing? Why does the space where "YOU" existed appear white like the rest of the page? The answer is that your brain made something up and filled in the empty space, your blind spot, with what makes sense to you—what you will accept and what's familiar. That is, with no information available, your brain fills something in using the information around it. Our imagination is very powerful indeed. After all, it would be a bit jarring to suddenly see a black hole or picture of a long-deceased relative occupying the blind spot where the "YOU" disappeared.

As strange and disconcerting as it may seem, you, I, and the rest of humanity have, metaphorically, a multitude of blind spots based on our unique beliefs, and we all fill in those blind spots with things that we would never question. Are you getting the picture? Based on our previous experience, we make huge assumptions and go beyond the call of duty to make things up. In fact, the Rider makes up a *lot* of stuff, and then believes it's true, even though most of it isn't.

One of the primary causes of this kind of perceptual blindness is something called the reticular activating system (RAS). The RAS consists of a bundle of densely packed nerve cells running through our brain stem that connects with various parts of the brain. It is a control system that is designed to keep out everything that is unimportant or goes against what we believe or for which we have no model. As such, it is part of the Elephant's self-protection mechanism. Its functions, however, are many and varied. Among other jobs, the RAS contributes to the control of sleep, sex, eating, walking, and elimination. Its most important function, though, is its control of consciousness. It can be seen as a chief gatekeeper that monitors and filters the type and quality of information that is allowed into your awareness.

For example, imagine walking through a busy, noisy, and chaotic airport passenger terminal. There are constant announcements, the drone of hundreds of people talking, and the blast of music. It would be impossible to listen to every separate sound; therefore you will only be aware of a general background noise. That is, unless an announcement comes over the PA system stating your name loudly and clearly, calling you to the gate. Suddenly your attention becomes laser sharp. Your RAS has done its job. This automatic mechanism inside your brain has brought the information that is important to your attention. In a very real sense, you remain blind to everything else.

The RAS, then, is the filter between your Elephant and Rider, and it allows only two kinds of information to reach the Rider—information that is important to you right now and information that alerts you to real or perceived danger. Although the potential benefits of this are obvious, it can also create blind spots that have negative consequences. For example, it may make it impossible for you to see unhealthy and self-destructive habits. It may make you unable to recognize energy-draining relationships. It may also keep you from seeing the truth of the way things are, particularly if the way things are is threatening.

The good news is that the RAS can also be influenced by the Rider, and therefore influence the Elephant. This opens up interesting possibilities. It means that you can deliberately program the RAS and influence the Elephant by choosing the exact message you want it to receive. The even better news is that most of our blind spots are not due to our genetic programming or any physiological phenomenon. They are the result of our conditioning, our beliefs, and our expectations—that is, the Elephant. Even more important, it is possible for you to bring a great many blind spots to conscious awareness—that is, to the Rider's attention. You can do this by asking the right questions of yourself, challenging your assumptions about what you believe to be true, surrounding yourself with others who are willing to tell you the truth, or choosing a therapist or coach to play the role of questioner. That, in short, is how you get a glimpse into your blind spots. You ask questions. And once you see the truth about your life, you can never *not* see the truth again.

Speaking of which, the sentence in which I asked you to look for Fs earlier in this chapter actually has six of them. And now that you know, you can never *not* know. Take another look: FINISHED FILES ARE THE RESULT OF YEARS OF SCIENTIFIC STUDY COMBINED WITH YEARS OF EXPERIENCE.

Artists of Possibility Make the Invisible Visible

Another trait of the Artist of Possibility is the ability to make the invisible visible. As in the color exercise earlier in which red became the mindset and therefore visible in a conscious awareness, Artists of Possibility make what is nurturing, healing, comforting, and loving visible by the way they think and believe, and therefore what they notice and attract.

Earlier I spoke of how hypnotism can help us develop a better understanding of how we perceive of and deal with the world, and provided the first of two demonstrations of the technique. This second demonstration illustrates how our beliefs can render potential possibilities virtually, if not literally, invisible. Again, I present it as I do in front of an audience.

Link Alert: Enter the URL **https://vimeo.com/mapes/4-2** in your web browser and then the password "**invisible**" to see and hear this demonstration as I presented it at Alice Tully Hall in New York City.

THE INVISIBLE NUMBER

Having put a woman into a deeply relaxed state, I make the following suggestion to her: "You cannot remember the number seven. In fact, you cannot say the number seven, see the number seven, or hear the number seven. In your reality, the number seven does not exist, but you will have no memory of my giving you this suggestion."

Then I have her open her eyes. She is fully conscious, awake, and aware. I ask her to count from one to ten. Without hesitation she counts up to six and then proceeds directly to eight. That is, she skips the number seven, apparently without realizing that anything is amiss.

I then ask the audience to yell out the total of four plus three. A loud roar of "Seven" fills the auditorium. I ask her what she has heard, and she answers, "Nothing" or "A noise." The Rider is already justifying this sharp twist of reality.

Next, I write a series of numbers on a flip chart and ask the woman what she sees. She identifies "two," "five," and "eight." I then write and ask her to identify the number "seven." What do you think happens? She cannot recognize it as a number, or sees nothing at all. For all intents and purposes the number is invisible. Of course, everyone else in the audience can perceive the number "seven." In a sense, the woman is living in another reality, an alternate reality, but one that is as real to her as everyone else's is to them.

This may seem impossible to you, but it's true. I have done this demonstration hundreds of times, and the result is always the same. Just in case, though, you still have doubts about the concept of invisibility, here are a few additional examples.

In Stephen Simon's book, *The Force Is with You*, the Hollywood producer relates this story. During Ferdinand Magellan's trip around the world in 1519, when his fleet of enormous ships arrived at primitive islands, the natives usually fled in fear. However, writes Simon, "One day, the fleet sailed into the bay of an island, and to the amazement of all aboard, the natives onshore paid no attention whatsoever. They simply went on about their daily chores without the slightest shred of concern for these foreign invaders."[8] Even more interesting was that when the crew transferred to the much smaller longboats and headed toward the island, the natives did react with great fear. After Magellan's priests learned the language of the locals, they discovered something amazing. These islanders did not react to the large ships because they could not physically perceive them! While they could see the longboats, which frightened them, their filter, their belief system, and their paradigm could not "let in" the images of the ships. These massive structures remained literally invisible to them!

Another, if slightly less dramatic, example comes from my own experience.

My wife and I were on a two-week tented safari in Kenya. The first day we ventured out early in the morning in search of what is referred to as the "big six," the larger animals that form the core of the experience. (And I can assure you that it was only the expectation of seeing these animals that motivated us to get out of a comfortable cot at 4:00 a.m.!) As dawn broke on the Masai Mara, our guide scanned the horizon and asked us, "What do you see?" We looked, straining to see shapes or movement on what seemed to be an empty plain. We informed him that we saw very little. "Let me tell you what I see," he said, then proceeded to point out all the animals and their camouflage. I was amazed at how blind my wife and I were to what was right before our eyes. "Give it a little time," he continued, "and you will see what I see. You will develop 'safari eyes' and I will help you do it."

My final example concerns my wife's apparently uncanny ability to find parking places on the streets of New York City. Is this some kind of magic? No. It's all about the mindset. She visualizes the end result, sees it taking place, believes it will happen, and then lets it go. She has, unknowingly, put the Elephant in tune for what she wants to happen. (She also has a deep commitment to achieving her goal of not having to pay forty dollars for parking!) For that reason, with all these factors in place, and her perceptual antennae on full alert, Susan is able to see clues and notice what she might have missed if she had a different mindset. Her expectation guides her to notice someone walking toward their automobile, a car door opening, brake lights blinking, or an empty space. Her belief, combined with her mental movie or visualization of finding a parking place, almost always becomes her reality.

She is able to do this because, in a sense, we see with our brain, not our eyes. The more we learn, experience, and develop our awareness, the more we will be able to notice specific patterns, make predictions, and tap into the intuition of the Elephant. Seeing is active, not passive. Still not convinced about something being invisible to you? Do you think you are immune to having blind spots and that your personal mental map of the world doesn't limit what you perceive? You might want to think again.

YOUR TURN

Where you choose to focus is your reality. What you focus on, positive or negative, renders everything else essentially invisible. What you must do, then, is learn to make what you want—but don't have—visible. You can start with this exercise.

Close your eyes, then summon up a mental picture or image of an object that you believe to be in your immediate environment, something that up until this moment you have not focused on. Take your time. Once you have the image clearly in your mind, open your eyes and look around. Can you instantly see the object that matches your mental image? Did you notice how your focus narrows?

Practice this both indoors and outdoors. Repeat the exercise until you "see" something that you had not previously noticed. Once you've become accustomed to doing it, you will understand that in order to become aware of potential choices, you must first have the mindset, positive expectation, and mental picture, image, or belief of what can be before you can actually see it.

 LIFE THOUGHT: YOU SEE AS YOU THINK.

Have you ever lost your car keys only to discover that they were hiding in plain sight, or overlooked a garment for which you were searching only to later find it right before your eyes? We've all had the experience. It is neither wrong nor uncommon to be blind to what is right in front of us. But this doesn't apply only to physical objects. If you don't see a possibility at this present moment, it is most likely because you haven't prepared your mind to see it. As brain science has shown, learning to manage your mind allows you to see new possibilities. When your mind is prepared, you truly do make the invisible visible. In a sense, you de-hypnotize yourself from old, limiting mindsets.

So what reality do you live in? No matter what information, communication, opportunity, or relationships exist, you notice only what your paradigm, your mindset, and your perceptual filter allow into your awareness. But when you learn to shift your thinking and make the invisible visible, you soon begin to notice something quite wonderful and exhilarating—you realize that everything you have ever wanted may be immediately available to you right now. Because you see as you think, changing the way you think will change what comes into your life.

Artists of Possibility Grow through Discovery

Artists of Possibility learn from the past and apply the lessons to creating the future. They learn what their emotional triggers are—those events or circumstances that prompt the "fight" response of anger, blame, and fear—as well as the beliefs that underlie them. And they accept responsibility as the creators of their own experience. Because you are an Artist of Possibility, I'm again going to ask you do something a little out of the box, perhaps out of your comfort zone. I'm going to ask you to re-create another negative emotional experience from your past to help you learn about you.

Are you ready? The way you are going to learn about you is to find fault with yourself. As startling as that thought may be, it's an extremely effective means of gaining insight into how you are the creator of your experience and responsible for your actions. You can accomplish this by using a specific "fault-finding" process that will help "de-bias" the way you see yourself and help clear the lens of your perceptual filter. The exercise will call upon you to mute your inner justification and rationalization voice. Fortunately, you have an effective tool at your disposal by which to do this—saying "Isn't that interesting."

Before you start to re-create the negative experience, though, for the sake of objectivity I think it would be advantageous for you to get some mental distance. So here's a suggestion: Pretend that you are a "detective of the mind" who is gathering evidence to solve a puzzle. In doing so, it's important for you to keep some important guidelines in mind.

- Record your observations. Every good detective knows how important it is to record information so that you can reflect back on your observations and discoveries. Have your journal or computer ready.

- Cast aside all need to justify or blame yourself or others. Recognize and set aside your judgments until all the information is in. You know that when you blame, you are blind, so if you find yourself placing responsibility on someone or something outside yourself, stop it! And if you become aware that you are blaming yourself, put on the brakes, take a couple of deep breaths, observe, and say to yourself, "Isn't that interesting."

- Face the reality of "what is" and let go of "what you want to be." We all live in our own form of illusion. I don't mean that as some metaphysical musing but rather that our conditioning, beliefs, myths, and history color our thinking, perceptions, and experience—that is, what we consider reality. But in order to solve this puzzle, you must recognize that it is not about wishful thinking. It is about honestly, truthfully, and totally facing your life without rose-colored glasses and making friends with reality. It is about having the courage to momentarily set aside your dreams and your hopes in order to examine every aspect of your life—mental, physical, spiritual, emotional, and social.

- Get tough with yourself. As you get ready to solve this puzzle, you must recognize that you are examining emotionally charged negative aspects of your life and that there is a possibility that your Elephant may go into survival mode. You must understand, too, that if that occurs, the Trickster will attempt to dominate your consciousness. So you must make the decision to resist all temptation to justify, and to shut down the voice of the Trickster before you get swept away in rationalization. You must commit yourself to being brutally honest, tough-minded, and brave. After all, the mind you save may be your own.

Recreating a Negative Experience

Now let's begin. Take your time, scan your past, and choose a major emotionally charged event that led to a negative outcome, specifically one in which someone was hurt or diminished in some way. It could be a disagreement with a friend, sibling, or parent, or an argument with your child, spouse, boss, or financial planner. Maybe it was a divorce, rejecting or betraying someone you love, being passed over for a promotion, or passing someone over for a promotion. If you prefer you may also choose a current life circumstance with which you are feeling dissatisfied, unhappy, disappointed, angry, resentful, bitter, or incomplete. Doing this does take courage, but remember that you are only playing a game, and the game is to glean information about how what you said, didn't say, and did, or didn't do contributed to the negative outcome. Once you have recalled the circumstance, write it down. It may be a few sentences or a paragraph. Writing it or typing it in your computer helps bring the memory back as vividly as possible.

Now I want you to read over what you've just written and, being conscious of how you feel, ask yourself the following questions:

- What choices might I have made that could have contributed to this negative result?
- What might I have said or done that led to the creation of this negative outcome?
- What might I have said that would have led to a positive outcome?
- What did I miss? What might I have paid more attention to?
- How did I separate myself from others by the actions I took or the words I said?
- What old patterns of behavior led me to this outcome?
- What negative or destructive habits do I have that might have contributed to this event?
- What view do I have of other people that might have contributed to this outcome?

Remember that the point of this self-questioning is discovery. There is nothing you have to do or say. Just notice if what you discover could be a pattern. What doesn't get acknowledged doesn't get changed.

Here is a very straightforward discovery that a client of mine made. Every time his wife asked him to do a household task for the third time—just as his mother had when he was a boy—he snapped back in anger, just as he had snapped back at his mother. It had long since become a habit. However, once he discovered this pattern, he sat down with his wife and gently let her know that he hears her the first time she asks, and that he will gladly perform the task as long as she gives him a little time to do it at his own pace. Issue resolved. Of course, many issues are not that simple or straightforward, but discovering our old habits and emotional triggers based on past beliefs can pave the way for loving relationships.

Once you have exhausted this self-interrogation, do your best to answer the following questions:

- What other choices could I make in the future knowing what I now know?
- What do I need to believe in order to change my old behavior?
- What do I need to change in order to break the pattern of old behavior?
- What do I need to communicate to others so as not to repeat my old behavior?
- What support do I need to make these changes?
- What is the payoff for hanging on to resentment or anger?

The purpose of asking yourself these questions is to discover a belief or behavior that you can recognize as being a problem, and that you will, hopefully, commit to changing. Discovery begins with awareness. Once you have the information, you have a goal. And once you have a goal, you can develop an action plan to achieve that goal. If you are honest with yourself in doing this exercise, it is likely that you will find and accept responsibility for at least one fear-based thing you said or did that was hurtful, insensitive, mean, rude, or unkind, and that contributed to a negative outcome. If you can make amends in any way, please do so. If you can, you will discover that, along with the feeling of discomfort, you will get a sense of satisfaction. In fact, you will in all likelihood not only feel gratified but maybe even a little proud for taking responsibility for your own behavior.

"If you look for the truth outside yourself,
it gets farther and farther away.
Today, walking alone,
I meet him everywhere I step.
He is the same as me,
yet I am not him.
Only if you understand it in this way
will you merge with the way things are."[9]

—TUNG-SHAN (807-869)

TRANSLATED BY STEPHEN MITCHELL

• • •

As you can now see, Artists of Possibility are those who choose to be accountable, commit to examining their paradigm, learn how to clean up their perceptual filter, become aware of their blind spots, learn how to make the invisible visible, and grow through discovery. As you can also see, becoming an Artist of Possibility isn't easy, but the difference it will make in your life is incalculable.

Of course, there are times in life when "stuff" happens. People accidently bump their heads, break down, get sick, or depart this earth. Fear grips the market, stocks plummet, and gas prices soar. Tornados and hurricanes strike. Things happen that you can't control. But you can always control your reaction to what life throws your way. Imagine that!

THINKPOINTS

- You are the artist of your life, the sculptor of your reality.
- There are three kinds of reality sculptors—Artists of Restriction, Artists of Possibility, and those who are somewhere in between.
- You are accountable for every aspect of your life at every moment of your life.
- When you blame, you're blind.
- You must believe in the possibility *before* you can see it.
- You see as you think.
- You create your own experience by and through the choices you make at every moment.
- You cannot always control what happens to you, but you can control your reaction to what happens to you.

5

MEET YOUR NEEDS

"Fulfillment can only be achieved through a pattern of living in which we focus on two spiritual needs: 1) the need to continuously grow; and 2) the need to contribute beyond ourselves in a meaningful way. All dysfunctional behaviors arise from the inability to consistently meet these needs."
—TONY ROBBINS

How many people really have their needs fulfilled? How many have given up hope that their needs will ever be met or have subjugated their needs to others and feel lost, bitter, resentful, angry, or hopeless? How many individuals are afraid to ask for what they need or attempt to gratify their needs in totally inappropriate ways? More important, how many have stopped long enough to even identify their needs?

When clients first walk through my door, the majority of them absolutely believe they know what their needs are. Before long, however, many of them discover that their energy has been consumed in a futile attempt to satisfy what they have been led to believe should be important. And that's because most of them have not yet taken the time to differentiate between what they want in the moment and what they need in the larger frame of their life to feel loved, creative, and fulfilled.

Needs are complicated and sometimes difficult to define because they often include your goals, dreams, core values, and lifestyle. Determining exactly what our needs are is also complicated by the fact that even the effort to do so can be very unsettling to the Elephant and therefore to the

Rider. This is because, while the Rider may be the great visionary, problem solver, and pathfinder, the Rider also has issues of denial and the tendency to worry and overanalyze. In addition, the Elephant makes instantaneous decisions as to whether it likes or dislikes something and does not like to be observed. You can see the challenge. If you add the Rider's and the Elephant's weaknesses together, the freedom of—and ability for—self-reflection are clearly a challenge. You can overcome this challenge, but in order to do so you must learn and use the mental tools necessary to play to the Elephant's and Rider's strengths. You can calm down the Elephant by choosing to pause and relax, while at the same time help guide the Rider to analyze and problem solve by asking specific questions.

In order to make the choices necessary to live your exceptional life, you will want to have a clear understanding of who you are and what you want at your deepest level, the level of your values and needs. Once you have this data you will have a better understanding of what motivates the Elephant. Only then can the Rider create a clear and vivid picture of what will serve you best in the future and guide you to focus on completing the goals that will help you get there. This is how to play to the strengths of both the Rider and the Elephant.

The "Twenty-Five-Square Game"

The process of self-discovery can be tricky, and for that reason I've devised a game that enables you to take an indirect approach to defining your needs by first having you identify what is most important to you now. Only then can you determine whether the actions you are taking are in accordance with your life priorities. It is very important to approach this exercise with the correct frame of mind—that of playing a game. As with all games, though, there are rules. If you break the rules, the game is point-less and the results useless. The beauty of this game is that you can only win. Like opening a box of Cracker Jack, you always get a prize, even though you will have no idea what the prize is until you get it. In order to play the game most effectively, make sure you will not be disturbed for the ten to fifteen minutes it will take you to complete it.

Link Alert: Enter the URL **https://vimeo.com/mapes/5-1** in your web browser and then the password "**squares**" and I will guide you through the game. Or you can simply follow the instructions below.

SETUP

On a journal page or blank piece of paper, draw four vertical lines dividing the paper into five equal sections, or as close to equal sections as you can. Next, draw four horizontal lines also spaced equally apart. You now have twenty-five squares or rectangles of fairly equal size in the form of the chart below.

THE RULES OF THE GAME

- *Play the game with the courageous soul of a warrior and with 100 percent commitment.* The game requires you to make choices, and you may find them difficult to make. But make them you must, even if in doing so you feel uncomfortable, frustrated, or experience pangs of guilt or loss. It is important to notice your emotions and feelings—your experience is the soul of the game. It is also important to finish the game and get your personal information down because you will need that information to answer what I call a "Magic Wand Question" in the next chapter.

- *Provide the information as instructed.* You are going to list five specific pieces of information in five different categories of your life, one in each of the twenty-five spaces. Make each answer as short as possible.

- *Write the requested information in each category in any order you choose.* You can fill in all five spaces in each category horizontally, vertically, or randomly among the twenty-five spaces. In the end it will not matter how you choose to position your information. If you are unable to think of anything to write, place a "0" in the box so you know the space cannot be used for any other answer.

- *Make your choices even when those choices are difficult to make.* Once you have written your choices, you may not go back and change them.

THE GAME

Now let's get started. In five of the spaces I would like you to write down the names of the five individuals who represent the most important relationships in your life, whether they are living or deceased, positive or negative. Put one name in each space. You may include a pet if you wish, but you may not write down a group like "my family" or "my friends." If you have six children and a spouse you must make a choice, even if the choice is difficult. If you cannot think of five relationships, put a "0" in any empty spaces. Upon completion you will have five spaces filled in.

In the next five spaces I want you to write five plans you have for the future, with one plan in each space. When I refer to plans I don't mean something as trifling or mundane as having dinner tonight, getting your hair cut, or taking the car in for servicing. I am talking about plans that are more meaningful, such as vacationing in that place you have always dreamed of seeing, visiting a loved one who you have not seen in a long time, or writing a novel. You are only limited by your imagination. Again, if you cannot think of five plans, put a "0" in any empty spaces. Once you are finished you will have ten spaces filled in.

Next, I would like you to write down five material possessions to which you feel attached. How do you know if you are attached to a material item? It's easy. Ask yourself, "If this item was lost, stolen, or destroyed, would I be upset?" If your answer is "yes," you're attached to that item. (By the way, should you have any doubt, a person is not a possession.) If you cannot think of five material possessions, put a "0" in the empty spaces. Upon completion you will have fifteen spaces filled in.

Now I want you to list five character traits you have that you admire. These might include honesty, integrity, being a good friend, loyalty, reliability, charitableness, enthusiasm, etc. Again, if you cannot think of five character traits, put a "0" in any empty spaces. When you are finished you will have twenty spaces filled in.

At this point I would like you to list five elements of your lifestyle that you consider important. What I am talking about here are such things as spirituality, creativity, sociability, healthfulness, etc. How do you know if an element of your lifestyle is important? Imagine if that element was somehow suddenly taken away from you. If you feel that such a loss would diminish the quality of your life, then it is important to you. If you cannot think of five important elements of your lifestyle, put a "0" in the empty spaces. Once you have finished you will have all twenty-five spaces filled in.

Now comes the tricky part. Please pay attention and follow the next set of instructions to the letter. Once you begin, plunge ahead with speed. If you over-think this part of the exercise, you will inhibit that part of your mind that already knows the truth about your deepest desires and beliefs—that is, your intuitive self. In this final step of the game you are going to eliminate the twenty-one items that are the least important to you at this moment in your life, leaving the four that are most important. Again, it is essential that you do this quickly. If you feel guilty as you let go of items in making your choices, experience it, let it go, and keep moving. No one is judging you but you. Now . . .

1 Quickly scan the page of twenty-five spaces.

2 As rapidly as you can, start eliminating the spaces in groups of three by putting an "X" through the square. I suggest you begin by eliminating any space you previously marked with a "0." Pause and take a breath in between each set.

3 Eliminate the first three spaces. Now, take a breath and . . .

4 As fast as you can, eliminate the next three. Take another big breath and . . .

5 Eliminate the next three.

6 Move on, eliminating groups of three until you have only four boxes remaining.

7 When you are finished, circle the four remaining boxes.

EXPLORING YOUR RESULTS

Out of the twenty-five filled-in squares, you now have only four remaining. Take a moment to contemplate your results. Are you surprised? How do you feel about what you eliminated? How do you feel about your remaining four choices? How did you feel about the exercise? The exercise may churn up a great deal of emotion, but it can also give you enormous insight into why and how you made your choices.

In order to help you do that, on a separate page of your journal, I want you to list your four choices horizontally across the top of the page. Under each choice list as many thoughts, insights, or observations as you can about each choice. Go for quantity, and ask yourself the following:

If one or more of the remaining choices was a future plan, ask yourself:

What do I need to do in order to achieve what I say I want? What steps can I take right now to move toward my goal? How can I make what I now have even more meaningful?

If one or more was a material possession, ask yourself: Why am I attached to this possession? How does it make me feel knowing I own it? How would I feel if this possession were taken away?

If one or more was a relationship, ask yourself: Do I give enough attention to this relationship? How can I further enhance and nurture this relationship? How would I feel if this relationship disappeared?

If one or more was a personal character trait, ask yourself: Do I always act in accordance with this personal attribute?

If one or more was an element of your lifestyle, ask yourself: Do I consistently take the steps necessary to support this lifestyle? What can I do to enhance this lifestyle?

There are two reasons that I wanted you to complete the "Twenty-Five-Square Game" at this point in the book. The first is that I wanted you to determine your top four life priorities. The second is that I wanted you to take a hard look at the way you live your life and do the best you can to answer this question: Are the actions I am taking in my life in accordance with what I say is most important to me? By determining whether or not they are, you will be performing a reality check, which will in turn enable you to determine if where the Rider is focused is leading you in the direction of living an exceptional life. If not, you can make a course correction.

A Personal Wake-Up Call

A reality check can occur without doing an exercise. Sometimes life just gives you a wake-up call, and if you are mentally prepared, you can use it to your advantage.

My aortic valve replacement was certainly the biggest wake-up call I ever had. But in spite of, or because of, all the fear and emotional turmoil, the experience gave me an opportunity to grow emotionally. In fact, recognizing the magnitude of this event early on, I made a decision to use it as a growth experience, which I would then incorporate into my coaching and speaking. As a result, what could have been a psychologically agonizing experience instead led to my developing a program called Patient Pre-Op/Post-Op Healing Therapy™, which I subsequently transformed into the program "Mind Over Body: Harness Vision to Create a Wellness Strategy." Although originally designed to help pre-op and post-op patients, the life lessons that form the core of the program—"The Five Keys to Living an Exceptional Life"—can actually be applied to all areas of life. In addition, they are perfect tools to assist you in fulfilling your needs, achieving your goals, and creating your future.

 Link Alert: Enter the URL **https://vimeo.com/mapes/5-2** in your web browser and then the password "**fivekeys**" to see and hear me speak about the "Five Keys to Living an Exceptional Life." This is also explained below.

The Five Keys to Living an Exceptional Life

1 *Make friends with reality.* If I had slipped into denial when I was first diagnosed with an aortic aneurism, or refused to have surgery quickly, I wouldn't be here today. The lesson is clear. Making friends with reality and acting based on "what is" give you an enormous opportunity to turn fear into positive action, prepare, seek out the best help possible, make a plan, and execute it. The bottom line is that making friends with reality gives you the edge in controlling what can be controlled and letting go of the rest.

2 *Adjust your attitude.* I'm sure that virtually everyone has heard about the importance of having a positive attitude. However, I'm not sure that everyone realizes that attitude is both a choice and a tool for healing. While I was in Yale/New Haven Hospital I received incredibly wonderful care from the staff, which prompted me to do a small

study about attitude. Approaching five of the senior nurses, all of whom had been on the cardiac floor for over twenty years, I asked each one, "Have you noticed that attitude influences a patient's recovery?" Their responses (as well as those of hundreds since) were almost identical. "I have seen patients," they said, "who should have recovered without incident but had severe issues. These were patients who berated the nursing staff as well as family members who visited. They complained constantly, blamed everyone for their situation, and didn't express their gratitude for the care they were receiving. Then there were patients whose physical situation suggested they would have a terrible recovery or even worse, but who recovered and healed faster than expected. These were also patients who were calm, loving, and expressed their gratitude for the care they were getting." The lesson is that attitude is a choice. As trite as this may sound, you choose to focus on the glass being half-full and to express your gratitude for your caregivers. In life, your attitude affects everyone from your coworkers, team, and clients to your family, friends, and social network. You can choose to be a life enhancer.

3 *Create a solid support system.* I have encountered people who either find the idea of a support system to be too "touchy-feely" or believe they can handle everything alone. This is a misguided view on many levels. Having a support system doesn't mean that you must have an individual or group constantly hovering around you. It simply means that you have people who are available to support you, and all you need to do is have the courage to ask for help, be willing to receive it, and say "Thank you." A few of my dear friends kept my wife company during the seven hours of my surgery. But the real support came into play when I returned home to recover. Every day for well over two weeks my wife arranged for friends to drop by for thirty minutes. I cannot tell you how joyful I felt. In spite of my physical limitations and blurred thinking, their visits brought me peace and gave me comfort. I know beyond a shadow of a doubt that it positively influenced my healing. Having support will serve you in every area of life. It gives you the opportunity to be with like-minded people, share

information, and learn. It can help you process feelings and communicate your ideas without being judged. Knowing that you have a support system lets you know that you are not alone. Of course, the key is to carefully choose the people with whom you surround yourself. The lesson, though, is to make sure your support group is in place before you find yourself in a crisis. In your personal life that means having friends and acquaintances, while in business it means surrounding yourself with the best team possible. But how do you create a support system? It's simple. We are wired in our DNA for reciprocity, meaning we are programmed to return favors. So look around for those who need help and support and give it to them. If you do that, when you are in a crisis you will have all the support you need.

4 *Ask for help and express your gratitude*. Friends, coworkers, and caregivers really do need to know you need them. You would be surprised how hurt, useless, or ignored others can feel when they don't feel needed and, of course, appreciated. Expressing gratitude is equally important. Rest assured a simple "Thank you" goes a long, long way. So set aside your ego and ask for help, and be sure to let people know it when you appreciate something they've done for you. It will be a win/win for everyone.

5 *Create a vision that will carry you through a crisis*. For many years I've created customized programs to help people achieve their goals as well as to assist individuals in preparing for surgery and aid them in their healing. The program for presurgery patients that I call the "closed-eye process" consists of three parts that are designed to calm the Elephant, mute the Rider's tendency to worry, and release our natural healing process. While the program, as it's described below, includes some form of coaching, either in person or through an audio program, the skills it requires can be easily mastered and applied to any goal-achievement process. In the first part patients go through stress reduction and imagery exercises to ensure they will go into surgery both relaxed and calm. In the second, a positive expectation is set up by having patients imagine going through surgery successfully and

coming out on the other side already on the way to healing. The third and final part helps instill hope for the future by enabling patients to visualize a vivid, emotionally charged mental movie of being with people they love, going on an adventure, or already having achieved a dream goal. This part of the process acts as a kind of positive tension pulling them into a joyful, exciting, imagined future. As with any successful relaxation/visualization process, it is essential to reinforce the emotionally charged "future" mental programming by visualizing twice a day for one to two weeks before surgery. This reduces negative stress and changes the brain, so instead of experiencing fear the patient experiences hope, relaxation, trust, and positive expectations.

The most important thing to take away from this key is to recognize the monumental importance of applying your imagination through visualization. Throughout the remainder of this book you will be asked to apply your imagination or visualize a number of scenarios. When you do, you must remember that the Elephant cannot tell the difference between a real experience and one imagined by the Rider. So, visualization—that is, seeing a goal as already accomplished—puts the brain in gear to take the necessary steps to achieve that goal.

• • •

This wake-up call not only gave me the gift—Five Keys to Living an Exceptional Life—that I could pass on to others, it also prompted me to examine my life as it was at the time and how it might change when I recovered. I had to ask some tough questions. Have I made the most of my life? What do I regret? What would I have done differently? What relationships do I need to heal? Are my wife, family, and close friends happy? Have I helped and supported them to achieve their needs? What does my work give me besides an income? How much is enough? What could I do to be happier? How much of my time do I want to give away? And, if all went well with the surgery and I totally recovered, what would I do differently?

Since identifying these Five Keys, I have made them the cornerstone of my efforts to help others take an active part in their overall wellness on a daily basis. If you take the time to reflect on your life—mentally, physically, spiritually, emotionally, and socially—through the lens of the Five Keys, you will open up possibilities for taking your life to the next highest level.

You can begin right now. Commit to "making friends with reality" by *honestly* looking at the choices you are making now and asking yourself how you can make even better choices about such things as your relationships, how you deal with fear, what you input into your brain and body, and how you meet your needs. Examine your attitude and, if needed, learn how to adjust your thinking so it is as positive as it can be, and ramp up your passion and motivation for life. Create a solid support system by doing as much good for others as possible, putting yourself out in the world by being part of a group, networking, volunteering, and paying attention to your most valuable relationships. Have the courage to ask for help from others when you need it. Do a gratefulness exercise before you go to sleep every night, and always express your gratitude to those who help you in life. Make it your mission to catch family, friends, and those whose paths you cross "doing something right" every day. Project into the future and identify at least two things you are really looking forward to doing—or something you really want to do—that make you feel enthusiastic and hopeful. This could be either a short- or a long-term plan or dream—anything that gives you a sense of joyousness, delight, or excitement when you imagine doing it. If you make these Five Keys to Living an Exceptional Life part of your skill set, you will find yourself having taken a quantum leap in the quality of your life.

Defining Your Needs

Thus far I've been talking primarily about what you want or would like to have. Now, however, I'm going to talk about what you need, that is, what you *must* have to live what I have described as an exceptional life.

Just like your genetic coding, needs simply *are*. They are neither good nor bad, and regardless of how much you may deny them, they insist on being fulfilled. If, however, you want to live an exceptional life, it's going to be up to you to fulfill them. You can do this, first, by being clear about your personal needs, and second, by communicating those needs to the people whom you trust for support in fulfilling them.

I've gotten a lot of flak for encouraging people to make their needs a priority, because at first it appears selfish. That's simply not true. I am unwavering in my belief that your ability to take care of yourself is of paramount importance to the well-being of everyone in your life, and is one of the main ingredients in nurturing healthy relationships. It's also very logical. How can you fully and joyfully support others to fulfill their needs if you secretly harbor feelings of neglect, resentment, guilt, anger, or sadness because, consciously or not, your needs are not being met? (Although you should not dismiss the possibility that being of service to others may be one of your primary needs.)

In order to effectively identify and explore needs, I've found that it is helpful to divide them into five different categories: physical, mental/emotional, spiritual, security, and social. To help you start thinking about your own needs, I have listed a number of them in each of these five categories. These lists are based on a survey I took of more than one thousand people over a period of many years, both the survey and list having been inspired by Dr. Phil McGraw's book *Relationship Rescue*. These are by no means all the needs that exist, and are only meant to open up and stimulate your thinking, not limit you. Some of them may resonate with you and others may not. But it's difficult to see the picture when you live in the picture frame, and I want to help you see the frame in which you live.

Before you read the lists, though, I would like you to open your journal; and across the top of a new page write the five categories of needs: physical, mental/emotional, spiritual, security, and social. As you read through the lists, write down those needs that resonate with you under the appropriate category. It will also help if you write a short comment or observation as you list them. Think big! Go for the good stuff. Dig deep, look, and explore your feelings. Note your judgments. Find the needs that have been hidden or fallen in the bin of neglect or hopelessness. Those are the ones that may have the greatest impact on your life.

As you make your list, you may find your voice of judgment kicking in and saying things like "This needs thing is silly." "Meeting my needs seems selfish." "It doesn't apply to me." "I'll never have my needs met anyway." If you find your negative mind chatter getting in the way of the exercise, just stop, let go, say, "Isn't that interesting!" and go on recording your needs. Don't worry if some of your needs overlap. This isn't a test—you can't be wrong and you can't make a mistake. Just do it!

PHYSICAL NEEDS

- To be hugged
- To be held in a nonsexual way
- To feel physically welcomed by both your partner and friends
- To feel joyfully embraced when encountering your partner
- To be treated with tenderness
- To be gently touched or stroked
- To have a satisfying sexual life
- To have fresh air and open space
- To exercise and feel physically fit
- To be in good health
- To have physical closeness
- To be able to snuggle
- To be without chronic pain
- To get enough sleep

MENTAL/EMOTIONAL NEEDS

- To feel loved
- To feel unconditional love
- To be told that you are loved
- To feel respected for who you are and what you do
- To feel respected for the contributions you make to a relationship
- To have your differences valued
- To feel appreciated for what you do
- In you are in a relationship, to feel your partner is your best friend
- If you are in a relationship, to feel you are totally trusted by your partner
- If you are in a relationship, to totally trust your partner
- To feel needed
- To feel desired
- To feel you can express emotion without being judged
- To feel passion

SPIRITUAL NEEDS

- To feel your spirituality is accepted without judgment
- To worship
- To share a spiritual life with others
- To feel your partner respects your spirituality and spiritual life, even if it is not shared

SECURITY NEEDS

- To make a specific amount of money
- To know that you can take care of yourself independent of anyone else
- If you are in a relationship, to know that your partner will always be there for you and have your back in times of stress and conflict as well as in good times

- If you are in a relationship, to have absolute total trust in your partner
- To know there is enough money for the unexpected and for you to retire comfortably

SOCIAL NEEDS

- To have companionship
- To feel appreciated
- To feel accepted
- To have someone you feel you can communicate with without being judged and who can be counted on in tough times
- To feel a sense of connection or belonging in a community, club, or group
- If you are in a relationship, to share a social life with your partner and feel included in your partner's plans
- If you are in a relationship, to feel you can have friendships independent of your partner
- To have time to spend with friends and family
- To make a contribution
- If you are in a relationship, to be shown affection and know you are important to your partner in social situations

Assuming you have now made a list of your needs, you are entitled to congratulate yourself. Identifying and acknowledging your needs is not always an easy thing to do, but it is vitally important in creating positive change. That's because once you have identified your needs, you will be able to identify a specific personal goal and take action to achieve it. Now, as you look over your list of needs, you should ask yourself, "Are they all being met?" If the answer is "yes" you can just go on reading. If, however, the answer is "no," the next step is for you to think about what you can do to make it so—that is, to take action!

LIFE THOUGHT: YOU AND YOU ALONE ARE RESPONSIBLE FOR HAVING YOUR NEEDS MET.

The satisfaction of your needs is not dependent on anyone else but you. As tough as this may sound, if in your secret heart you believe that others are running around thinking about your needs, you are sadly mistaken. Even those who deeply love and respect you often get so caught up in their own whirlwind that they become totally focused on their own survival. That's just the way life works. So if you are lucky enough to have someone who knows your needs and supports you in fulfilling them, you should treasure that person with all your heart. You have a wonderful partner in life.

Fulfilling your needs, however, is still your responsibility. Over my years of coaching I've met people who actually do assume that others should be held responsible for meeting their needs—and I'm not referring to children! The major downside of this assumption is that there is no upside. Even if depending on others to meet your needs doesn't result in disappointment, resentment, or anger, it will most certainly stifle emotional growth and put an undue burden on them. That's the bad news.

But there is good news as well. Just because you are responsible for having your needs met doesn't mean that you have to do it entirely alone. Most needs can be met with the support of someone who cares for you and has your best interests at heart. That's why I related the life lesson about the power of support I learned from my heart surgery. Although in my case that support came from my wife, it can also be provided by a friend, family member, or acquaintance.

If you do want support from another individual, however, it is essential that you communicate it. You would be surprised at just how many of my clients, in both their personal and professional lives, expect others not only to know what they need but also to automatically help them achieve it—without even having to ask! There are other people, too, who are simply too afraid of rejection to ask, but then feel victimized when they don't get what they didn't ask for.

In the case of relationships, "Ask and ye shall receive" will *almost* always give you positive results. By almost I mean most of the time. Yes, there is always risk in asking for support because there is always the possibility of rejection. But regardless of the outcome, you can always learn and grow. Act boldly, take the leap, and if you are fearful of asking for help, ask yourself, "What's the worst that can happen? Can I take what life throws my way?" Yes, you can!

Take a Breath

The information and exercises I've given you so far were meant to shift your thinking, just as turning the picture of the clown sideways enabled you to see things from a different angle. At the beginning of the book I suggested you move forward at the pace that feels right for you. I hope you are following that advice. Although I may prod and support my clients to take action, I am also acutely aware that individuals can take only so much change and intake only so much information before they short-circuit. I don't want that to happen to you. I do want you to give yourself time to process and practice.

It's impossible to do calculus until you have an understanding of basic math. You will also find it useless to attempt to qualify for a black belt in martial arts until you learn and practice your basic combinations and forms. You will similarly find it difficult to have close friends until you have put time into nurturing those friendships. In other words, you need a solid foundation before you can go to the next level in any endeavor.

There is no standard grade school, middle school, high school, or college course that teaches you how to manage your thinking, become an Artist of Possibility, meet your needs, communicate with love, discover what makes you and others feel loved, or let go and forgive. In a world devoid of such assistance, you basically have four choices: You can learn from your mistakes and successes; learn from the mistakes or successes of others; find appropriate role models; or go on repeating fear-based behaviors. What I have attempted to do so far is to lay the groundwork for communicating with love, transforming fear into love, and letting go and forgiving by providing you with the insights and tools you need to do so. So review what you have written in your journal, decide when you want to move forward, and get ready to stretch. Imagine that!

THINKPOINTS

- Identify your priorities (relationships, future plans, material possessions, personal character traits, and lifestyles) and ask yourself, "What is my next level?" "How can I enhance every aspect of my life?"

- Identify your needs (physical, mental/emotional, spiritual, security, and social) and determine if they are being met.

- Remember that if you are a mature, healthy adult, you and you alone are responsible for having your needs met.

- If you are in a relationship, make sure your partner knows your needs and, if necessary, ask for help in meeting them.

- Contemplate the Five Keys for Living an Exceptional Life and ask yourself: "Have I made friends with reality?" "Do I need to adjust my attitude?" "Do I need to create a stronger support system?" "Do I ask for help when I need it and express my gratitude when others help me?" "Do I have a strong, positive vision of the future that can carry me through any life crisis?"

- Be aware that change is never easy and requires courage, commitment, and support.

6

CREATE A STRETCH GOAL

"The reason most people never reach their goals is that they don't
define them, or ever seriously consider them as believable or achievable.
Winners can tell you where they are going, what they plan to do along the
way, and who will be sharing the adventure with them."

—DENIS WAITLEY, AUTHOR, *THE PSYCHOLOGY OF WINNING*

Sitting atop a lumbering elephant on the outskirts of New Delhi, India, I
was absolutely convinced I was heading to my doom. I was also expend-
ing all my energy in a futile attempt to get the massive beast to move
either left or right instead of straight down an amazingly steep hill. The
elephant, however, was determined to trudge down the well-trodden path
that it had taken hundreds of times with unsuspecting tourists like me. In
a metaphorical sense, what happened to me is exactly what might happen
to you if you don't have the skills necessary to influence your Elephant to
stretch, that is, to take a new path and venture into unexplored territory.

Let me give you a personal example. In order to remain relevant as a
speaker, I have to essentially reinvent myself and my presentation no less
than every two years. This large, time-consuming, and challenging task
requires achieving a variety of smaller goals, including writing, working
with my webmaster to redesign my website, scripting and shooting new
video footage, and planning and executing a social media campaign. In
other words, it is a major change, and no easy mission for someone who

doesn't even like it when his wife so much as moves a chair in the living room! Like many people who face a daunting undertaking, my tendency is to put it off. And to support that delaying tactic, my Rider just loves to come up with logical excuses to procrastinate.

So how do I surmount this obstacle and influence my Elephant to move off its comfortable path? I do it by creating a "stretch goal," that is, the kind of goal or vision of the future that blasts you with energy and causes you to think differently, act differently, and therefore achieve an extraordinary result. Because it can take anywhere between one and five years to achieve, a stretch goal is supported by smaller short- and long-term goals and anchored in the "bigger" picture of your life—large enough to make a major difference, challenging enough to inspire, learn, and grow, but not so overwhelming as to demotivate the Elephant.

Link Alert: Enter the URL **https://vimeo.com/mapes/6** in your web browser and then the password **"stretch"** to see and hear me speak about stretch goals. This is also explained below.

Over the last several years the idea of creating a stretch goal has become increasingly common in business, education, and other areas. For example, a salesperson might set a stretch goal of increasing the number of her sales calls by 20 percent. An educator might develop a stretch goal of helping students increase their study time by fifteen minutes every night. And a stay-at-home parent might establish a stretch goal of making more health-conscious meals for the family every day. All of these examples, while difficult, are doable. That is the key to achieving success with a stretch goal. It is also where willpower can be successfully applied to jump-start the Elephant into action and get it moving on a new path until it stretches into a new comfort zone.

When I want to create a stretch goal myself, I do it by following a process specifically for that purpose. Since I know I have a tendency to put off making changes, one of the first things I have to do is make friends with reality. That is, I become aware of, and take responsibility for, the fact that I am stalling. I do this by acknowledging and writing down the potential damage I will do to my career by not taking positive action. Next, even though I don't particularly like it, I accept the fact that I am going to be uncomfortable for a period of time, because it is likely I will be upsetting my comfortable routines with my family, my social life, and other day-to-day activities.

Then, because in order to take action I must influence my Elephant to move out of its comfort zone, I identify and write down the exact stretch goal I want to achieve. This ignites my imagination and enables me to mentally jump into the future and see, feel, and essentially live what has changed for the better. Once I have created this mental movie fantasy, at least twice a day every day I take the time to close my eyes, rerun it in my mind, and imagine the joy and satisfaction of having achieved what I wanted. Finally, I develop the short-term goals, action steps, and needed support to attain that goal, and then I put them into motion to make my dream come true.

In developing such a goal it's important to remember that if the new path does not have a crystal clear and precise destination, the Elephant will insist on sticking to the status quo—the most familiar path. If the destination is fuzzy and uncertain, the Elephant will grow anxious and resistant. In order to grab and hold the Elephant's attention and influence the stubborn beast to move in the correct direction, it is essential that the Rider craft this kind of positive, vivid, emotionally charged mental movie, because the process of visualization forms new connections in the brain and therefore influences behavior. Such a movie not only provides fuel for the Elephant, it also acts as a compass and provides direction. Simply put, you have to craft a stretch goal that has the power to compel and propel the Elephant into action, and then keep it moving forward by breaking your big-picture goal down into smaller, easily achievable goals, and then visualizing those too.

Greg Anderson, founder of American Wellness Project, puts it best. "When we are motivated by goals that have deep meaning, by dreams that need completion, by pure love that needs expressing, then we truly live life."

Even before you set a stretch goal, though, you must be willing to recognize and accept the fact that change will happen only when you stretch out of your comfort zone and move your life to the next level of possibility. It will also help if you understand and accept that change actually happens twice—first in your imagination, your brain, and then in reality. To accomplish such change, however, you must also choose to be willing to think outside the box of your comfort zone. As the great physicist Albert Einstein once said, "The significant problems we face cannot be solved at the same level of thinking we were at when we created them."

Edward de Bono's "Six Thinking Hats"

It is very easy for me to suggest that you set a stretch goal by thinking differently, but thinking differently is not necessarily a simple task. It may help you do it, however, if you know something about the work of Dr. Edward de Bono, one of my favorite writers on the subject of creative thinking, and the author of two important books on the subject, *Lateral Thinking* and *Six Thinking Hats*.

The de Bono Hats system (also known as "Six Hats" or "Six Thinking Hats") is a magnificent thinking tool for individuals and groups. Put simply, it helps you, your staff, or your team view and explore a problem, challenge, or goal from a 360-degree perspective. Its basic premise is that the human brain thinks in a number of distinct ways. These can be identified, deliberately accessed, and accordingly used in a structured way that allows groups and individuals to develop strategies for thinking about particular issues. Dr. de Bono identifies six distinct states in which the brain can be "sensitized." In each of these states the brain will identify and bring into conscious thought various aspects of any issue being considered, such as gut instinct, pessimistic judgment, and neutral facts. These states are represented by six differently colored hats; and by imagining wearing these hats, individuals and groups employing de Bono's system can shift points of view and therefore states of thinking. The six different hats also represent the six different states needed to reach a goal. They are as follows:

Blue Hat (Thinking): This is the first step in the process, because wearing this hat gives you the perspective you need to define how you or a group will approach your goal or challenge, and helps you remain objective. As a result, when wearing the Blue Hat, you think about the "big picture," which includes determining where you are now, setting objectives, and defining the path you must take to attain those goals. This is how I begin the process of reinventing my speaking topic whenever I want to update my presentation or create a new one. When you are wearing a Blue Hat, your Rider uses logic and projects into the future.

White Hat (Facts): When either a group or individual is wearing this hat, it enables them to identify those resources, information, and facts they need, which of them are available, and what can be learned from them. When I am in the process of reinventing my career or creating a new product, this means identifying which members of my team will handle what task; what additional help, if any, I will need; the research and writing required; and the budget for the project.

Red Hat (Feelings and instincts): Wearing this hat essentially gives you permission to tap into the Elephant's intuition and emotion and express your gut feelings and instincts. In a group setting, people are allowed to express their feelings in either a negative or positive manner. They have permission to exhibit all kinds of feelings, everything from ambivalence to mild interest to unmitigated enthusiasm, and there is no need to justify their feelings or judgments. This step is important because unless you know what feelings and emotions people have there is no way of dealing with them. It is accordingly an opportunity to do your best to understand people who do not understand your reasoning or are not buying into your idea. In terms of time, it is a very brief part of the process. Since it is about gut reaction, each person is allowed only a few words to express their feelings, e.g., "I feel it will be too expensive," "This doesn't sound very exciting," "I feel the timing is wrong," etc. When I am revising my presentation or creating a new product, asking my group for their gut reaction often prompts me to look at an issue in a new way, as well as to examine my intention and the clarity of my communication.

Black Hat (Being cautious): Wearing this hat basically gives you full permission to be judgmental, critical, and skeptical. For that reason, this is a great time for the Rider to identify possible risks, hazards, problems, and barriers. I use Black Hat thinking to get rid of the really impractical ideas my group or I come up with when wearing the Red Hat, and to closely examine the feasibility of the most practical ideas. Hiring a publicity agent and learning how to use social media were two ideas that came out of my last rebranding.

Yellow Hat (Being positive and optimistic): If wearing the Black Hat enables you to be skeptical of new ideas, wearing the yellow one lets you look for reasons to move forward. While you have this hat on you are positive, but not blindly optimistic, and are able to determine both what is working and what is not working. The advantage to Yellow Hat thinking is that it enables you to purposely look for what has been successful in the past and do more of it. For example, during one reinvention, because the monthly newsletter I had been producing generated a lot of web traffic, we decided to put more focus on expanding the use of social media.

Green Hat (New thoughts): Green Hat thinking, which focuses on creativity and innovation, enables you and your team to quickly express and investigate new creative possibilities, alternatives, ideas, and solutions without judgment, so you have the freedom to see where an idea might go. I truly love wearing the Green Hat because this part of the creative process gives me—and my team—permission to dream without restrictions or limitations. It also gives us a great excuse to get together and brainstorm. In fact, I love the freedom of saying, "Let's put on the Green Hat!"

Wearing these hats, going through this process, enables me and my team to consider new possibilities as well as deal with problems by looking at them through six different filters or lenses. And in doing so, it gives us a unique advantage not only in creating and refining a stretch goal but also in spotting and dealing with potential roadblocks or barriers. As you explore setting your own stretch goal it might help to pay a visit to Edward de Bono's website—www.debonogroup.com—and try on each of the six hats.

The "Magic Wand" Exercise

It is now time for you to choose and craft a stretch goal, and the purpose of the six-step "Magic Wand" exercise is to guide you through that process—that is, to assist you in identifying a goal that is challenging, achievable, and will make you happier in some way. Please approach this exercise with a lightness of spirit. You are not carving a goal in stone. You can tweak or refine it all through the process. In fact, you may well decide to change it before you even finish reading this book. What is important is that you make a decision based on what you feel you want to achieve, and that you establish a deadline of from one to five years. Also, before you begin the exercise, I would suggest that you review your answers in the first exercise under "Feelings Determine Actions" in Chapter Three that best describe what makes you feel frustrated, angry, loving, and happy. I would also suggest that you review the four individuals, plans for the future, material possessions, lifestyle elements, and personal character traits that you considered most important to you in the "Twenty-Five-Square Game" in Chapter Five. You will want to carefully consider these as you complete the process.

I encourage you to dream big. Small dreams get small results. Peak performers in general, and great leaders in particular, create their future by developing a vision. This is your opportunity to dream big, move that dream forward mentally with your imagination, and then come back to the present and begin working on what is possible now to make that dream a reality by developing the steps you need to take to get there.

STEP ONE: IDENTIFY YOUR STRETCH GOAL

All self-motivated insight and growth begins with a question. The writer and philosopher William S. Burroughs said, "Your mind will answer most questions if you learn to relax and wait for the answer." So after you read the "Magic Wand" question below, and review the rules, feel free to ponder the answer for as long as you need to. Here is the "Magic Wand" question:

> If I could wave a Magic Wand and instantly change one thing that would have a major positive impact on my life—personally and/or professionally—what would it be?

It's a very important question to ask. Before you answer it, though, here are the rules. For the purposes of this exercise you can only wish for something that is possible. That is, you can't make someone disappear, you can't control the weather, you can't be six feet tall if you are only five feet, and you can't be thirty years old if you are fifty years old. A magic wand may be a powerful tool, but there are certain things that you simply cannot change with it. On the other hand, there are a great number of things you can change, because you can *always* change your perception of *how* you experience what you experience.

In this first step all I am asking you to do is identify a single stretch goal, that is, one thing you would like to change or improve in some area of your life. Be bold in making your choice. Remember, too, that while all decisions need some course correction, you cannot correct a decision that has not been made. Life is a continuous series of adjusted decisions. That is part of the process. As you contemplate your stretch goal, ask yourself the following questions:

- Is this goal something I personally really want?
- How realistic is my goal?
- How much time do I need to reach my goal?
- Do I currently have the skills and/or knowledge required to reach my goal?
- How flexible am I prepared to be in achieving my goal?
- Are there any financial issues that will impact achieving my goal?
- How will I reward myself when I achieve my goal?

These questions are designed as a reality check to help you in several different ways. First, it will help you make sure your goal is something you really want rather than something you have chosen out of guilt or obligation. It will also help you eliminate any potential barriers or fears you may unconsciously put in the way of achieving your goal. Third, it will help you identify what types of partnerships you may need to form in order to reach your goal. Fourth, it will also help you examine your finances and determine if you need to take out a loan or refine your plan. And, finally, it will help you visualize a reward for accomplishing your goal, which will help spur the Elephant forward.

STEP TWO: SET A DEADLINE FOR YOUR STRETCH GOAL

A goal without a deadline is just a dream. As Paul J. Meyer, author and founder of the Success Motivation Institute, wrote, you have to "Crystallize your goals. Make a plan for achieving them and set yourself a deadline. Then, with supreme confidence, determination, and disregard for obstacles and other people's criticisms carry out your plan." Once my private clients have chosen a specific goal, I have them choose a deadline they think will work for them. Sometimes they resist making a commitment for fear of not meeting that deadline. When they do, my response is simple: "Make your best guesstimate and set a time limit. If you finish before your deadline, great. If you need more time, reset your deadline." Every client who sets a deadline eventually succeeds at achieving his or her goal, and setting a deadline is mandatory for success. Deadlines create a sense of urgency for the Elephant. Deadlines create movement. So take the leap. Will you need one year? Two? Three? Make a choice, and write it down.

STEP THREE: VISUALIZE YOUR GOAL AS IF IT HAS ALREADY BEEN ACHIEVED

In this step I want you to visualize the area of your life you would like to change and how the result of that positive change would look and feel, that is, exactly how your life would be different than it is today. Use your imagination and step into the future—one year onward or whatever time frame you choose—and visualize the change as if it had already taken place and your goal had been achieved. How do you do that? Perhaps the best way to start is by asking yourself: "What would have to have happened for me to attain my ideal outcome?"

Answering this question, of course, depends on which area of your life you have chosen to change. It could be your health, your relationships, your career, or any of a number of other areas. In order to help you home in on exactly how it would feel to have achieved your goal, I have provided below examples of the type of questions you should ask yourself. Now, what I would like you to do is close your eyes for a few moments, step into your imaginary movie, and look around. See, feel, and live your goal as if you had already achieved the ideal outcome in whichever area you want to change, and then answer the questions. These questions were inspired by my colleague Brian Tracy, author of *Goals! How to Get Everything You Want—Faster than You Ever Thought Possible.*

PHYSICAL HEALTH

- How does my body look?
- How much do I weigh?

- How do I feel?
- How much do I exercise each week to stay fit?
- What foods do I eat to stay healthy?
- What changes did I make in my diet, sleep habits, exercise, and attitude to achieve my ideal health?

FAMILY AND RELATIONSHIPS

- Who is my partner or spouse?
- Who is no longer my partner or spouse?
- Who is my perfect partner or spouse?
- What does my family look like? Do I have children, and if so, how many?
- What changes did I have to make in my mindset, attitude, and behavior to have my ideal relationship?

CAREER AND BUSINESS

- What are my top skills?
- What, exactly, am I doing to earn money?
- Where am I working?
- Am I working for someone else, in a partnership with someone else, or in my own business?
- What level of responsibility do I have?
- What did I have to learn and what new skills did I have to acquire to attain this position?
- What changes did I have to make in my mindset, attitude, and behavior to achieve success in my career?

FINANCIAL HEALTH

- How much am I earning?
- How much in savings and investments do I have?

- What kind of car do I drive or how many vehicles do I own?
- How much financial freedom do I have to do what I wish?
- What kind of home do I live in?
- What changes did I have to make in my mindset, attitude, and behavior regarding money to achieve my ideal financial goals?

LIFESTYLE

- What hobbies do I pursue?
- What type of events do I enjoy attending?
- How many weeks a year do I take for vacation?
- Where have I traveled? Where do I intend to travel?
- What is my favorite activity to do on weekends?

SOCIAL LIFE

- What causes do I support?
- Do I volunteer my time for something in which I believe?
- What types of organizations am I a member of?
- What types of organizations do I contribute to financially?

Remember that the Elephant is a captive audience for the movies—the visualizations—that you create. Even more important, when the subconscious Elephant watches these movies taking place in the conscious Rider's thoughts, it accepts that it is actually happening in the moment, which triggers either a negative (fear) or positive (pleasure) reaction and, in turn, movement either toward or away from what is being visualized.

Finally, once you have created the imaginary movie of what your life is like after achieving your stretch goal, I suggest you write it down or type it into your computer in as much detail as you can. This mental movie script will give you a quick reference point as to where you began in the process as well as provide written reinforcement for your imagined outcome.

Once you have crafted and practiced your visualization, I guarantee you will be astounded at what a positive impact it has on your brain and therefore what you bring into your life.

STEP FOUR: BECOME AWARE OF THE POSITIVE EMOTION YOU FEEL WHEN YOU VISUALIZE YOUR GOAL AS ACHIEVED

Achieving your stretch goal requires moving the Elephant onto a new path, and positive emotion anchors that goal and moves the Elephant to action. So becoming conscious of how you feel when you imagine your life after you've accomplished your goal will help you attain it. In what is now considered a classic study, "What Good Are Positive Emotions?," psychologist Barbara L. Fredrickson cited several examples of the benefits of doing so. These included the fact that doctors experiencing positive emotions solve tricky medical dilemmas more flexibly and quickly, students in a positive mood devise more innovative solutions to technical challenges, and negotiators in a positive state of mind are more creative and, as a result, more successful; that is, they find "win-win" solutions more often.

An additional benefit of anchoring your stretch goal with a positive emotion is that it energizes you and opens up your curiosity. Emotions such as enthusiasm, excitement, and joy make us want to get involved, become part of something, and create. Others like pride and satisfaction motivate us to strive and grow, and in the process boost our self-esteem. In other words, positive emotions solidify and cement the visualization of your stretch goal and add power to motivate and move you forward. They speak directly to your Elephant's emotional center. Perhaps even more important, by reinforcing your positive emotion you buffer your brain against any fear-based thinking or negative emotions that might creep into your imaginary movie. You always want to avoid sending the Elephant into a fight-or-flight mentality. You do want to keep it curious, engaged, excited, and centered on the desire to move toward pleasure and good feelings. Fear-based negative emotions may work for short-term goals that require quick action; but when it comes to stretch goals, you want to blast the Elephant with positive, hopeful, and encouraging emotion.

But exactly how do you anchor your stretch goal with a positive emotion? You can start by asking yourself, "When I visualize my goal as having been achieved, how do I feel? Am I happy, proud, grateful, excited, energized, fulfilled, relieved, unburdened, or something else?" If your visualization is clear, the emotion usually makes itself known. How could it not? You're already successful! You have created a mental movie of success that the Elephant interprets as real. All you have to do now is remember that positive emotion.

If you have difficulty summoning up a positive emotion, here is a hint. Go back into your past and recall an event or situation where you experienced excitement, pride, or unabashed joy. It could be the feeling you had from winning a prize, being congratulated for a job well done, achieving a high grade on an exam, or any other positive experience. I'm sure you have your own unique positive memory, and once you recall it you can use it as your positive emotion in your stretch goal visualization. In my own case, I recall years ago being presented with an award for "Campus Entertainer of the Year" by the comedian Red Skelton. I felt such pride and accomplishment that I can summon up that feeling whenever I need a boost for my brain, and I incorporate that emotion into my stretch goal when reinventing my career.

STEP FIVE: BECOME YOUR OWN SUCCESS COACH

In order to become your own success coach, you need to gain some distance from yourself, become an actor of sorts, and enter the world of make-believe. For the purposes of this exercise, you have to pretend you are the wisest mind coach in the world, and that you are enormously respected because of your insight and intuition. Now I want you, as that coach, to reread the "Magic Wand" question and the ideal outcome you envisioned, and then step back and look at that outcome through the coach's eyes. In other words, act as if you are the coach and your client is you! It may seem challenging or strange at first, but if you take your time and are willing to approach this exercise with a lightness of spirit, it can actually be a lot of fun. The purpose of this exercise is to help your client—you—come up with at least one simple, straightforward, doable action step that could help your client—that is, you—move forward to achieve a positive result today. Once your first action step is in place, you will be able to move forward and break your stretch goal down into weekly and daily achievable action steps. Go ahead and try it! Trust your instincts. I suspect you will come up with some excellent advice and, perhaps, even be surprised at your ability to help yourself create solutions.

STEP SIX: TAKE ACTION

Now, in this final step, you cast off your role as a coach and step back into yourself. Record in your journal or on your computer the action step or steps you just decided on, read them over again, and make a commitment to take the first step, whether large or small, within the next twenty-four hours. Write down: "I will take the action step_____ by_____." Now do it! And remember that taking action is mandatory if you want to achieve growth. Action takes the dream from your imagination and makes it real. With action you get feedback. With feedback you can make course corrections and learn. And when you learn, you grow.

The reality is that peak performers are invariably action-oriented. While staying centered, they are always moving forward, and always in the process of achieving. If an idea occurs to them, or an opportunity presents itself, they take action immediately. They write down a plan, make a phone call, do research, or seek support. And if they don't have the knowledge or skills to achieve their goal on their own, they learn it or partner with someone who does. Many people live their dreams in their imagination without taking the action needed to manifest them in reality. You don't want to wake up years from now and suddenly realize that all you needed to do was take the first step.

The "Magic Wand" exercise is a major creative step toward becoming a peak performer and creating an exceptional life. It frees and focuses your imagination, shines a light on what you can change, and prompts you to let go of what you cannot change. By creating your own personal "as if" script you are essentially reprogramming your brain and influencing your perceptual filter to allow in people, communication, circumstances, and opportunities that will make your imagined future a reality, and the invisible visible. Imagine that!

THINKPOINTS

- In order to grab the Elephant's attention and influence it to move in a new direction, you have to develop a stretch goal.
- A stretch goal is usually a one- to five-year goal that moves you out of your comfort zone, is realistic, encourages you to "stretch" your capabilities and skills beyond your usual performance, and does not overwhelm the Elephant.
- Dr. Edward de Bono's "Six Thinking Hats" can help you develop a stretch goal by enabling you to view your future from many different perspectives.
- To achieve such a goal you must craft a vivid, emotionally charged mental movie of an ideal outcome that is challenging but realistic.
- Once you have developed such a mental movie you should visualize it a minimum of twice a day.
- You can launch yourself toward achieving your stretch goal by choosing your first action step and taking it today.
- Once you have moved the Elephant to action, you can keep it on the new path by writing down and committing yourself to taking weekly and daily action steps.

7

SET THE STAGE FOR LOVING COMMUNICATION

"While we do not have to agree with [people], we do have to acknowledge
their right to think and feel as they do; and we do have to acknowledge and
give value to their sense of justifications (in their terms) that they have a
right to think and feel the way they do. We must let them know that to us
they have worth, value, and dignity in who and what they are—even if we
do not see eye to eye on every issue."

—DR. GLENN FOSTER AND MARY MARSHALL, *HOW CAN I GET THROUGH TO YOU? THE TRIED-AND-TRUE
METHOD FOR ACHIEVING BREAKTHROUGH COMMUNICATION IN PERSONAL RELATIONSHIPS*

Imagine what life would be like if for some mystical, magical reason the
seven billion people on this planet suddenly found it impossible to communicate. I don't believe there is a word to describe the chaos that would
ensue. Fortunately, we can let go of this strange fantasy because virtually
every human being on this planet is capable of communicating in some
form, even if, as in the movie *The Diving Bell and the Butterfly*, it's only
with the blink of an eye. Of course, this doesn't mean that everyone is an
expert. There are untold numbers who have never had the opportunity to
learn communication skills, and still more who have never realized the

importance of—or taken the time to develop and refine—those skills. As a result, there are times when a special kind of chaos reigns—miscommunication, misunderstanding, confusion, dysfunctional relationships, and worse.

Much has been written and said about all the various means of communication that technology has made possible in recent years, and it is most important that you familiarize yourself with them. However, even a mastery of the most advanced communication devices doesn't ensure that you will be an effective communicator, nor does it guarantee that you will have meaningful relationships. There is a different kind of competency that is required to build, nurture, and keep exceptional relationships. That competency is what I call "loving communication." Before I explain what I mean by loving communication, however, it is important that you first understand something about communication itself.

Communication As an Art

Communication at its best is an art. In that ideal form, communication is saying what you mean, expressing how you feel, and making sure the other person understands. It is also proactively listening to what the other person says and making sure you have received the information accurately. In practice, however, communication is not always an art, and it is important to recognize the differences among its various levels. In order to help you better understand, I have divided communication into three categories—technical communication, discussion, and dialogue. While these categories may overlap on occasion, they all have their own distinct characteristics.

Technical communication occurs when someone is simply providing information, that is, facts—such as that the earth is 24,901 miles in circumference; that as of this writing the world's population is 7,293,611,20; or that the square footage of a room is determined by multiplying its length by its width. Such information can be communicated verbally or in writing and, as a rule, does not require any response from the recipient.

It is either accepted or not, understood or not, and acted on or not. In other words, there is no up- or downside to technical communication—it simply is.

The second category, which I refer to as discussion, is usually extended, interactive communication that deals with a particular topic, examines the pros and cons of some subject, and/or seeks to explore possible solutions. The upside of discussion is that it can expand the knowledge of those involved, enable them to solve a problem or meet a challenge, increase their self-awareness, expand their perspective, and help them gain insight. There can, however, also be a downside to discussion. If, for example, there is even one individual involved in the discussion whose self-confidence depends on being right at the cost of others being wrong, who is competitive or combative by nature, who is neither empathetic nor has good listening skills, or who does not know how to control his or her emotions, a simple discussion can turn into an out-of-control argument and end up doing more harm than good.

It's also important to note that most of our communication takes place in discussions, and that they are often essentially disguised monologues within our own heads. That is, without even realizing it, during discussions we are often rehearsing our replies to what others are saying without really listening to what is being communicated. It's another example of the primitive survival mechanism of the Elephant's fear of rejection. Therefore, if we are not mindful, we may unconsciously and without malice play out our plans, impose our opinions, or run scripts of defense or justification.

The third category of communication, which I call dialogue, is a step above technical communication and discussion. The word dialogue has its roots in the Greek word *dialogus*, meaning to speak alternatively or converse. A dialogue, in this sense, is a nonjudgmental, free exchange of ideas or opinions on a particular issue with the purpose of reaching an amicable agreement or settlement. It is only in this form that communication achieves the level of art, and it does so because it is in this form that the participants engage in loving communication. Realistically, of course, we cannot always communicate through dialogue, nor am I suggesting we can. Therefore, in a sense, dialogue is an ideal, something to strive for, the touchstone of loving communication.

Loving Communication

What do you think the response would be if I stopped someone in a store, on the street, or in an executive conference room and said, "Do you communicate with love?" At best, they would probably think I was a bit eccentric. At worst, they might think I was mentally ill. That's because in our society if you insert the word "love" into any phrase, most people get uneasy, giggly, starry-eyed, serious, or even defensive. Why is that? It may be because the word itself is confusing. It may also be because, as Plato wrote, "Love is a grave mental disease." And yet, communicating with love is a vital ingredient to living an exceptional life.

What, then, does loving communication mean? Again, as the highest form of communication—the artistic form—at its most basic it means making sure that you are expressing what you mean and how you feel in a way that the other person understands. It means proactively listening to the other person so you are sure that you understand what he or she means and feels and can respond accordingly. It also means letting go of the need to be right or approaching communication as a form of combat. But it is really much more than that. It is choosing to recognize and accept that human beings are vulnerable, sensitive, fragile, and delicate. It is doing everything you can to keep from negatively impacting your communication. And it is honoring others and respecting their point of view. Is it idealistic? Maybe. Is it possible? Absolutely.

Ultimately, loving communication means respecting the dignity of the individual. Psychologists believe that a fundamental need of humans is to be socially accepted, and that the consequences of social rejection impact us negatively on many levels. Although it has not yet been proven, I suspect that the desire to be respected and appreciated is also part of our DNA. When you neglect or refuse to value another's point of view you are essentially making the statement, "What you say doesn't matter." Valuing the point of view of others doesn't necessarily mean that you agree with them or refrain from debate—it means that you respect them regardless of who they are or what your relationship to them may be. And showing respect for the dignity of others is not only a basic tenet of loving communication, it is the lynchpin of successful win/win negotiations and compromise.

The remainder of this chapter is designed to help you set the stage for loving communication essentially by two means. First, I will show you how to establish and maintain rapport by creating the mindset that, regardless of judgment, everyone is right. Second, I will show you how to support the art of communication by becoming an active listener.

Link Alert: Enter the URL **https://vimeo.com/mapes/7** in your web browser and then the password "**stage**" to see and hear me speak about setting the stage for loving communication. This is also explained below.

Learn to Develop and Maintain Rapport

Webster's New World Dictionary defines the word "rapport" as "a sympathetic relationship; harmony." It is a word that I want you to burn permanently into your mental hard drive, because it is the bond or connection that is established between people that allows them to hear and be heard. It is a mutual understanding of trust and agreement between people—a bond of safety. It is also an emotional dialogue based on mutual caring and respect. Given these definitions you should be able to understand how critical it is to create and maintain rapport, because when rapport is broken, the art of communication slams to a halt.

Rapport does not only happen on a one-on-one basis. Motivational speakers like myself, as well as all those who address audiences—politicians, comedians, storytellers, religious leaders, and many others—must establish rapport if they want to have their message heard or their impact felt. As a clinical hypnotist and Neuro-Linguistic Programming practitioner, the first skill I was taught was how to instantly create rapport. And if you want to live an exceptional life and communicate with love, it is essential that you make it a priority to establish and keep rapport. The first step in doing so is adopting the mindset that everyone is right from his or her point of view.

Recognize that Everyone Is Right from His or Her Point of View

The same fact may tell different stories to observers who wear different spectacles or look through different filters. Look at the pictures below. Is (b) a bird or an antelope?

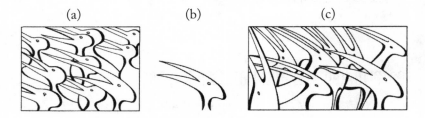

Bird antelope among birds, Bird antelope, and Bird antelope among antelope
PATTERNS OF DISCOVERY: AN INQUIRY INTO
THE CONCEPTUAL FOUNDATIONS OF SCIENCE
Copyright © 1958 Cambridge University Press,
Reprinted with the permission of Cambridge University Press. [1]

When (c) is covered up, most people think it is a bird. But when (a) is covered, most will see it as an antelope. So which one is it? Now imagine you are looking at it with another person. You say, "I see an antelope," and he or she says, "I see a bird." Which of you is right? In fact, taking into account each of your points of view and the context in which you process information, both of you are right.

Whether we like it or not, there are seven billion people in the world and, putting ethics and morals aside for a moment, every one of them is always right—from his or her point of view. If you don't believe it, just ask them. While I want to bring a smile to your face with that statement, I am quite serious. We are all right from our own point of view.

Think about this. How do you feel when someone attempts to invalidate you by making you wrong or making fun of what you believe? How do you feel when other people attempt to force their beliefs on you? What emotions do you experience? When this happens to me, my very first survival instinct is to take on a defensive posture. If I followed through, I would attack, defend, or pull away. Luckily, experience has taught me that if I act on this initial knee-jerk, fear-based, self-protective instinct, I will most certainly trigger the other person's survival self, even if that was not my intention. However, I have learned that, when I feel myself going down this path, the best thing to do is stop, take a deep breath, reframe, and make a more loving choice. It is the Rider's skill that can choose to communicate with love rather than follow the Elephant's inclination to respond with fear.

Ultimately, then, creating and maintaining rapport is about not letting your ego get in the way of your communication—and your relationships—with those around you. Left to its own devices, the ego desperately needs to be right, to have the last word, and to win, even if it means creating separation between you and others. But when you recognize that everyone is right from his or her point of view, you can let go of the need to be right, make peace your highest priority, and transform your survival self into your loving self.

Of course, in spite of all your good intentions you will sometimes feel the tug of the ego, that overwhelming need to be right at the expense of making someone else wrong. If this happens, what you should do, as I've already suggested, is stop, take a couple of deep breaths, come to the present, choose peace, and ask, "Why do I need, right now, to prove that I'm right? What's the payoff?" You can do this little exercise in the blink of an eye. By questioning the ego, fear loses its grip on you. It works. Test it out.

You might also consider taking a suggestion from Dr. Helen Schucman's *A Course in Miracles* and ask yourself what I consider to be the million-dollar question: "Do I want to be right or do I want to be happy and experience inner peace?"

The point is that you are in control of your communication. You can always let go of the necessity to prove you are right, even when you are. That doesn't mean that you allow yourself to be a doormat or betray your principles. You can debate without attacking. You can be firm and self-confident without being hostile and belligerent. You can agree to disagree. All it takes is a shift in your thinking and behavior. So the next time you're tempted to attack and diminish someone's viewpoint, remember the bird and antelope illustration. While you don't have to agree with others, you can always choose to honor them.

As your coach, I ask you to make a commitment, right now, to never purposefully diminish the point of view of your communication partner. You can listen, recognize the value of others, and make others right for what they believe without sacrificing your integrity. And when you forget and fall back into old, destructive patterns of communication, make others wrong, lose your temper, attempt to control by bullying, or shy away because you are afraid of being rejected, you should make amends, and do it immediately. How do you make amends? What can you do to reestablish the bond if rapport is broken? It's easy; all you have to do is apologize. Simply say, "I'm sorry." Let go of your need to be right or the erroneous belief that apologizing is a sign of weakness, and tell your ego to take a hike. When you apologize, you are expressing love. Apologizing goes a long way to reestablishing rapport.

Although it is relatively easy for me to tell you to restrain your ego, I know that in practice it can be very challenging. Communicating with love can be particularly difficult when you find yourself having to deal with people who are looking for confrontation. Their egos need to be fed by putting you on the defensive, but you can refuse to buy into other people's negativity and fear. You can choose to make them right. Here are two tools to help you tame the ego and maintain rapport.

"YOU'RE RIGHT"

When someone aggressively confronts you with his or her self-righteous point of view, daring you to disagree, simply say, "You're right." How does one argue against "You're right"? Like an Aikido master, you can disarm a potentially explosive moment by taking away all resistance. This very useful tool will squash the ego and bring a potential confrontation and "no-win" argument to an abrupt halt. Test it out.

THE MAGIC "AND"

Imagine someone has just expressed his or her opinion to you, and you respond by saying either "I hear and appreciate what you believe, *but* here is what I believe," or "I hear and appreciate your point of view, *however* here is my point of view . . . " Although people often express disagreement this way, the problem with using the words "but" and "however" is that they always make the listener feel you are trying to invalidate whatever he or she is saying, even if you do not intend to do so. Both words are guaranteed rapport breakers.

What is the solution? Just substitute the word "and" for the rapport breaking words "but" and "however." "I hear and appreciate your point of view *and* here is my point of view." You are not agreeing with the other person, but you are respecting him or her. And by doing so, rapport is maintained and communication remains open. Use it in both your personal and professional relationships. You will find the results are quite magical.

Learn to Listen Actively

Because communication—particularly loving communication—is a two-way street, the second means of setting the stage for it is active listening. Listening is much more than just sitting still and looking at the other person. Although I will discuss communication at greater length in a later chapter, here are three basic ways to listen actively.

- Always keep your attention on the speaker. Maintain eye contact and refrain from checking your watch, fidgeting, or showing impatience in any way. Studies show that the majority of communication is non-verbal, that is, expressed through facial expressions, gestures, posture, etc. So use your body language to show you are paying attention—lean forward, make sure your arms and legs are uncrossed, and nod occasionally.

- Listen for the important points and, when appropriate, mirror back what the speaker has said by restating or paraphrasing what you have heard. Use statements such as "So, I'm hearing you say that . . . " or "Am I correct in understanding that you want . . . ?" Doing so not only shows you understand but also keeps you from making erroneous assumptions.

- Part of active listening is making efforts to avoid breaking rapport. One way to do so is to wait for the other person to finish speaking before you start to think about your response. Another is to avoid trying to dictate what the other person should feel or do. Statements beginning with "You should . . . "or "You must . . . "are instant rapport breakers. Do not give advice unless you are asked to, and even then it is best to respond by saying "What do you feel you should do?" or "What would make you most comfortable?"

"PLEASE LISTEN"—A POEM BY A SURVIVOR

When I ask you to listen to me and you start giving advice,
you have not done what I asked.
When I ask you to listen to me and you begin to tell me why
I shouldn't feel that way, you are trampling on my feelings.
When I ask you to listen to me and you feel you have to do
something to solve my problems, you have failed me,
strange as that may seem.
Perhaps that's why prayer works for some people.
Because God is mute and He doesn't offer advice or try to fix things.
He just listens and trusts you to work it out for yourself.

So please, just listen and hear me. And if you want to talk,
wait a few minutes for your turn and I promise I'll listen to you.
—ANONYMOUS

YOUR TURN

This exercise is intended to help you become aware of how you communicate, practice communicating with the mindset that everyone is right from his or her point of view, and listen actively. I would like you to do this exercise for the next three days, beginning with writing the following statement in your journal or entering it in your computer. By doing so you are giving a suggestion to the Elephant to be alert and aware. Read it once at the beginning of each day.

I will do my best to set the stage for loving communication and create rapport at all times. I will be aware when I feel the need to prove I'm right at the expense of making others wrong, and will choose to always respect the dignity of others. I will notice when I am not proactively listening and will refocus my attention.

If you read this every morning, as you communicate over the next three days you will become aware of exactly how you communicate, and notice not only when you are trying to be right by making others wrong, but also when you are absorbed in the self-dialogue of judgment instead of proactively listening with an open mind. And soon, almost before you realize it, you will be setting the stage for loving communication. Imagine that!

THINKPOINTS

- Communication at its best is an art.
- There are essentially three types of communication—technical communication, discussion, and dialogue—each with its own particular characteristics.
- Dialogue, the highest form of communication, is a nonjudgmental, free exchange of ideas or opinions on a particular issue with the purpose of reaching an amicable agreement or settlement.
- Loving communication is the result of creating rapport by recognizing that everyone is right from his or her point of view, and learning to listen actively.
- Recognizing that everyone is right from his or her point of view means respecting the dignity of others even if you don't agree with them.
- Active listening means concentrating on what is being said rather than just passively "hearing" the message of the speaker, as well as exhibiting both verbal and nonverbal signs of listening.
- Loving communication stems from the single-minded desire to experience peace.

8

COMMUNICATE

"Words are, of course, the most powerful drug used by mankind."
—RUDYARD KIPLING

How often have you blamed someone for the way you were treated? How often have you felt that people were taking you for granted, ignoring your needs, steamrolling over your desires, or showing you, as Rodney Dangerfield complained, "No respect"? If your answer to either of these questions is "Very often," there is a reason for it. And the reason is that people treat you the way they do because you teach them to treat you that way. You teach them by tolerating inappropriate, rude, crude, and cruel behavior, or not doing so. You teach them by lying or telling the truth. You teach them by asking for what you want and need or not asking for it. You teach them through your assumptions. You teach them by micromanaging or empowering them. You teach them through your fear or love. You teach them by your silence. You teach them through your attitude. You teach them through your actions and your words.

In other words, you teach them through your communication. It is through your communication that you impact the subconscious Elephant of others. That is, the way you communicate, the words you use, how you say them, and your body language all impact the emotional center of the subconscious Elephant by sparking its imagination with either love or fear. Impressions are received, judgments are made, and beliefs are formed about you, and people treat you accordingly.

 LIFE THOUGHT: PEOPLE WILL TREAT YOU THE WAY THEY PERCEIVE YOU.

Do you know how most street muggers select their victims? They look for people who appear to be weak and frightened. Remember the bully in school? Who did he or she pick on? Just like a mugger, the bully also looked for weakness and fear. But there is one thing of which I am fairly certain—neither he nor she continued to torment anyone who refused to tolerate it.

Here is an example of an individual being treated the way he or she is perceived. An acquaintance of mine was complaining that the job of babysitting his grandchildren always seemed to fall on him, even when it was inconvenient. He further lamented that he'd had to make loans to family members that were never repaid, and was often steamrolled into running errands because other members of the family didn't want to. When I pointed out that perhaps it was because he always said "Yes" when asked to do any of these things, his reply was, "What else could I do?" In other words, he didn't see any other alternative. Despite his frustration and growing bitterness, he was stuck being a victim, and was unable or unwilling to see that he contributed to his circumstances by the choices he made. But his family treated him the way they did because he had taught them to treat him that way.

I have counseled thousands of individuals in all walks of life who feel overburdened, under compensated, ignored, or just plain taken advantage of. When I inquire as to whether they have ever clearly communicated their displeasure, the answer is often something like, "Well, not in so many words." They are simply unaware of how their communication or—more often—lack of communication affects others. Eventually clients do reveal their reasons for not speaking up, and it is almost always because of fear—fear they will be punished, rejected, yelled at, demoted, or fired. So if, like these individuals, you feel people use you, break their word, or take advantage of your good nature, you may need to make some new choices. Step out of denial, let go of anger, stop feeling sorry for yourself, and communicate! You do not want or need to be an unintentional professional victim. You want to respect yourself and, starting now, focus on learning how to teach people how to treat you.

It is important to note that, while I advocate taking responsibility for teaching others how to treat you, I don't mean to imply that you should stand on a soapbox and preach. The only thing that will do is teach people to avoid your moralizing or complaining. Nor do I mean to suggest that you should be aggressive. Being aggressive or combative will only trigger the Elephant's primal defense mechanism in others and create more fear. As your coach, I simply want to encourage you to become confident and in control. I want you to be assertive and to educate people about how you want to be treated or don't want to be treated. I want you to "speak your truth," but I want you to do it in a loving way.

My intention in this chapter is to help you communicate in a way that will create positive outcomes. To paraphrase the Rolling Stones, you may not always get exactly what you want, but you will often get what you need—the feeling of control that comes with being proactive and putting communication into action. You must bear in mind, though, that sometimes people will learn quickly and sometimes you will meet with resistance. We humans are uncomfortable with any kind of change, especially when it comes to relationships. But eventually they will learn, as long as you are patient.

Four Strategies for Successful Relationships

Over the last three-plus decades of coaching clients, I have discovered four somewhat out-of-the-box strategies that can enhance the quality of relationships. Although not often spoken about or explored, these tactics, when applied, can elevate the quality of your relationships, whether business or personal, to a much higher level, and therefore help you toward living an exceptional life.

> **Link Alert:** Enter the URL **https://vimeo.com/mapes/8-1** in your web browser and then the password "**strategies**" to see and hear me speak about the Four Strategies for Successful Relationships. This is also explained below.

RELATIONSHIP STRATEGY NUMBER ONE: SET STANDARDS FOR WHAT YOU WANT FROM YOUR RELATIONSHIPS

If you don't know how you want to be treated, you will be unable to ask people to treat you that way. And unless you provide people with your rules, they will treat you by theirs. Why shouldn't they? So it is essential that you get clear about what you want so you can communicate it. The following exercise is designed to help you do that.

YOUR TURN

The following series of questions will assist you in quickly identifying what you are receiving or not receiving in a relationship. Choose one of your most important relationships (friend, acquaintance, boss, spouse, or lover) and write down the answers to the questions as honestly as you can. Answering them truthfully will give you the opportunity to look at what you believe you deserve through the mirror of that relationship.

- What do I expect from this relationship?
- What do I feel I deserve from this relationship?

- What am I getting from this relationship?
- What do I want that I am not receiving from this relationship (intimacy, time, communication, respect, support, etc.)?
- What am I giving to this relationship?
- What am I withholding from this relationship?

Were you surprised by any of your answers? Did something become apparent to you that you have been avoiding or denying? Is there some action you can take or something you can communicate today that would enhance the quality of your personal and/or business relationships?

RELATIONSHIP STRATEGY NUMBER TWO: DETERMINE YOUR "RULES FOR RELATIONSHIPS" AND COMMUNICATE THEM

Although we may not think of them as such, we all have rules for relationships. These are the conscious or unconscious expectations we have about how we will treat those around us and how they will treat us. Of course, the rules are not the same for every relationship we have. You certainly wouldn't have the same expectations of your spouse as you would of your boss. (Although I suppose that might depend on your boss—and your spouse!) You should never, however, assume that people know your rules, even those closest to you. This is certainly true of people with whom you are just beginning a relationship, but it is even true of those you know well. After all, we change and grow, as do our relationships, and if your expectations change, you can't expect others to know what they are unless you tell them. This is important because if you don't clearly communicate your rules (your desires and needs), your closest relationships may suffer. Of course this presupposes that you are not a tyrant, your rules are not destructive, and you don't communicate like a dictatorial, militaristic general who demands to be obeyed at every moment!

Here's a personal example. With my best friends it is perfectly acceptable to communicate every two to four weeks. Sometimes it's more, sometimes less. My rule does not require a daily or even a weekly conversation. Therefore my feelings will not be hurt if I don't hear from a friend every day or even for a few weeks. This is one of my rules for friendship, and I act in accordance with it unless some new information alters my thinking. With my wife, not surprisingly, I have a different rule. When I'm on the road we speak several times daily, and we are seldom apart for more than a week. When I am home, though, the rules change. During our working day we leave each other alone to write or do whatever needs to be done. If I interrupt her writing, she lets me know—in a loving way—that it is not what she wants or needs, and I do the same if she interrupts me. Fortunately our rules are the same, which is obviously a good thing in a marriage.

Of course, unless you know what your rules are, it is impossible to communicate them. The following exercise is designed to help you put into words some of the things you expect from others in a relationship.

YOUR TURN

Choose any one of your closest relationships, write down the person's name, and then list at least three underlying rules you have set for this relationship. This exercise will require self-reflection to uncover exactly what your rules are. Some of the questions you might want to ask yourself are: "How much time do I expect to spend in this person's company?" "How frequently do I expect to communicate with this person?" "How honest do I expect this person and I to be with each other?" "How much can I and this person expect to rely on each other for support?"

Once you have determined and written down at least one to three rules, ask yourself, "Am I absolutely certain they are aware of them?" If the answer is "No" or "I'm not sure," the next question you have to answer is, "What do I need to communicate that I have not communicated to this person?" And once you've determined what that is, you need to communicate it in a gentle, loving, caring way. Do it soon!

RELATIONSHIP STRATEGY NUMBER THREE: WHEN SOMEONE IGNORES YOUR STANDARDS AND PUSHES YOU OVER THE LINE, COMMUNICATE YOUR CONCERN IMMEDIATELY EITHER VERBALLY OR IN WRITING

One of the many lessons my clients have taught me is that great damage can occur in a relationship when you let unexpressed anger and resentments accumulate without open and straightforward communication. Suppressed anger will *always* come out in the most unexpected and inappropriate ways, such as a sudden blow-up, hurtful name-calling, sabotaging behavior, or even stress-related illness. You do both yourself and others a great service when you choose to communicate your dissatisfaction, concerns, anger, and resentments in a responsible way. Be logical. If others don't realize when they are bulldozing over you, how can you expect them to behave differently in the future? How can they learn if you are not willing to teach them? Let the other person know that he or she is loved and valued, and then express your upset as soon as possible *without* anger or blame.

YOUR TURN

Consider your closest personal relationships and recall a time when you did not express your hurt, anger, or resentment for the way you were treated, and then answer the following questions.

- What was your payoff for not speaking the truth?
- What did you think you were accomplishing by not communicating?
- Were you fearful? If so, why?
- Did your lack of communication work in the long term?
- Was the same negative behavior repeated because you didn't communicate?
- What lesson did you learn that you could apply in the future?
- Could you now express your negative feelings, either in a letter or in person?

Now consider your business relationships. Think about the times you did not express your concerns with your employees or your boss, and answer these questions.

- What was your payoff for not speaking your mind?
- In retrospect, was it the right thing to do?
- If not, what would have been a more effective approach for communication?
- Specifically, what did you learn and how can you apply it in the future?

If you are unclear as to what is or is not acceptable in a relationship, it's time for you to get clear now—right this minute. If you haven't communicated your rules for a relationship, do it today!

RELATIONSHIP STRATEGY NUMBER FOUR: IF YOU HAVE GIVEN EVERYTHING YOU CAN TO THE RELATIONSHIP AND IT STILL DOESN'T WORK, BE WILLING TO LET IT GO

All successful relationships require continuous compromise. However, even with compromise, commitment, and clear and loving communication, sometimes a relationship just doesn't work. When you have given it everything you've got, when another person is draining your energy and joy, you must summon the courage to make changes. Loving someone does not require that you suffer. You can love and still let go. Remember that letting go doesn't mean giving up, it means accepting that there are some things that simply cannot be. Change in a relationship is never easy, but the alternative is even less acceptable—for both parties. You have to know when it's time to play and when it's time to fold, and have the courage to make the more empowering choice.

YOUR TURN

Write down any relationship that is draining the joy from your life and visualize your life without that relationship. Then ask yourself the following questions.

- How might my life improve by letting this relationship go?
- What is the payoff for holding on to a destructive or dead relationship?
- What is my fear about letting it go? How do I think I would feel if I did let go?
- What is the worst that can happen if I let go of this negative relationship?

Letting go of any relationship is a challenge. Fear of hurting another or fear of being alone is common when considering ending a relationship. But you can confront and break through any fear once you recognize that you can handle whatever life throws your way. If you reflect on the tough patches in life that you have survived and learned from, you will know that you will be able to face whatever you may have to deal with in the future.

Nine Approaches to Achieving Exceptional Communication

My dictionary defines communication as "a process by which information is exchanged between individuals through a common system of symbols, signs, or behavior." That is, what you say and how you say it to others, including your spouse or partner, your children, your employees, the waiter who served you lunch, and anyone else you may come in contact with throughout the day. Broader definitions given in some dictionaries include body language, speaking and writing skills, and listening as core components of successful communication.

While all this is true, to my mind communication is actually far more expansive than even the broadest dictionary definition might suggest. In fact, in addition to communicating with all those you come into contact with during your waking hours, you also communicate with yourself—your subconscious Elephant—through your self-talk and what you visualize. Through this self-communication, you can spark your own emotions, both negative and positive, which in turn may affect your attitude and therefore how you interact with others. How you communicate with yourself also influences your expectations and therefore how you perceive things.

The nine approaches that follow are by no means intended to provide solutions to every communication challenge. In fact, while many of them can be effective in any human interaction, I have chosen to concentrate specifically on communication with those who have the greatest immediate impact on your life, including your spouse or partner, your children, your closest friends, and your business associates. I have focused on these particular relationships because they are the ones my coaching clients and workshop members have expressed the greatest interest in improving, and the ones that most contribute to living an exceptional life. This is of course not to say that you needn't be concerned about communication with others. There have been many volumes written on the art of communication, and it would be to your advantage to read whatever you can on the subject.

COMMUNICATION APPROACH NUMBER ONE: WHEN YOU LISTEN, LISTEN WITH YOUR WHOLE BEING

I've had the privilege of meeting many extraordinary people in my life, but if I were pressed to pick three individuals as shining examples of superior communication skills they would be President Ronald Regan, Frank Sinatra, and Academy Award–winning actor Eddie Redmayne. When engaged in conversation with any one of these three men, I always felt as if I was the most important person in the world. Their attention was absolute. Unfortunately, that's not the norm.

How many times have you been in a conversation when suddenly you notice the other party is glancing around or observing someone else? How often have you felt that what you were saying was unimportant because the other person was more absorbed in his or her own opinion? How often have you done these things yourself?

If communication is really important and you want the person you are speaking with to feel special, don't look at something or someone else.

There is nothing more aggravating than watching another person's eyes darting around the room or glancing at an iPhone when he or she is supposed to be connecting with you. So raise the bar for yourself. When you engage in conversation, make the other person your total focus. Yes, it does take a conscious, mindful effort, but the payoff is enormous.

COMMUNICATION APPROACH NUMBER TWO: REFRAIN FROM INVALIDATING OTHERS' BELIEFS

Developing the communication habit of refraining from invalidating what others feel or believe is both a choice and a developed skill. In the last chapter I gave you two tools to help you maintain rapport—"The Magic 'And'" and "You're Right." Here I simply want to reinforce the value of not invalidating others' beliefs as a means of keeping your communication exceptional.

What we think and feel is our reality—it is what the Elephant believes to be true in the moment. Having your reality invalidated can be very unsettling, as can having someone make fun of or dismiss your thoughts and feelings as irrelevant. So when it happens, it can be not only extremely troubling, but it can also break rapport. And while it's bad enough when strangers make snide remarks about our beliefs and observations, it is even worse when it comes from those who love us. At the very least, being invalidated may cause us to question ourselves. At worst, it can result in anger or bitterness.

Invalidation comes in many forms besides verbal digs. For example, imagine you are attempting to communicate and as you speak the person you are talking to turns away to do some chore, buries his nose in the newspaper, glances at the TV, or checks her email on a smartphone. How would that make you feel? Very likely it would make you feel invalidated and diminished.

Whatever people think, feel, or see is their experience. It's real to them. As challenging as it may sometimes be, your job is to give validation and love, not take it away by consciously or unconsciously invalidating. Your mission is to *always* respect the dignity of other individuals. You don't want to be a life-diminisher. You want to be a life enhancer! Of course, this does not mean that you have to put up with rude or disruptive people. There are times when you must take a stand to protect yourself, but there are always positive choices you can make instead of falling into the trap of another's fear and anger.

COMMUNICATION APPROACH NUMBER THREE: CRITICIZE WITH THE TOUCH OF A FEATHER

"People say I don't take criticism well, but I say, what the hell do they know?"
—GROUCHO MARX

My wife, Susan, is a movie and theater critic, journalist, and speaker, and it was in her professional capacity that I first met her. A number of years ago I was performing my one-man show, *Journey into the Imagination*, at a local university and was intent on improving the presentation. Knowing of her insight as a critic, I thought she would be an ideal resource for ideas, so I asked her to watch the show and give me some feedback. I recall very clearly her asking me, "Do you really want to hear the truth?" "Of course," I replied. So she watched the show and gave me some suggestions—in a kind and loving way. I tested her ideas out and found that some worked and some did not. I then asked her to watch the show a second time, and then a third. "What do you want," she asked, "your own critic?" "Yes," I answered, and the rest, as they say, is history.

The point is not, of course, that providing criticism in a gentle way will lead to a marriage proposal, even if it did in our case. The point is that criticism does not have to be negative. Nor does it have to inflict damage. So if you are going to criticize, it's always best to do it with love. Never intentionally bruise or hurt the dignity of another. Regardless of how confident someone may appear, everyone's self-esteem is delicate, and we need to take special care. So make sure the person knows he or she is respected, valued, and/or loved *before* you talk about the issue at hand.

For example, when criticizing a significant other you might say something like, "You know I love and respect you, and I would like to speak with you about something you did that really bothered me." In criticizing a friend, you could say, "You know how much I care about you, and there's been something on my mind that I need to talk to you about." Finally, if you need to criticize a subordinate at work you might say, "You're a valued member of my team, and I need your advice on something that has been troubling me."

Perhaps the most important thing to remember is that you should always separate the problem from the person. By making sure that the other person doesn't feel you are attacking them, by showing that you respect his or her dignity, you leave the door open for ongoing dialogue. You will find, too, that the respect you show others will flow back to you in ways you least expect in both your personal and professional lives.

COMMUNICATION APPROACH NUMBER FOUR: ASK FOR WHAT YOU WANT AND NEED

In your most intimate relationships, having both your and your partner's needs met is central to living an exceptional life. When core needs are expressed, supported, and pursued, the breeding ground for bitterness, jealousy, anger, resentment, and hopelessness is destroyed. But asking for what you want and need in a gentle, loving, non-threatening way is important in any kind of relationship, whether it is with a partner, a family member, a friend, or a coworker.

How do you make sure your needs are met? Here is a good rule of thumb: Don't believe the delusion that human beings are mind readers, even if they love you dearly, much less if your relationship with them is primarily a professional one. In my coaching practice I am often surprised by how many people believe that others should somehow cosmically know what you want and need, and provide it without them even having to ask. There is nothing as erroneous as thinking, "If he loved me, he would have remembered our special day," "If she really cared about our friendship, she would have remembered to call," or "If he really understood how important this project is to the success of the team, he would have offered to put in some extra time." Faulty thinking! By our nature we are self-absorbed creatures who often focus on our own survival or that of our loved ones. So if you want relationships that will endure, you have to cut people some slack. Someone can love you dearly and still forget those important dates. We're all just human.

Ultimately, though, you are responsible for yourself. So you should ask for what you want and need, and you should do it in a loving way. Although you will not always get want you want, most of the time you will. Before you ask, however, it is always a good idea to consider the pros and cons of doing so. As with everything else in life, there are benefits and drawbacks to asking for something. The most important thing to remember is to make sure that you have established rapport with the person to whom you are making the request, and to be gracious if the response you receive is "Not now" or "No."

COMMUNICATION APPROACH NUMBER FIVE: COMMUNICATE TO OTHERS HOW MUCH THEY ARE VALUED AND LOVED

Never assume others know they are valued and loved. Everyone needs affirmation. If we don't get it, we feel empty. Although psychologists say we must seek validation from within rather than from others, in many cases, unless someone lets us know we are valued and loved in a language we understand, we don't know it. So it is important that you affirm your love and appreciation of others through your words, your gestures, and your actions. You should let your partner and your close friends know how valued and loved they are, and do it continuously. But expressing your appreciation shouldn't be limited to those closest to you. I regularly let my travel agent know how much my wife and I value him, tell our local auto mechanic how much we appreciate his excellent work, and let our favorite waiter at a local restaurant know what a good job he does. By communicating like this you can make someone's day!

By letting others know they are valued and loved, I do not mean that you should dance up and down the street shouting how much you love your partner, or run around your workplace telling your coworkers how much they are valued. That would probably send a different kind of message—and one you wouldn't particularly want to send. Of course, the way you express how much you love and value someone is a very personal matter. There is no rule book for how to do it. You just have to use whatever approach makes you comfortable. No matter how you do it, though, communicating positive feelings about others speaks directly to their Elephants' need to feel safe, accepted, and cared for. So the only questions you have to ask yourself are: "To whom can I express my love?" and "To whom can I express how much I value him or her?"

COMMUNICATION APPROACH NUMBER SIX: LET THOSE CLOSEST TO YOU KNOW WHEN YOU ARE LONELY, IN PAIN, FEARFUL, OR FEEL MISUNDERSTOOD

"Trouble is part of our life. If you don't share it; you don't give
the person who loves you a chance to love you enough."
—DINAH SHORE

How can your partner, spouse, or close friend have the experience of comforting you if you don't let them know when and why you are troubled? How can you have the satisfaction of comforting others if they don't share their pain, sadness, or disappointment? Many people make the mistake of assuming that sharing their painful feelings is a sign of weakness, or is the same as complaining. But there is a major difference. Complaining about your problems is often a sign of victimization. Sharing your emotions is a sign of intimacy. Sharing your emotions is healing.

Research has shown that the quality of your closest relationship is directly related to the quality of your communication skills. This does not mean that you should continually sit around and talk about your troubles. It does mean that if you and those who are close to you are willing to talk about things that really matter, and are not afraid to express what you think and feel, your relationship is likely to be considerably better. As you have probably noticed, however, most women seem to be much more open to this kind of dialogue than men. A major grievance of many of my female coaching clients is that a friend, partner, or spouse does not share their emotional pain, fear, or troubles. And as a result they often feel ignored, left out, or not trusted. At the same time, I have also discovered that many women—out of fear of judgment, and for their own self-protection—have been forced to shut down their emotions and are accordingly unable or unwilling to share them. There are, however, several steps you can take to improve relationships with those close to you.

- **Look at things from your partner's or close friend's point of view.** You don't need to always agree with either your partner or your friends. You should, however, take time to understand their underlying concerns. A lot of arguments stem from trying to solve problems, and there are lots of ways to do that once you know what is really at issue. As soon as you have both stated your worries and desires, it's much easier to work together to find a satisfying solution. Being flexible is a key part of communicating well and is critical for making a relationship last.

- **Develop the skill of talking about yourself.** You may lack confidence in expressing your feelings, or find it difficult for some other reason to tell your partner or friend about your emotional turmoil. If so, you want to learn how to use the "I" language—that is, "I feel . . . ," "I want . . . ," and "I need . . . " Doing so will help you express yourself and let those who care about you know your emotional state in a non-threatening manner. Practice in your imagination, then mentally run through your script before you start a dialogue.

- **Respect and support your partner or friend.** This is a choice, an attitude, a mindset. When you make the commitment to respect others, you communicate in harmony. When you respect each other, you avoid being nasty and refrain from calling each other names or putting each other down. You are courteous, and use "excuse me," "I'm sorry," "please," and "thank you" as easily with those you are close to as you do with strangers.

COMMUNICATION APPROACH NUMBER SEVEN: COMMUNICATE TO OTHERS HOW MUCH YOU VALUE THE PEOPLE YOU LOVE

The way you speak in public about those you love, value, and respect reflects on you. Imagine yourself, for example, in this social situation. You are at a cocktail party engaged in conversation with someone you have just met. The topic of relationships comes up and, out of nowhere, the other person makes a negative comment about his or her spouse, significant other, or close friend. What would be your opinion of that individual? I always find that comments like this are immensely embarrassing, and make me question how compassionate, caring, and loving the person could be to speak of a loved one in such a way. It also makes the person look like a bit of a fool. And don't kid yourself—people do notice.

So you should never, ever communicate in a way that denigrates your partner or close friend in public. In fact, since public affirmation is one of the highest compliments you can pay to anyone, if the opportunity arises, you should speak of them in the most loving way possible. Tell a story that reflects their kindness and love. Praise their accomplishments and talents. Speak of their intelligence and acts of caring and consideration. What you say in public about others always affects how others see you.

COMMUNICATION APPROACH NUMBER EIGHT: NEVER THREATEN A RELATIONSHIP DURING A CONFLICT

If you voice your opinion and stand up for what you believe is right, you will on occasion encounter conflict. It's inevitable. In their book *Maximum Success*, James Waldroop and Timothy Butler write: "Conflict, although painful, serves a useful purpose. The clash of opposing ideas and strategies is a dynamic, creative process that reveals the strengths and weaknesses of each and leads to reconciliation at a higher level."[1] In other words, you can't cook without heat. Conflict can, however, be dealt with in a loving manner without attacking, blaming, or attempting to instill guilt in the other individual. The important point to remember about conflict is that no matter how intense the disagreement, you should never, ever threaten the relationship.

There are always what the British call "rough patches" in all relationships. There are also always times when a partner, spouse, or coworker either intentionally or otherwise tries to wound you with words or actions. It is at times like this that you may be tempted to threaten your relationship by presenting ultimatums. If you do, however, you are playing a very dangerous game, one that could inflict a deep wound—if not an irrevocable breach—in the relationship. The major danger an ultimatum presents is that the other person may call you on it. Imagine being so filled with fear that you say, "If you don't do what I want, I will leave," when what you really mean is, "I feel lonely and afraid, I want to be heard, and I need validation." But the other party, not understanding how you really feel, and responding to his or her own fear, may say, "OK. Leave." Then what do you do?

If, however, you remember the importance of always respecting the dignity of the individual—if that value has become part of who you are—you will be able to resist attempting to control another person by threats, intimidation, ultimatums, or name-calling. And you will avoid finding yourself in a situation in which, by expressing your anger rather than your respect, you will have lost a valued partner or friend.

COMMUNICATION APPROACH NUMBER NINE: SHOW GRATITUDE, SHOW APPRECIATION, AND ALWAYS SAY, "THANK YOU"

"Let us each give thanks for this beautiful day.
Let us give thanks for this life.
Let us give thanks for the water without which life would not be possible.
Let us give thanks for Grandmother Earth who protects and nourishes us."
—LAKOTA INDIAN DAILY PRAYER

Link Alert: Enter the URL **https://vimeo.com/mapes/8-2** in your web browser and then the password "**gratefulness**" to see and hear me speak about gratefulness. This is also explained below.

You might be surprised to hear it, but showing appreciation in both your relationship with yourself and with others has been shown to positively affect the brain, attitude, performance, and even health. According to the article "Boost Your Health with a Dose of Gratitude" by Brunilda Nazario on MedicineNet.com:

> Throughout history, philosophers and religious leaders have extolled gratitude as a virtue integral to health and well-being. Now, through a recent movement called positive psychology, mental health professionals are taking a close look at how virtues such as gratitude can benefit our health. And they're reaping some promising results.

In a 2012 report on some of the studies that have been done, "The Grateful Brain: The Neuroscience of Giving Thanks" in "PreFrontal Nudity," Dr. Alex Korb discusses some of these promising results.

> One study by . . . American researchers assigned young adults to keep a daily journal of things they were grateful for (Emmons and McCullough, 2003). They assigned other groups to journal about things that annoyed them, or reasons why they were better off than others. The young adults assigned to keep gratitude journals showed greater increases in determination, attention, enthusiasm and energy compared to the other groups. . . . The same researchers conducted a separate study on adults, which showed that even a weekly gratitude journal was beneficial. Subjects assigned to journal weekly on gratitude showed greater improvements in optimism. . . . But that's not all; it also influenced their behaviors. Keeping a gratitude journal also caused greater improvements in

exercise patterns. Lastly, it also caused a reduction in physical ailments . . .

A third study . . . did not require a gratitude journal, but simply looked at the amount of gratitude people tended to show in their daily lives (Ng et al., 2012). In this study, a group of Chinese researchers looked at the combined effects of gratitude and sleep quality on symptoms of anxiety and depression. They found that higher levels of gratitude were associated with better sleep, and with lower anxiety and depression. . . . The wide variety of effects that gratitude can have may seem surprising, but a direct look at the brain activity during gratitude yields some insight. The final study . . . comes from the National Institutes of Health. NIH researchers examined blood flow in various brain regions while subjects summoned up feelings of gratitude (Zahn et al., 2009). They found that subjects who showed more gratitude overall had higher levels of activity in the hypothalamus. This is important because the hypothalamus controls a huge array of essential bodily functions, including eating, drinking and sleeping. It also has a huge influence on your metabolism and stress levels.[2]

In other words, those who show gratitude also take better care of themselves and engage in more productive health behaviors. In addition, grateful people tend to be more optimistic, which has been shown to boost the immune system. Perhaps most important, focusing on gratitude can be a buffer to all the negative garbage life may thrust at you, so when you focus on being grateful, you are happier. But how do you do that? One way is to tune into your "Gratefulness Channel."

The Gratefulness Channel

When you are watching television you have a choice of which channel you want to watch. You can flip to AMC and watch a romantic tearjerker, switch on the SyFy channel and watch a horror film, or choose Comedy

Central and laugh your head off. Imagine, though, what would happen if, as you flipped through the stations, you landed on one showing a violent or depressing movie, and when you went to change it you discovered that the cable box had frozen and you could neither change the channel nor turn off the set. Now, time passes and you still can't change what's on, but you become so used to living with the negative images and sounds that they become normal, a way of viewing reality, and a habit. To make matters worse, you may not even realize it, but what's showing on your television also begins to negatively affect your health by increasing your level of stress.

The same would hold true if your mental channel was tuned to sadness, dismay, or hopelessness. It would become so familiar that you wouldn't even know your life was being diminished. Is it possible that at this moment you are stuck on a life-diminishing mental channel and don't even know it? Or you do know it and can't seem to get unstuck? Can it be that you are unconsciously focusing on self-pity, scarcity, hopelessness, resentment, victimization, jealousy, failure, rejection, or worry? The only way to find out if you are is to look at your life. Examine your attitude. Are you focusing on what you have or what you don't have? If you are experiencing more negativity and conflict than peace and love, you are probably stuck on the wrong channel. But unlike the television nightmare I asked you to imagine, you can get unstuck by learning to shift your focus to gratitude. When you are tuned into your Gratefulness Channel and appreciate what you have, you cannot dwell on the channel of your frustration, hurts, or fears.

When you change to your Gratefulness Channel, you shift your focus from scarcity to abundance. Gratefulness fills up your spirit and awakens something special deep within you—your ability to let abundance flow outward into the world. It is by being grateful that you learn to share, to give of yourself, and to be of service. It may manifest itself in any number of ways—giving someone a compliment, praising someone for his or her success, smiling at someone who is lonely, taking a friend out to lunch, or working in a soup kitchen. As your coach, I want to prompt, poke, and prod you to focus on the limitless number of things for which you can be grateful.

You tune into your Gratefulness Channel by recognizing and focusing on what you have to be grateful for. Even in the darkest lives there are things we can and should appreciate, if only we are conscious of what they are. It can be your health, your family, your friends, your social life, the food you have to eat, flowers and nature, your pets, your work, your home, music, books, movies, the beauty of the world . . . the list is literally endless. I would suggest that in order to remind yourself of what you have to be grateful for, you list as many of these items as you can in your journal. There are also, however, two other very effective ways of tuning into that channel.

THE THIRTY-DAY GRATEFULNESS EXERCISE

I started using this exercise with my private clients twenty years ago to help them recognize what they were grateful for, and literally every one of them has reported truly dramatic results. Perhaps one of the most remarkable things about it is how incredibly simple it is.

Over the next thirty days, just before you go to sleep, I want you to review your day and list in your journal five things for which you are grateful. Each night you can draw on the gratefulness list you've already compiled, or you can come up with additional items that weren't included there. It doesn't matter what you choose, as long as it's something you are grateful for. Then, immediately upon awakening, jump-start your day and reboot your brain with a positive mindset by quickly reviewing the list you wrote the previous evening, briefly focusing on one of five things for which you are grateful, and then circling it. That's it! This is all that is required of you. Try it, and if you are like my clients, I suspect you will choose to make it part of your on-going daily routine.

THE "THANK YOU" LIST EXERCISE

Gratefulness goes two ways—it's not just about what you are grateful for, it's also about expressing your gratitude to others. You never want to take a person or what that person does for granted. It is very easy to get used to loving acts others do for you, but it is important to remember that they are gifts, and you want to avoid becoming complacent. So, as the last exercise in this chapter, I would like you to make a short list of those people who have done loving acts for you and ask yourself, "Did I give them my heartfelt thanks? What can I do or say today to express my gratitude?" It is never too late. And remember as you go forward in life that a simple "thank you" goes a long, long way.

. . .

Learning how to communicate with love is similar to learning a new language. When you get it, you get it. And in the meantime, the more you practice, the better you become. As you put the Four Strategies for Successful Relationships and the Nine Approaches to Achieving Exceptional Communication into practice, and incorporate them into your life, you will find that they will become part of your daily interpersonal communication. And in turn they will not only open a new world of relationships, but they will also help you attain an exceptional life. You do teach people how to treat you, so teach them well. Imagine that!

THINKPOINTS

- You teach people how to treat you—others will treat you as they perceive you.
- Set your standards for what you want from your relationships.
- Communicate your rules for relationships.
- When others ignore your standards or rules, let them know.
- Be willing to let a bad relationship go after you have given it your all.
- When you listen, listen with your whole being.
- Refrain from invalidating others' beliefs.
- Criticize with the touch of a feather.

- Ask for what you want and need.
- Communicate to others how much they are valued and loved.
- Let those closest to you know when you are lonely, in pain, or feel misunderstood.
- Communicate to others how much you value those you love.
- Never threaten a relationship during conflict.
- Show gratitude, appreciation, and always say, "Thank you."

9

TRANSFORM FEAR INTO LOVE

"In order to create, there must be a dynamic force,
and what force is more dynamic than love?"
—IGOR STRAVINSKY

Attaining an exceptional life is something like a treasure hunt in which one clue leads to another until you reach your ultimate goal. The next clue you must follow in order to reach this particular goal is to recognize that the Elephant ultimately experiences only two pure emotions—love and fear. When it is experiencing love it cannot experience fear, and when it is experiencing fear it cannot experience love. One totally cancels out the other. "But wait," you say, "There are many other emotions besides love and fear. What about happiness, excitement, and pleasure? What about anger, depression, and jealousy? If there is only love or fear, where do these emotions fit in?" That is certainly a logical question, and there is a relatively simple answer. If you peel away the layers of the emotional onion, what you find at the core of all the positive feelings is a reflection of love. And if you peel away the layers of all the negative feelings, what you ultimately find is a reflection of fear.

What is perhaps even more important to recognize, however, is that on some level, you have a choice about whether you allow love or fear to rule your life. If you choose fear, that is, if you let the Elephant be controlled by fear, you will not only have stress, internal conflict, and disharmony, you will also be unable to forgive. If, however, you choose love, that is, if you learn the art of forgiveness, which is what transforms the Elephant's primitive survival fear into love, you will be able to create harmony between the Elephant and the Rider, and ultimately attain the exceptional life you want to live. But before we start looking at how you can achieve that exceptional life, it's necessary for us to first determine exactly what we mean by love and fear.

The Meaning of Love

"Unconditional love given on a daily basis can melt mountains."
—JAMES TAYLOR

In its purest form, love has absolutely nothing attached to it, neither desire nor expectation. It is unconditional and given freely. Pure love goes beyond intimate relationships, sex, family, or marriage. I'm sure this concept is not new to you. In fact, you may well have done your best to live this way only to decide that it's simply too much work, or that people don't respond the way you want them to. If that's so, however, you should reread the definition, think again about whether or not you have really lived this way, and, if necessary, shift your thinking.

Ultimately, whether or not you are capable of experiencing pure love depends on how you experience reality. The easiest way to determine this is to ask yourself a simple question: "Do I experience the majority of my life in peace, abundance, and love, or do I spend just a little too much time experiencing anxiety, scarcity, and fear?" If your scale tips to the negative, you are seeing the world through the lens of fear, and what you need to do is stop, reframe, and transform fear into love.

And how do you do that? You do it essentially by exploring and challenging the Elephant's old, limiting paradigms and belief systems about love. While doing so may at times make the Elephant feel uncomfortable, the payoff is well worth it. In fact, if you give yourself the chance to embrace the possibility of pure love, you will transform your life. How do I know that's true? I base it on the research and experiences of many experts in the field, my own experience working with thousands of people, and the fact that giving myself that chance enabled me to overcome my own challenges.

Another path to transforming fear into love is through spirituality. Although it is not mandatory, spirituality can play a role in living an exceptional life. Unfortunately, people tend to use "spirituality" and "religion" interchangeably, even though they are not the same thing. Religion, in its purest meaning, is a system of practice that connects us to the divine; often it is a formal organization that not only organizes spirituality but also purports to have an exclusive interpretation of God. Spirituality, on the other hand, is a personal interpretation of something greater than yourself and what that might mean to you personally.

What does something "greater than yourself" mean? For some it does mean traditional religious beliefs, but it is really limited only by your imagination. I have some friends who for years have been volunteer teachers in a local kindergarten class. I have others who give their time to local charities. Stars who use their celebrity status to draw attention to the plight of others are also embracing something greater than themselves. There is literally no end to the possibilities. The point is that whether it is through traditional religion or through other choices, when you feel you are a part of something, you shift your attention from yourself to something more. And that, in turn, enables you to open yourself to the restorative and healing power of forgiveness, and to have an exceptional life. Before, however, you can take the next step toward attaining that life, it's important that you understand exactly what fear is.

The Meaning of Fear

Love, relatively speaking, is simple; fear is much more complicated. It is also, unfortunately, much more common—so much so, in fact, that it pervades our lives. Just to give you an idea of exactly how pervasive it is, attorney Michael Fitzsimmons, a partner at the law firm Duensing, Casner & Fitzsimmons located in St. Thomas, U.S.V.I., once told me that, as a litigator, understanding the extent to which people are motivated by fear provides "a very useful perspective from which to assess situations and to plan strategies. Because of the nature of litigation, fear predominates as a core motivator. In litigation, everybody, on some level, is fearful of something—the plaintiff, the defendant, the plaintiff's attorney, the defendant's attorney, witnesses, and the judge. In short, all the actors are in fear to some degree." By recognizing this reality, he added, "a lawyer better understands the terrain in which he operates."

Ultimately, there are three categories, or faces, of fear. The first is "delicious fear," the kind you may feel before going scuba diving, ballooning, or shooting the rapids. It's a fear that creates natural excitement and energy, and is one of the reasons reasonable risk-taking is important. The second is "primitive fear," the kind that's programmed into our DNA and has kept us alive as a species. However, unless you are a soldier, a firefighter, or a police officer, this type of fear actually works to your disadvantage. This is because the Elephant in each of us is genetically designed to interpret even benign situations (someone cutting in front of us at the checkout counter or well-intentioned criticism) as a threat to our survival, and therefore reacts in the "fight" mode. The third and final type of fear is "illusory fear," which includes our fear of failure, rejection, success, change, commitment, and poverty, and is the kind of fear in which we essentially trick ourselves into creating the very thing we fear—a "self-fulfilling prophesy."

Delicious Fear

Delicious fear is the kind of fear you want to have. It's what you feel when you take the plunge into a new adventure. It is more intense than excitement but not as excruciatingly stressful and potentially self-defeating as primitive fear. It focuses, highlights, and brightens your experience. I experienced this kind of fear while on a safari in East Africa when four of us decided to go out on a morning walk with our guides. As we moved silently and slowly through the verdant bush, I felt it. It was the anticipated thrill of encountering a dangerous animal, yet knowing that I was protected. I also felt this fear when I began skiing, learned to scuba dive, went for a hot-air ballooning license, and took race car driving lessons. I feel it when I embark on learning a new skill or speak in front of an audience. In fact, I experience delicious fear whenever I venture into any new and unfamiliar territory. This face of fear heightens our sense of aliveness, creativity, and pleasure. Delicious fear is a form of fear to be celebrated.

Primitive Fear

Primitive fear isn't nearly as much fun as delicious fear, and it is the real thing. It's inborn, automatic, and hard-wired in the brain; that is, it's programed into the DNA of the Elephant. Of course, at one time our very survival depended on our defense-related emotions and reactions. Back in those wild days when a very large animal might have taken a bite out of one of your ancestors, or someone bonked his neighbor over the head and stole his food, fear served a very useful purpose. It allowed humans to detect danger and their fight-or-flight instincts gave them the edge to respond quickly to all threats.

This primitive fear is triggered in the reptilian part of the Elephant's brain and activates the sympathetic nervous system. With the assistance of the creative imagination, the survival response can be amplified to powerful and dangerous levels. As potent hormones are released into the bloodstream, the heart beats faster, blood pressure rises, and blood flows to the muscles. At the same time, our feet turn cold, our sweat glands churn, our vision narrows, and the pupils of our eyes dilate so we can see better. We prepare to do battle! We are at the ready to throw the spear, ward off the enemy, or run like the dickens.

However, while the human nervous system has not changed very much in the thousands of years since it developed, our needs have. For most of us living in the twenty-first century our fears reflect something slightly different. Some of these fears, of course, are realistic—it's entirely possible that we might be beaten up, mugged, stabbed, shot, or otherwise harmed. There are also the looming threats of terrorism and disease. All of these things can occur, even if they are not particularly likely to. And because of that, primitive fear serves a purpose when it prevents us from putting ourselves in physical jeopardy by walking down a dark alley in a shady neighborhood or balancing on one leg atop the Eiffel Tower. In fact, fear gives us an early warning when we are in true danger and prepares the body and mind to act unconsciously and quickly to protect us from potential disaster.

Unless you are a soldier in the midst of war or involved in law enforcement, it's fair to say that you needn't be afraid of most of these things happening. I'm not suggesting that you should try to eliminate primitive fear. That would be a foolish waste of time, as well as quite impossible. The Elephant is, after all, you. However, I strongly advise you to learn to recognize the difference between primitive fear and the third type of fear—illusory fear.

Illusory Fear

Most of the fear we experience is based on the illusion of a threat to our survival. In other words, it is a trick of the imagination. Even so, once our minds see the illusion as real, the brain goes into action. The Rider's thinking becomes exaggerated and distorted, and we become focused only on short-term survival. Prompted by fear, we go on the lookout for every possible danger, overreact to slights, and tend to perceive everything in our environment as a threat. The fact is, though, that the person cutting you off at the intersection really isn't trying to spear you, and the individual who gets the last piece of steak from the meat case isn't really going to put you in any danger of starving. Neither is being caught in rush hour traffic, bouncing a check, having a disagreement with your spouse, being rebuked by your boss, or missing a deadline. The problem isn't the actual event; it is the Rider's perception of the event. In fact, if would be helpful if you looked at this kind of fear as *False Evidence Appearing Real*. Your job is to recognize that, and to develop the skill to push the "pause" button long enough to discern the difference and reframe the situation.

Link Alert: Enter the URL **https://vimeo.com/mapes/9** in your web browser and then the password **"transform"** to see and hear a demonstration of an illusion in which both the appearance of a circling green dot and the disappearance of other dots are totally created by your mind. They don't exist—just like illusory fear.

Credit: Green Dot illusion, "Hinton's Lilac Chaser" © Jeremy L. Hinton.

Think about illusory fear this way. If you were to smear a gooey mass of molasses over the lens of a movie camera, the filmed footage would be clouded and distorted. Fear works the same way. It clouds the perceptual filter through which you view and experience the world. You then project your fear outward onto the world, and by doing so trick yourself into believing that the false evidence is indeed real. And since this false evidence for our fear justifies our outlandish response, we see our negative behavior as totally appropriate. Unfortunately, when we see the world this way we feel compelled to act or react without considering the consequences of our actions. We compete, become defensive, procrastinate, make excuses, hoard, feel superior, put down, blame others, and exhibit a whole raft of other negative behaviors. In addition, illusory fear feeds on itself, and when our fear triggers fear in others, the result is often a mirror image of our own fear-based behavior, which in turn further fuels that fear. In order for you to break out of the warped reality of illusory fear, however, you must want to recognize and confront the fear head-on. And by doing so you can become a peacemaker rather than a fear enabler.

"A thousand fearful images and dire suggestions glance along the mind when it is moody and discontented with itself. Command them to stand and show themselves, and you presently assert the power of reason over imagination."

—SIR WALTER SCOTT, *THE JOURNAL OF SIR WALTER SCOTT, 1825-1832*

How much control do you actually have over fear? You have a lot more than you may believe, and you can exercise that control by managing your thinking. You do that by learning to distinguish between fears that are reasonable and those that are not, fears that manipulate you into making self-destructive choices and fears that simply prod you to pay attention. Equally important, you must recognize that none of us operates in a vacuum. Fear-based thinking impacts others' Elephants just as love-based thinking does. That's why it is so important for you to understand the destructive nature of what I call "The Dances of Fear."

The Dances of Fear

I'm sorry to have to report that The Dances of Fear are not the latest reality show craze. Nor are they graceful, and they are most certainly not fun. These dances, instead, are executed to a pounding beat in which one person's fear-based steps trigger another's fear-based defense moves, and they fall into six types. These six Dances of Fear represent fear of rejection, failure, change, success, commitment, and poverty. There are, however, many cousins in the family of fear. The fear of abandonment is a cousin to fear of rejection. The fear of being inadequate—whether emotionally, physically, sexually, spiritually, or socially—resides side-by-side with fear of failure. Fear of the unknown is a relative to the fear of change, and fear of being found out as a fraud is connected to the fear of success. The fear of being part of a group may be related to the fear of commitment, and the fear of loaning money to a friend may be linked to the fear of poverty. In other words, fears wear many disguises, and sometimes the layers must be peeled back to identify the actual fear. This is the purpose of exploring the Dances of Fear.

THE REJECTION TWO-STEP

One of the most common fears is the fear of rejection. On some level, everyone is afraid of rejection, and I suspect everyone has experienced it sometime in his or her life. It might have been being rejected by someone with whom you wanted a relationship, being turned down for a job, or even being denied membership in an organization. It is also natural to fear that we might be rejected, and there is nothing wrong with feeling that way. When I stand before an audience, attempt to sell a new idea, or open up to a new friendship, I still feel a little nibble of this fear. Instead of resisting, I've learned to feel the fear, stop, recognize it for what it is, reframe my thinking, and use the fear itself to give me energy to focus on what I need to do. The problem comes when the fear triggers the Elephant's fight-or-flight mode, which in turn dictates your behavior.

This kind of fear can keep people from doing many things they might otherwise wish to do, such as asking someone out on a date, starting a business, or asking for a promotion. But avoiding rejection not only disables us from doing things we want to do, it can also create damaging patterns of behavior. It can make us doubt ourselves and even cause us to feel that we are not good enough and don't deserve what we want.

Like all The Dances of Fear, though, the Rejection Two-Step has mirror image steps; that is, the fear of rejection can trigger others to actually make the very choices you fear, thereby giving you the "proof" that what you suspected is true. For example, becoming jealous, obsessive, or clingy can drive others away before a relationship has even begun. If this fear goes unrecognized and unexamined it can, and often does, create separation. However, when acknowledged and investigated, the fear of rejection dissipates in power. Most important, regardless of the form any such fear takes, when confronted with it, it might be worthwhile to recall Eleanor Roosevelt's suggestion that "no one can make you feel inferior without your consent."

THE FAILURE SAMBA

Like all fear, the fear of failure can manipulate you into a trap of your own making. It can keep you from taking the risks necessary for personal growth. It can inhibit you from voicing your opinion, learning new skills, trying out new ideas, and forming strategic alliances. The Trickster can also sway the Rider into making up and believing the worst-case scripts of doom and gloom. "What if I fail?" "The odds are against me so why even try?" "I'll only put the weight back on so why should I diet?" "Everything bad always seems to happen to me." "I know my boss is going to reject my ideas so why bother suggesting anything?" Simply put, the fear of failure can keep us stuck.

The Failure Samba also has its mirror image steps. Fear of failure can manipulate you into taking foolish risks that will guarantee your failure. It might, for example, make you rush blindly into a promising investment opportunity only to find out it's a scam. It might lead you to choose untrustworthy business associates or refuse to take advantage of a lucrative opportunity. Fear of failure can also lead you to surround yourself with "yes" people who won't challenge you even if you are on a destructive path. It can also manipulate you into focusing your time and energy on activities that keep you from facing a problem. The good news, though, is that recognizing, confronting, and examining the fear of failure can lead to taking well thought-out risks, learning from failures, growing, and moving forward on a positive path.

THE FEAR OF CHANGE MAMBO

Every time I mention to a dear friend and business associate of mine the possibility of him personally changing something in his life, he puts both his hands on his cheeks like Macaulay Culkin in the first *Home Alone* movie and screams, "Change! Noooooo!" The truth is that many people feel the same way, even if they don't express it quite so dramatically. Others fall victim to their fear without even realizing it. The Elephant likes the status quo. It is afraid of loss.

The reality, though, is that change is something that happens to us in subtle ways every day. People come and go in our lives. Shops and restaurants close and new ones open. Roads we travel frequently are shut down for repair and new roads are built. In fact, small changes happen so often that we don't usually recognize the stress they create. Of course, when the change is major, we stress mightily. Change that radically alters or even threatens to alter our physical or mental health, environment, relationships, or situation challenges our existing paradigm of how things have always been and should be.

If left unrecognized and unchallenged, the fear of change can affect you in every area of your life. It can block you from creating positive mindsets and adapting new life-enhancing behaviors. It can prohibit you from letting go of negative baggage from your past and block your ability to forgive. Fear of change can also prevent you from projecting into the future and identifying what the upside or downside of making a change might be. Finally, it can also keep you from eliminating destructive habits and behaviors such as excessive drinking, drugs, or poor eating habits.

In addition, in the mirror image steps of this dance, fear of change may manipulate you into creating change for the sake of change by deceiving you into believing that your happiness and satisfaction depend on what you have or who you know. For example, some people move from one social circle to another hoping they will then be perceived as more credible or upwardly mobile even though, in fact, it may only serve to give others the impression that they are unreliable or unwilling to commit. It may also influence you to move from one relationship to another in the false belief that the next change will give you what you want—the perfect mate. Fear of change can also enable you to procrastinate by making you believe that just being "busy" is moving you forward when all it is actually doing is avoiding change. Finally, it can prompt you into avoiding communicating with a partner, friend, or business associate and thereby manipulate them into avoiding you, becoming aggressive, or taking some other action.

When it comes to living an exceptional life, the most important thing for you to know is that the larger your goal, the more you will be required to change, and the greater your resistance to change will be. In order to grow, however, it is essential that you do whatever you need to do to step out of your comfort zone. Psychotherapist, author, and expert on self-esteem Nathaniel Branden said, "The first step toward change is awareness. The second step is acceptance."

THE FEAR OF SUCCESS WALTZ

Over my years of coaching I have made a variety of discoveries about human nature. One of the most amazing of these is that a large number of people who believe they have a fear of failure actually have a fear of success. Doesn't that seem odd? Why would someone be afraid of success? Here are some of the reasons clients have provided: "I don't really deserve to be successful." "If I'm successful, I don't think I can I maintain it." "If I'm successful, I'll have too much responsibility." "If I'm successful, people will demand more of me." "If I'm successful, I'll have to work harder and I'll have even less time for myself." Do any of these "reasons" sound familiar to you? Do you have a fear of success that you have mistaken for a fear of failure? Ultimately, however logical the justification for *not* being successful may seem, the underlying belief is invariably "I cannot handle what may come my way." So what may seem like fear of failure turns out to be fear of success.

In order to understand this, we must go back to the Elephant's need to stay in its comfort zone. Some people actually feel comfortable with success and will work extremely hard to turn a failure into success. Others, however, are more comfortable with failure, and if the opportunity to succeed presents itself, or by some miracle they succeed, they will sabotage their success by turning it into failure. Even the thought of success, let alone actually achieving it, makes people who are manipulated by this fear feel unbalanced, and it topples their equilibrium. The Elephant, then, takes over and finds a way to feel safe; that is, it steps back on the familiar path by helping the Rider confirm what the Rider already knew, that he or she is a failure. As Marianne Williamson put it in *A Return to Love*, "Our deepest fear is not that we are inadequate. Our deepest fear is that we are powerful beyond measure. It is our light, not our darkness, that most frightens us. We ask ourselves, who am I to be brilliant, gorgeous, talented, and fabulous?"

Those who have a fear of success are likely to not accept invitations that would put them in the company of successful people, or take advantage of opportunities for advancement because they subconsciously associate success with something they consider evil, such as money or competition. As with the other dances, the waltz has its mirror image steps. Individuals who suffer from this kind of fear are frequently late for appointments, miss deadlines, break their word, rebuff offers of help, constantly pick fights with those they work with, and, in general, display behaviors that are likely to ensure their failure.

THE FEAR OF COMMITMENT TANGO

James P. Womack, founder of the Lean Enterprise Institute, says, "Commitment unlocks the doors of imagination, allows vision, and gives us the 'right stuff' to turn our dreams into reality." That's the positive result of having the courage to commit. The fear of commitment, however, can make the difference between settling for what you have and attaining what you really want. Of course, most individuals relate this fear to the avoidance of long-term partnerships, romantic relationships, or marriage. In reality, though, it actually covers a much broader spectrum and can easily affect a person's work, home, and academic life. More important is the fact that, at its extreme, this fear can be both destructive and exhausting.

This is a peculiar type of fear because, at its most basic, the Elephant wants connection and love—to be part of something bigger. However, along the journey of life, as a result of negative input or programming, a belief that commitment means being trapped, or perhaps betrayed, has become part of the Elephant's makeup. And since this belief is so much stronger than the need for love and connection, when it is triggered the reaction of the Rider is often one of indecision and confusion, resulting in self-destructive behavior. This behavior—simply running away from a relationship, a partnership, an agreement, or making a decision—is essentially an effort to avoid the responsibilities, duties, and obligations required with commitment, even while the individual secretly desires the very thing he or she is pushing away.

Like the other dances, though, the Fear of Commitment Tango has mirror image steps. Those who have this fear sometimes overcommit, that is, are unwilling to say "No more! Enough!" But as a result they are then unable to fulfill their obligations to others. The most common negative outcome of this dance is on potential long-term relationships. Individuals with this kind of fear often have an impossibly long list of requirements for the "perfect" mate, tend to be most interested in people who are unavailable (such as those who are already married), and are likely to end relationships before they get too serious and, in the process, hurt both themselves and others.

If you find yourself confronted with the fear of commitment, it would be helpful to remember the words of William Hutchison Murray, a Scottish mountaineer and author of *The Scottish Himalayan Expedition*, who wrote, "Concerning all acts of initiative (and creation), there is one elementary truth the ignorance of which kills countless ideas and splendid plans: that the moment one definitely commits oneself, then providence moves too."

THE FEAR OF POVERTY FOX-TROT

The sixth and final major fear is the fear of poverty. I am not, of course, ignoring the very real poverty that exists on our planet. What I am concerned with here is how our perceptions and behavior can be manipulated by the fear of poverty. The primary symptom of this fear is constantly worrying about not having enough money, even when you have as much money as you need. It often clouds people's vision of the future, and keeps them from learning from failures and bouncing back from adversity. It is often at the root of criminality, such as stealing, refusing to pay taxes, and other dishonest behaviors.

Above all, this kind of fear can hold you back from achieving success and living an exceptional life. It can, for example, keep you from seeing and seizing opportunities that would bring prosperity, such as starting a new job or a new business, because you believe that making such a change would result in your losing everything. It can also keep you from making decisions by leading you to overanalyze everything. The mirror image steps for this fear include pushing yourself into making self-defeating and life-diminishing choices, such as saving all your money and denying yourself what gives you pleasure, the result of which is to make you feel poor.

This fear is often the result of an extremely negative event from the past that has been stored away in the Elephant's memory bank. Let me give you a personal example. While my mother was a terrific, bright, and loving person, she carried with her, as many of her generation have, a poverty mentality stemming from the Depression. She would constantly complain, expressing her worry about not having enough money, and shopping at a multitude of stores to save a few pennies on food or clothes. Despite my father assuring her and reassuring her that we would "get by," she would verbally paint her disaster scenarios. My subconscious Elephant paid attention, and as a result it has had a profound effect on me. For many years I worried constantly and worked every job I could so as to "have enough." Even when I was making a good income, I scrimped and saved, refused to take vacations, and worried, worried, worried.

In fact, I didn't begin to turn my negative belief system around until I was able to identify my fear, admit that I needed help, and open myself to examining that fear. My breakthrough came when a friend recommended two books, Napoleon Hill's *Think and Grow Rich* and Phil Laut's *Money Is My Friend*, both of which provided examples and stories that helped me recognize my fear as well as strategies, such as visualization and affirmation, that enabled me to release its hold on me. Once I understood where my fear came from, I was able to recognize that while my mother's fear was the right thing for her, it had nothing to do with my circumstances. I also took a class in abundance thinking and eventually used my Rider to help me eliminate a poverty mentality and develop an abundance mentality.

• • •

Please do not blame yourself for having fears. Not only does it serve no purpose, it limits your ability to act. Fear is part of the Elephant, so it's natural and normal. What is important to recognize is that almost all—if not all—our fears are illusory. Now that you understand how The Dances of Fear can keep you from doing things you would like to do, and make you do things that are not necessarily in your best interests, the next step in the process is to determine exactly what your own fears are, deconstruct them, and use the tools in your mental tool kit to break through them.

Identifying Your Fear

"You gain strength, courage and confidence by every experience
in which you must stop and look fear in the face. . . .You must do
the thing you think you cannot do."

—ELEANOR ROOSEVELT

We all have fears, whether or not we recognize them, and whether or not we admit to having them. This was dramatically demonstrated to me some years ago when I was presenting a program to a sales group of five hundred men and women. After I had defined the nature of fear to them, I said, "I want all of you who are afraid of rejection to raise your hands." At first there was total silence as everyone scanned the room waiting for that first person to confess. And then it was like popcorn popping. Two, three, ten, twenty, fifty, one hundred, two hundred, four hundred, and finally five hundred hands went into the air. It was amazing to me, and startling to them. What it demonstrated was that even though on some level every human is afraid—in this case of rejection—we all feel unique and alone in our fear.

If, though, we are ever going to overcome those fears, it is necessary that we both identify and admit them. Unfortunately, it is not always easy to pinpoint exactly what they are. For that reason, I have listed below a number of common fears. Read the list and use it as a springboard for discovery. Take your time and make use of your Tool for Truth—that is, pay attention not only to what your mind is telling you but to what your body is saying as well. When something resonates with you, write it down, and do it immediately. Identifying your fears is the first step to silencing the Trickster.

YOUR TURN

Read through the following list and determine if you are afraid of:

- forming a relationship because you have been rejected in the past?
- speaking in front of an audience for fear that people will laugh at you?

- taking a new idea to your boss because he or she may think you are stupid?
- starting your own business because you may fail?
- letting go of a negative or abusive relationship because you believe it is safer than stepping into the unknown?
- letting go of a job you hate because it is safer than the unknown?
- intimacy because you're easily embarrassed?
- spending money because you feel poor?
- committing to something because you may want to change your mind?
- being successful because you may not be able to maintain that success?
- being successful because people won't like you?
- being taken advantage of?
- confronting health issues?
- having responsibility because you believe you can't handle it?
- telling someone the truth because you want to avoid conflict?
- committing to a relationship because you will feel trapped?

Recognizing the "Payoff" for Fear

Once you have identified a fear, or possible fear, there is an important question you have to ask yourself: "What is the payoff?" That is, what do you get out of this fear? "But what kind of payoff can there be?" you may ask. After all, you don't want the bloody fear. Well, perhaps. But the fact is that for every choice you make there is always a real or perceived payoff. And the deeply embedded hidden assumption that colors all of our decision making is an underlying belief that whatever decision we make will ultimately help us avoid pain and gain pleasure. "But why," you ask, "would anyone make a self-defeating decision?" Think about eating a giant candy bar. You know it's loaded with bad stuff, but you also know that it's going to taste good and satisfy you. You may feel guilty afterward but you still eat it, because you want the payoff more than you want to give away the candy bar. The Elephant does not like to make a short-term sacrifice for a long-term payoff.

How do you determine the payoff for a fear? Again, you start by asking yourself the right questions: What does the fear let me avoid? Who does it let me avoid? What responsibility do I get to avoid? What does it let me hold on to, even if it's to my or someone else's detriment? Who does it let me blame for my problems other than myself? Answering these questions, understanding the payoff for your choices, helps you move closer to shifting your thinking and transforming fear into love.

Here are some examples of how fear can provide you with a payoff:

- If you are afraid of telling the truth, the payoff may be that you avoid confrontation or possible rejection.

- If you are afraid of asking someone out or of breaking off a relationship first, the payoff may be that you avoid being rejected.

- If you are afraid to break off an abusive relationship, the payoff may be that you can avoid the unknown.

- If you are afraid to ask for what you want and need, the payoff may be that no one can deny you.

- If you are afraid to open yourself up to love, the payoff may be that you believe you can avoid being hurt.

- If you are afraid to do what's necessary to lose weight, the payoff may be that you can avoid intimacy.

- If you are afraid to take risks, the payoff may be that you believe you can't fail.

- If you are afraid to commit, the payoff may be that you get to procrastinate.

- If you are afraid to try to be successful, the payoff may be that you can remain comfortable, avoid responsibility, and stay out of the limelight.

Do any of these things sound familiar to you? Some of them may sound silly, but the fact is that no matter how absurd the payoff may seem, it makes sense when you consider the malevolent intent of the ego and the self-fulfilling aspect of fear. And these are just a few possibilities. There are actually endless payoffs for both positive and negative choices. Again, the question you have to answer is, "What is the payoff?" That is, what do you get for holding on to fear? Once you have discovered the perceived payoff for not challenging your assumptions, not breaking through fear, not changing your behavior, and not having what you really want in your life, you will be on the path to letting go of powerlessness, helplessness, and victimization. And, most important, you will be able to transform fear into love!

Transforming Fear into Love

By now I'm confident that you have a clear picture of what fear is, how it works, what fear might be influencing your behavior, and what your perceived payoff is for retaining that fear. Therefore it's time for you to take the next step toward transforming fear into love. The following exercise is designed to help you accomplish that by launching you on the path of introspection.

Introspection is essentially a skill that enables you to get to know yourself at the core, and it is one of the most important skills you can develop. Even though the Elephant may resist being examined in this way, you can get past that resistance by making the choice to do it, and doing it often. You are much more than a leaf being blown wherever the wind might take you. No one makes you do anything or think anything. You have much more control than that. Even when something or someone pushes your buttons, you still have a choice. By tapping your inner wisdom, you can get in touch with, determine, and mute your fear; examine a present challenge, behavior, or feeling that is perplexing you; and take practical, well thought-out risks. Introspection is, however, challenging to commit to and build into your life. Here, then, are some guidelines to help you achieve it.

- Create a quiet space. This does not mean you have to seclude yourself in a room (although some people do). You can do it by staying in bed a little longer before you get up in the morning, sitting quietly with your favorite morning beverage, or taking a walk in the woods. I like to go fishing or walk on the beach. Being alone and relaxing is the key.

- Ask yourself questions. Exactly what these questions are depends on your own situation. They may be questions such as "What would I do if I had no fear?" or "What kind of job would I do if I could make a living doing what I love?" You know better than anyone else what sort of questions you need to answer.

- Set aside judgment. Although I can almost guarantee that you will get an answer to any question you ask yourself, even though the answer may be insightful, it might also be silly. Don't be judgmental. Just accept the answer and glean whatever information you can from it.

- Write your insights down. It's important to do this because thoughts are illusive, and you want to capture whatever information your subconscious Elephant gives up.

- Reflect. Reflection is a valuable tool. It's somewhat difficult to do, but it becomes easier with practice.

Ultimately, becoming an expert in introspection depends on your being able to recognize that your prejudices, biases, and assumptions dramatically influence your perceptions, and therefore your interpretation of reality. Like any skill, introspection takes work, but once you get it, you've got it. Then, like the intuitive and immediate defensive response of a martial arts master, you become introspective automatically whenever the need arises. And when that happens, you can break down the protective shell the Elephant creates to keep you safe and protect you from being hurt by what others do or say. You can also be open to take in advice, learn from constructive criticism, challenge your own assumptions, and ask the hard questions of yourself. The bottom line is that introspection gives you information and information helps you build awareness. It puts the Rider on alert to catch yourself when the Elephant's fear begins to manifest itself in action, to confront the things you fear, to smash them apart, and to live an exceptional life.

YOUR TURN

Although it is most important for you to think about the answers to the following questions, it will be helpful to you if you write them down in your journal or on your computer. That way you will have a record of how aware you are of your illusory fears and how they affect you today, and then in the future you will be able to measure how much your awareness and ability to be introspective have grown.

- What fear or fears do I have or believe I have?
- What expectations do I have about others that are causing me to feel these fears?
- What actions am I not taking because of these fears? That is, in what way are these fears limiting my ability to enjoy my life and have peace of mind?
- What actions am I taking because of these fears? That is, what am I doing because of the fear that I wouldn't do if I didn't have the fear?
- What is the payoff for holding on to these limiting behaviors? That is, am I protecting myself? Is it enabling me to avoid seeing or speaking my truth to someone, or is it limiting my ability to form a strong social network, be part of a group, or attend social functions?
- What would I have to change about my thinking to let go of my fears?
- What actions/risks can I take now that would take me out of my comfort zone and move me toward what I say I want?
- Am I willing to take those actions/risks?
- What's the worst that can happen, and am I willing to have it happen?

Once you have answered these questions, you should be able to stop the Dance of Fear by bringing to light your own beliefs and behavior. That's because once you are aware of the voice of the Trickster, fear immediately begins to lose its power. You also now have the tools to transform fear into love, and take the first step toward creating harmony between the Elephant and the Rider. You are becoming an Artist of Possibility, the sculptor of your own reality. Imagine that!

THINKPOINTS

- There are only two pure emotions—love and fear—and they cannot exist at the same time in the same space.
- There are three categories of fear—delicious, primitive, and illusory fear.
- Most fear is illusory, that is, it is *F*alse *E*vidence *A*ppearing *R*eal.
- There are six Dances of Fear representing the fears of rejection, failure, change, success, commitment, and poverty.
- Identifying your illusory fear is the first step toward silencing the Trickster, that is, breaking through the illusion, dismantling the fear, and releasing its hold over your thoughts and behavior.
- There is a payoff for every choice you make, even though it may be negative or destructive.
- You must recognize what that payoff is if you want to escape the trap of negative behavior.
- Awareness is ultimately what enables you to transform fear into love.

10

LEARN WHAT MAKES YOU FEEL LOVED

"To cheat oneself out of love is the most terrible deception; it is an
eternal loss for which there is no reparation, either in time or in eternity."
—SØREN KIERKEGAARD

Given the alternatives of walking down a dark, garbage-filled alley or
strolling along a broad, well-lit street, the subconscious Elephant will
always influence the Rider to choose the latter. That's because the Elephant, as the nonthinking part of the mind that basically runs from fear
(flight or fight), constantly influences the Rider to notice, seek out, and
choose what makes it feel safe. This is true of virtually every aspect of
life, but especially in regard to connecting with other human beings. In
fact, when it comes to relationships and love, connection is everything. As
Dr. Ned Hallowell, founder of the Hallowell Center for Cognitive and
Emotional Health, says, "A connected person feels positively involved in a
world larger than himself. He feels—and *feels* is the crucial verb—held in
place by loving and caring relationships. It is a feeling that precedes words
and goes deeper than beliefs or knowledge."

We may not be consciously aware of it, but those connections affect
us on a day-to-day basis. One way they do this is through what Stephen

Covey, author of *The 7 Habits of Highly Effective People*, calls our "Emotional Bank Account." What Covey means by this is that with anyone with whom we have a relationship, whether they are family, friends, coworkers, or those we interact with only on a limited basis, we maintain a type of bank account, but one that operates not with units of monetary value but with deposits of positive emotions and withdrawals of negative ones. That is, a kind word or act results in a positive emotional deposit, words or acts of anger deplete the account, and both impact on the Elephant and, therefore, on the experience of the Rider.

In order to help attendees at my workshops understand this concept, I take out a roll of fifty pennies and put them in a clear bowl that I label "Emotional Bank Account." The pennies represent positive units of love, each put in the account by a loving act. I ask a volunteer to tell me his or her story about feeling unloved, rejected, betrayed, or ignored. After the group hears this negative story, I take out a few pennies and explain that they represent a withdrawal that depletes the account. I then ask another volunteer to provide a negative story, which prompts me to take out a few more pennies, and then ask a third to do the same. Once it becomes obvious that the pennies are disappearing from the bowl, I switch and ask for positive stories. With each positive story of love, appreciation, gratitude, kindness, or forgiveness, I return some of the pennies, each time verbally acknowledging that they represent a deposit into the emotional bank account. It is not long before everyone understands why it is important to help others feel loved, and exactly how important positive connections are.

Of course, just because we both desire and need connection doesn't mean we will always have it, especially if our unconscious recognition system is not in tune with our expectations. But there is an absolutely guaranteed way to put the odds in your favor, and that is by learning what makes you and others feel loved. This is the job of the conscious, analytical, visionary Rider and can only be accomplished when the Rider develops the skill to recognize love. How do you know what makes you feel loved? How do you know what makes others feel loved? When you can answer these questions you will hold a powerful key to creating harmony between the Elephant and the Rider, as well as between yourself and others. And creating harmony not only enables you to elicit love from those around you but to share it with them as well.

Your Perceptual Love Filter

One of the many workshops and courses I attended in the 1970s was a course titled "NLP" or "Neuro-Linguistic Programming," conducted by John Grinder and Richard Bandler. Grinder and Bandler had coined the term Neuro-Linguistic Programming to emphasize their belief in a connection between the neurological processes ("neuro"), language ("linguistic"), and behavioral patterns that have been learned through experience ("programming"), and to explain how that connection can be organized to achieve specific goals in life. Their point, as translated for our purposes, was that you do not have to be a victim of your Elephant's programming, and that you have the potential to learn the necessary skills to change your behavior and influence the behavior of others.

I was very impressed with this idea, and over the next two years, mixing it into a stew with my knowledge of the subconscious and my training as a hypnotist, I let it simmer. Then one day, seemingly out of nowhere, I had an insight as to how we, as humans, know when we are loved. I spent the next year weaving this theory into my private practice as well as testing it out in social situations. As I tested, I refined. What was a somewhat complex issue was turning into a simple but extraordinarily effective communication technique that anyone can add to his or her communication skill set—a means of determining how you know when you are loved, and, just as important, how someone who is close to you experiences feeling loved.

Have you ever really thought about how you experience being loved? Have you considered that you and I might experience being loved differently? Have you ever wondered why the way you demonstrate love hasn't always been received the way you intended it to, or questioned why you don't feel loved even when you hear the words "I love you"? The answer to these questions will become clear when you understand the makeup of your personal perceptual love filter and how it is shaped by your basic beliefs.

Research shows that our basic beliefs, the way you and I see and experience the world, are substantially locked into place while we are still young children. In his article "Are You Programmed at Birth?" pioneer researcher Dr. Bruce Lipton writes: "The most influential perceptual programming of the subconscious mind occurs from birth through age six. During early childhood the brain is imprinting all sensory experiences as well as learning complex motor programs for speech, crawling, standing, and advanced activities like running and jumping. Simultaneously, the child's sensory systems are fully engaged, downloading massive amounts of information about the world and how it works."[1] In other words, all early-learned beliefs are a type of programming or software that has been installed in your brain by a combination of many elements. These include your physical environment, what you were taught, the manner in which you were spoken to, what you observed, and the way you were touched, held, or shown love as a child. All these events, and others, molded your Elephant and shaped your perceptual filter.

The mechanics of our mental programming work exactly like the expectation I set up in the exercise in Chapter Four in which the color blue essentially became invisible because I influenced the audience to focus on the color red. Acting like temporary software in a computer, my words subtly programmed and guided the "collective Elephant"—the perceptual filter of the audience—to create an unconscious mindset, a mental model for how they saw the world at that moment. As long as this temporary suggestion held and the filter was in place, the color blue was locked out. As I pointed out there, the makeup of your perceptual filter determines how you see and experience the world. It screens out some information and lets other information in. It governs your perceptions, choices, and actions. A perceptual filter is neither good or bad, right or wrong. It doesn't think, it doesn't care, it just does its job.

There is, however, another way to look at our perceptual filter. Consider the possibility that you actually attract certain people, information, and energy to you, and that the people, information, and energy you have in your life now are there because they resonate with the Elephant. That is, the Elephant's learned behavior and beliefs—its programming—influence what the Rider perceives, notices, and finds safe, familiar, and desirable. This presents the remarkable possibility that you can change or attract new, different, and healthier information, people, and energy. You can perform this seemingly miraculous feat by transforming the makeup of your personal perceptual filter. And this is where the idea of a love filter gets interesting.

What I refer to as your love filter is simply an aspect of your perceptual filter, and it works in the same way. The nature or quality of information allowed in through your filter depends on the integrity or makeup of the filter. If your earliest experiences are love-based, you will notice, attract, recognize, embrace, and be comfortable with information (actions, words, circumstances, and people) that are based in love. Conversely, if your earliest programming is fear-based, you will notice, attract, recognize, or be familiar with fear-based input. This is because the information that flows in through your perceptual filter becomes evidence from which you create your experience—the experience of being loved or unloved, and the experience of feeling whole and complete or incomplete and isolated. The fact is, though, that you do not have to be the victim of your programming. By examining and understanding the makeup of your perceptual filter you can learn to increase not only your experience of feeling loved but the experience of others as well. And you can do that by discovering your Love Trigger, and in the process open up a new path to positive change.

LIFE THOUGHT: THE MORE MENTALLY PREPARED AND OPEN YOU ARE TO RECEIVING NEW INFORMATION, THE MORE NEW POSSIBILITIES APPEAR.

Love Triggers

What exactly is a Love Trigger? It is essentially an experience—feeling, hearing, or seeing something—or a combination of such experiences, that makes you feel loved. Seems pretty simple, doesn't it? The problem is that we don't all have the same Love Triggers, and that can generate a great deal of difficulty when it comes to dealing with others. For example, I once had two clients, a husband and wife, who had very different Love Triggers. The husband, Roger, felt loved by being touched, so what he wanted, and expected, from his wife, Mary, was to be touched, hugged, and caressed. And because that was the way he experienced feeling loved, it was also the way he expressed his love. Physicality is what was allowed in through his filter. On the other hand, Mary experienced being loved through hearing. That is, what got through Mary's love filter was words, so she searched for verbal evidence of being loved, and of course expressed her love through words.

As a result, with only the best of intentions, Roger attempted to show love by touching, hugging, and stroking. However, since Mary's filter didn't allow her to receive the message, she felt unfulfilled, frustrated, and disappointed, and expressed it through both her body language and her words. Not surprisingly, hurt and confused, Roger became somewhat withdrawn, even while continuing to express love through his own model with even greater urgency, energy, and frequency. At the same time, he couldn't experience the love Mary was trying to show him because her verbal expression of love was literally falling on deaf ears.

Unfortunately, Roger and Mary are by no means unusual. In fact, the majority of couples' models for love are different because their past experiences and their filters have their own unique makeup. Paradoxically, both parties are right in their interpretation of the information—if you don't feel loved, you don't feel loved, period. And this doesn't apply only to couples, but to any individuals who feel love for each other. Perhaps not surprisingly, much of this problem stems from a lack of communication.

• • •

Any healthy, loving relationship obviously depends on good communication skills. Without the ability to communicate, the chances are that you will live in a world isolated and emotionally separate from others. Contrary to popular belief, communication isn't just projecting words. Many people talk but are unable to express their truth, their needs, their wants, or their desires—even to themselves. Nor is communication just a matter of listening. Many people listen but don't hear because they don't know how to be present—that is, mindful—in the moment. In his book *Loving Each Other*, Dr. Leo Buscaglia writes, "Communication, the art of talking with each other, saying what we feel and mean, saying it clearly, listening to what the other says and making sure that we're hearing accurately, is by all indication the skill most essential for creating and maintaining loving relationships."[2] Ultimately, it is the ability to feel empathy.

To be fair, one of the most challenging aspects of communication is letting others know what makes you feel loved, and eliciting from others what makes them feel loved. Why, when love is such a natural state, is it sometimes so difficult? The simple answer is that many people feel embarrassed, shy, or unworthy, are afraid of rejection, or project their method of feeling loved on another. There is, however, a key to solving this particular failure of communication, which is to understand, discover, and act on those Love Triggers. Fortunately, embracing this special communication skill set does not require you to make a drastic shift in your present beliefs nor does it demand that you embrace any particular philosophy. It only requires that you be willing to become aware of the makeup of your and others' love filters, learn how to request and accept what you need to feel loved, and learn to communicate to others in a way that makes them feel loved

"We have developed communications systems to permit man on earth to talk with man on the moon. Yet mother often cannot talk with daughter, father to son, black to white, labor with management or democracy with communism."[3]
—HADLEY READ, *COMMUNICATION: METHODS FOR ALL MEDIA*

What Makes You Feel Loved?

How do you know when you're loved? Is it instinctive? Is it cosmic? Is it chemical? The fact is that we all experience feeling loved through our senses—some primarily through hearing or sound (auditory), others through seeing (visual), and others through feeling and touching (kinesthetic). The majority of people, however, experience being loved through some combination of these senses. Like a treasure-finding metal detector, our built-in sensory radar system searches for the evidence of being loved, and if the evidence is there, we feel loved. If it is not, we don't. It's really that simple.

Since most of us show our love in the same way we would like others to show us their love, one way to discover what makes you feel loved is to be aware of, and note in your journal, what you do or say to express your love to others. This requires you to know, absolutely know, when you are coming from a state of love, when you are doing everything you can do to communicate your love, honor, and respect for the other person. Giving a gift, taking out the garbage, giving your time, supporting another with actions or words, cheering someone onward for success, celebrating someone's accomplishments, cooking a favorite meal, or forgiving someone for making a bad decision—that is, everything you do to show your love—are all clues to what makes you feel loved.

There is, however, a simpler and more direct method for determining exactly what makes you feel loved, and the following exercise is designed to help you do that. So open your journal or fire up your computer and we'll get started.

Link Alert: Enter the URL **https://vimeo.com/mapes/10** in your web browser and then the password "**loved**" and I will guide you through the "What Makes You Feel Loved?" exercise. Or you can simply follow the instructions below.

YOUR TURN

Because this exercise focuses on your sensory awareness, it is important that you make sure your environment is quiet and comfortable and that you won't be disturbed. Take your time, be curious, and have fun!

You have the ability to recall memories—especially emotionally charged memories—in clear and precise detail. You may be able to call up this image/mental movie instantly, or it may require you to relax and let the image come to you. In either case, what I'd like you to do is scan your past and recall a time when you felt totally, absolutely, and completely loved. This could be when you were a child, a teenager, or an adult. It could be a memory of being hugged, a look someone gave you, a feeling of safety and protection, a physical gift or letter you received, the gift of time spent with someone you love, or an acknowledgment for a job well done. It could be a moment when you were simply stroking a pet, resting your head on someone's shoulder, receiving a compliment, or having someone surprise you with a party. We all have our unique model for feeling loved. So try to recall that moment, and keep reflecting until you do.

Once you have captured the moment, you can make your picture, image, or feeling vibrant by asking yourself the following questions about it: How old am I? Exactly where am I? Who, specifically, am I with? What do I feel, see, smell, touch, or hear? It will also help if you see that image in your mind and imagine turning up the brightness, as you might on your television or computer screen, so the image becomes brighter and more colorful.

Once you can see the moment as vividly as possible, ask yourself the following questions. Consider each question carefully. There are no right or wrong answers. Since, as I mentioned, many people experience feeling loved through a combination of senses, it is possible that you may have more than one "yes" answer.

- Was it something someone said that made me feel totally loved, or because someone listened to me?

- Was it the way someone held me or touched me, or because they gave me a gift, either material or otherwise?

- Was it a look that someone gave me, or because they demonstrated some act of kindness?

The chances are that one of your answers/memories had a stronger emotional impact than the others, that is, that one of your senses sent a stronger message to make you feel loved. It is, however, also possible they all had equal—or nearly equal—power. In either case, you have now discovered your Love Trigger or triggers. This is important because understanding what your trigger is will enable you to ask for what you want and need to experience feeling loved.

What Makes Others Feel Loved?

"All persons are puzzles until at last we find in some word or act the key to the man, to the woman; Straightway all their past words and actions lie in light before us."

—RALPH WALDO EMERSON, *JOURNALS*

But what makes other people feel loved? What about your children, spouse, lover, or closest friends? Do you know their Love Triggers? As I mentioned, if you're like the majority of people, you will unconsciously attempt to use what makes you feel loved—your Love Triggers—as your strategy to make others feel loved. While this may seem logical, it's really a hit or miss proposition and could result in the other person feeling frustrated, dissatisfied, neglected, and generally unloved. There are, however, ways to discover—both directly and indirectly—what makes someone else feel loved.

The direct approach is to sit face-to-face with another individual and take him or her through the "What Makes You Feel Loved?" exercise as I did with you. The upside of this method is that it is straightforward and will give you immediate results. The downside is that many people resist participating in this type of intimate verbal interchange. Even couples who have been together for many years often find this open form of dialogue uncomfortable, especially if it is a change from the way they have communicated in the past. In addition, the Elephant can be very shy when it comes to expressing and examining feelings.

If the direct approach is simply too awkward, there are additional ways to get information. In order to discover the clues to what makes someone feel loved without making them feel uncomfortable, you will have to operate with stealth and become a love detective. In this role you will indirectly search out and uncover the clues to identify a person's Love Triggers. One way of doing this is by really listening to others describe their experience of life, as it will provide you with an abundance of information as to how they experience being loved. Since each category of sensory experience—auditory, visual, and kinesthetic—has its own clues, based on the extent to which an individual's language reflects one or the other type of experience, you should be able to determine to a fair degree of certainty what is likely to make him or her feel loved.

Those who are auditory, that is, more inclined to respond to what they hear, lean toward using words or expressions such as "ring," "sounds like," or "hear." "It rings a bell." "That sounds right to me." "Does it sound right to you?" "I hear what you're saying." For these individuals, the Elephant responds to words of support, encouragement, sincere compliments and praise, affirmations, and listening.

A visual person tends to use the words "see," "picture," "imagine," or "paints," such as "Do you see what I mean?" "I get the picture." "What you say paints a vivid image in my mind." Visual people feel loved when demonstrated or shown love. Eye contact when both listening and speaking is very powerful for visual people. Acts of service also resonate very strongly with the Elephant. Helping someone out in a time of need or crisis, being physically present, taking out the garbage, helping out with the housework, and helping a friend complete a task all resonate with love for the visually inclined.

People who are more kinesthetic will use words like "feel," "touch," "sensation," "heavy," or "light." Examples include "Does it feel right to you?" "What you said touches me deeply." "The decision weighs heavily on my mind." "I feel lighthearted." In this kind of individual the Elephant responds positively to loving, nonaggressive, and safe physical touch. Hugging, holding, stroking, and having sex resonate deeply. Also, receiving material gifts resounds on the "feeling loved" gauge, as does the reception of nonmaterial gifts.

Just in case you're wondering how much of a difference recognizing your own and others' Love Triggers can make, let me tell you about a couple who attended one of my workshops. Dorothy and James had been married for over twenty-five years when I first met them. They both felt unloved by their partner, and each had given up trying to understand the other. I told them about Love Triggers and guided them to recall their most loving moments. As each one heard the other describe his or her personal Love Trigger, looks of absolute amazement flooded their features. James learned that what Dorothy wanted was for him to spend a little quality time with her playing gin rummy or going for a walk. That is, his physical presence and willingness to give her time was her Love Trigger. Dorothy learned that James wanted her to stroke his head when they were watching television but was embarrassed to ask. Physical touch was what got through his love filter. By the end of the workshop it was as if each had discovered a new person inside the person they thought they knew so well.

Communicating with Love

Regardless of how you choose to determine what makes you or someone else feel loved, it can be difficult when you are not accustomed to doing it. But if you truly want to, that desire will fuel you with whatever courage you may need to say and do what may be unfamiliar or uncomfortable. I'm going to take a leap of faith and assume that you do have the desire, intention, and courage to discover how you and others feel loved. A word of caution: Even desire, intention, and courage will be wasted if people cannot receive what you are saying. Before you launch into your exploration, then, I want you to be aware of some basic concepts of communication that can help you be successful in your quest. The two things that are most important in asking your "love" questions in a way people will hear them are *timing* and the *environment*.

The timing of your communication is an essential factor in creating a positive result. It is not the right time to do the exercise if he feels rushed, distracted, busy, or is in a bad mood. And you certainly don't want to ask her how she knows when she feels loved if she has just come home from work exhausted, overwhelmed, or has recently received some painful or disturbing news. Be aware of the circumstances, and choose a relaxed time.

It is equally important to be aware of what's taking place around you—that is, your environment. Just because you want positive results quickly doesn't mean you're going to get them. If you don't seem to be achieving the results you want, take a step back and ask yourself, "Is there a better, safer environment where my communication would be more effectively received?" Sometimes you have to break people out of their comfort zone to find the answers you're looking for. Spontaneously take a walk together or go to a diner and have a cup of coffee.

Once you understand, practice, and master this very simple system you will become an accomplished love detective. By discovering love clues you will crack the code to both feeling loved and helping others feel loved. You will transform your relationships! So before you move forward to the next chapter, please make sure that you have practiced the system and recorded your observations and insights. Doing so will enable you to expand and maintain your awareness of one of the most powerful forces within us. Love! Imagine that!

THINKPOINTS

- In relationships with other human beings, connection is everything.
- It's important to keep your "Emotional Bank Account" full of positive feelings.

- What makes you feel loved—your "Love Trigger"—is one communication signal or a combination of signals that may be auditory, visual, or kinesthetic.
- What makes you feel loved may be different from what makes others feel loved.
- You can learn what makes others feel loved by becoming a "love detective."

LET GO OF THE ROPE

"In the beginning, it is difficult letting go. But as you get into the swing of it, you will feel lighter and fresher and better able to see what you really need. That is what I imagine spring cleaning is truly about."

—SUSAN JEFFERS, *END THE STRUGGLE AND DANCE WITH LIFE*

Link Alert: Enter the URL **https://vimeo.com/mapes/11** in your web browser and then the password "**therope**" to see and hear me speak about letting go of the rope. This is also discussed below.

You are engaged in a horrendous tug of war. You and your opponent stand on either side of a slimy, filth-infested, muddy pit full of unseen, unspeakable horrors, each of you gripping the end of a long rope. Suddenly, you feel yourself being pulled toward the black hellish hole. You have no idea who your antagonist is. In fact, you don't even know why you are engaged in this horrid contest, but you do know that you must resist with all your strength. If you are pulled into the pit you will die, and the only way to win is to annihilate your unknown enemy. It seems like there can be no positive outcome in the struggle. He will pull you into the deadly muck, you will pull him in, or you will continue fighting in vain. Your body screams with exhaustion as you are dragged closer to the edge. With a surge of inner strength, you regain your footing and pull with all your might. And then, suddenly, you wake up, exhausted and drenched in perspiration, and realize that you have relived the same nightmare you've had many times before.

Imagine, though, an entirely different outcome for the dream tug of war. Once again, you pick up your end of the rope and struggle against your opponent. Fearful of being yanked into the pit, you pull as hard as you can. Your opponent responds in kind. Then, as if by magic, the light bulb of *awareness* explodes. You suddenly see a new choice—a bigger picture. You realize this battle can never be won and, most importantly, you recognize that you can choose to end this senseless game. "Why not let go of the rope and walk away?" you ask yourself. You do! Suddenly, your anxiety and fear disappear. Your self-confidence rises. What a relief! You have finally let go. You have given up the struggle and you feel free! In your elation a question surfaces, "Why couldn't I have let go of the rope sooner?" The answer instantly comes to you. The possibility never occurred to you because you weren't yet *aware* that you had another choice.

ZIGGY © 2000 ZIGGY AND FRIENDS, INC.
Reprinted with permission of UNIVERSAL UCLICK. All rights reserved.[1]

For most of us, life is essentially a tug of war—with us pulling on one end of a rope and an invisible but powerful force pulling on the other. Unfortunately, sometimes we get so locked into that daily struggle that the struggle itself—whether it's over a career, a relationship, or our daily lives—becomes so familiar that we don't even notice it's happening anymore. Or we notice it but think we are unable to do anything about it. It is happening, though, and it's almost invariably a result of our inability to let go of something, even if that something is energy draining or destructive. So whether we want to reduce negative stress; break through a fear of success, failure, or rejection; heal ourselves; improve our athletic ability; raise our self-confidence; or deal with a myriad of other issues, the only way to accomplish it is to let go of the rope, let go of that baggage.

The baggage is the Elephant's programming, accumulated beliefs, and models of how the world should work, and much of our stress, exhaustion, and emotional anxiety stems from dragging it into every area of our lives. We let the Elephant's learned superstitions, biases, prejudices, stereotypes, fears, and old beliefs bog down our creativity and emotional and spiritual growth. Why do we do it? Why do we fight, struggle, and try to control the uncontrollable, when letting go may well be the easiest and healthiest choice? Is it habit? Is it the Elephant's fear of change and loss, or is it the need to stay with the familiar? Whatever the reason, the mere thought of letting go makes most of us feel as though we are about to jump into an abyss without a safety net. The Rider can learn to help the Elephant let go, but before that can happen, we have to understand exactly how the Elephant's resistance to change affects our ability to do so, what letting go is, and what we need to let go of.

How the Elephant Resists Change

In "The Myth of the Healthy Ego" section in Chapter Three, I offered some classical and contemporary definitions of ego. You may be familiar with another important theory, Freud's structural model of the psyche, the ego works as mediator between the id (responsible for instincts, impulses, and primary functions of the brain) and the superego (where the conscience resides). In this model, the ego is responsible for reality testing and personality. As I explained, I see the ego differently—as a Trickster that's powerful, full of deceit, and ultimately the source of all negativity in our lives. It's this negativity—the primitive, fear-based survival self of the

Elephant morphed into illusory fear—that acts as a barrier to letting go, and it does so in a variety of ways, including the following:

- Holding on to a fearful past and predicting a fearful future
- Deceiving the Rider into believing that being separate from others is safe and necessary
- Choosing competition over cooperation and "I" over "we"
- Encouraging us to define ourselves in terms of what others think of us
- Forming unhealthy attachments to people, ideas, and things
- Always being primed to attack or defend
- Needing to be right at the expense of almost everything
- Observing the world through the lens of fear
- Associating surrender with defeat
- Needing to blame, experience guilt, or feel anger
- Believing others should be responsible for meeting our needs
- Believing people and circumstances should conform to the way we think the world should be
- Always wanting more and never being more than temporarily satisfied
- Believing that controlling others is always effective
- Being terrified of letting go

What Letting Go Means

It is the final characteristic of the Elephant—being terrified of letting go—that is the ego's Achilles' heel. It is by focusing on this point of vulnerability that the Rider can influence the Elephant and create change by using its mental tools of mindfulness, acceptance, and forgiveness to transform fear into love. None of this is intended to suggest that letting go is easy. Like many important things in life, it can be very difficult, although the payoff is substantial. Realizing that payoff, in this case, requires going through a process of five steps, as follows:

1. Acknowledge the negative emotions that tell you what you need to let go of. Emotions are often signposts, but are also frequently ignored until they become destructive. Anxiety, stress, depression, anger, and heartbreak are all signposts of negative emotions, as are constantly revisited disheartening memories, grudges, and guilt from the past. Acknowledging our negative feelings fully is a powerful way to supercharge the process of letting go.

2. Recognize that you have complete control of letting go. Asking the right questions can help you do this, such as "Does holding on to negative thoughts, memories, people, or things serve a purpose?" "If so, what purpose does it serve?" and "Does holding on move me forward in a positive direction?"

3. Accept and trust that it is time to let go. This happens when you become grateful for the experiences you have had, negative or positive, and accept, with gratitude, that all experience has value. The more you accept what has happened and is happening in your life, the more peace of mind you will have.

4. Focus on what can be changed. As simple as this sounds, it takes honesty, patience, and courage to accomplish. As I mentioned previously, we humans spend an enormous amount of energy trying to change what cannot be changed. It's much more productive to focus on today.

5. Forgive those who need to be forgiven, including yourself. Forgiveness is the most powerful and remarkable tool the Rider has to let go of the past. You will be given specific instructions for forgiveness in the next chapter.

What We Have to Let Go of

As a concept, letting go seems fairly straightforward. In reality, it is a complicated issue as there are several areas that have to be addressed if you want to live an exceptional life. In order to begin the process of letting go, it's important that you become familiar with the most common unrecognized barriers that can keep you from doing so. These include the need to be competitive, being overly attached to things, the need to control others, judging, blaming others and being a victim, denial, and, finally, learning to live in the moment. The best place to begin is by examining traditional thinking about competition, the impact of low self-confidence, and how they are tied together.

LETTING GO OF BEING COMPETITIVE TO NO PURPOSE

"Competition, which is the instinct of selfishness, is another word for dissipation of energy, while combination is the secret of efficient production."
—EDWARD BELLAMY, *LOOKING BACKWARD*

The online *Merriam-Webster Dictionary* defines competition as "1. The act or process of trying to get or win something that someone else is also trying to get or win: the act or process of competing. 2. Actions that are done by people, companies, etc., that are competing against each other." In sports, of course, competition is a given. It's healthy and, as every successful athlete will tell you, it brings out one's personal best. It's essentially the same in chess or any other game. However, while competition is both mandatory and effective in the fields of athletics and games, that isn't necessarily true in other areas of life. In fact, while competition clearly has its place and its rewards, inappropriately exercised competition can have an extremely negative influence on you and your relationships.

In his book *No Contest*, Alfie Kohn writes, "The simplest way to understand why competition generally does not promote excellence is to realize that trying to do well and trying to beat others are two different things." Think about your own relationships. Are they cooperative, competitive, a little of both, or does it depends on the circumstances?

The reason I suggest the question is that the ideal classroom for learning about yourself is in the mirror of your relationships, past and present.

It is here that you will discover clues to how you view yourself in relation to others and whether you have fallen prey to the dark side of competition. As psychologist Carl Jung wrote, "Everything that irritates us about others can lead to an understanding of ourselves." Of course, there is nothing negative about the desire to challenge yourself, learn, and grow. But there is something inherently destructive about needing to affirm and define yourself at another's expense. Putting others down, as well as attacking, sabotaging, or attempting to control and manipulate others are the most obvious clues to low self-worth. This is where the very nature of competition can cut two ways, and there are several areas in life in which this can be demonstrated.

One of the areas in which competition can be extremely destructive is in the family environment. If parents pit one child against another they will often unknowingly create separation, guilt, and anger. This competitive model of behavior can also have an impact on future relationships throughout the siblings' lives, and can actually lead to low self-confidence. The social environment is another area in which competition can have a negative effect. People who compete in terms of their material possessions—homes, money, clothing, jewelry, or cars—and who constantly have to prove that they have the "best" or are the "most successful," are also often blind to the unconscious statement that they are making about their own self-worth. The reality is that you can always find someone who has more.

The classroom is also an area in which people sometimes compete to no purpose. In the classroom, the dynamics of interaction are a very important aspect of student motivation. In a competitive goal structure, it is assumed that learners understand that they will be rewarded based on comparison with others. However, while evidence shows that a competitive environment works well for extremely high-performers, it can actually be a disaster for average students. A reward system based solely on competition can have a negative impact on both motivation and self-esteem, and not only leave many children thinking and feeling like losers but also follow them through life.

Perhaps the most extreme example of destructive competition is in the business environment. In fact, the contemporary business paradigm has been constructed with competition at its core. And, as in sports, competition among businesses is healthy. A company wants to provide better products and/or services than its competitors, and the desire to do that can spur individuals as well as organizations to be creative and to excel. However, because many businesses also purposely or unconsciously structure their internal paradigm of competition on sports, pitting team against team or individual against individual, the very thing management wants and needs—creativity and innovation—is undermined. By only encouraging competition instead of cooperation within the company, creativeness and self-motivation slam to a halt. In other words, while competition may motivate some people, many of the silent majority simply give up. The competitive philosophy of short-term thinking goes hand in hand with short-term gains and long-term losses. You only need to look in the news to know the truth of that statement.

 LIFE THOUGHT: YOU DON'T ALWAYS NEED TO COMPETE TO WIN.

Does this kind of thinking sound familiar? Do you feel the need to compete with others even when there is nothing to win? Do you suspect people are always trying to get "one-up" on you? Are you determined to always be right even when there is nothing at stake? Like many of my clients, you may be unaware that you are extremely competitive, or that your need to compete is having a negative impact on your health and your relationships. However, unless you can recognize to whatever extent you are competitive, there is nothing you can do to alleviate the problems it can cause in your life. In order to do so, it's important for you to bear in mind that being competitive isn't just about others, it's about you—how *you* feel about yourself, what *you* feel you deserve, and what *you* feel others deserve. It is ultimately your willingness to take a good hard look at yourself that will enable you to put together the puzzle that forms your self-image and learn to let go of the rope.

YOUR TURN

This exercise is designed to help you determine how competitive you are by examining relationships in your past. As such, it will present you with an opportunity to recognize and, hopefully, let go of the need to define yourself through others. It will also encourage you to develop a healthier attitude toward your relationships, shift your mindset so that you can begin experimenting with new behaviors, and recognize that cooperation and compromise are not the same as being wrong or losing. Finally, it will show you that you can choose to give up the belief that you must always be right, dial back your need to be competitive, give up the struggle to compete, and let go of the rope.

First, list five of your most important relationships—either personal (friends or family) or professional (boss or coworkers). Then, on a scale of one to ten (ten being the most competitive) rate each relationship on how competitive you feel when you are engaged with that person. Once you have done the ratings, look at those with whom you feel most competitive, think about the feelings you hold toward them, and examine the actions you have taken and the choices you have made in the past when engaged with them. The ultimate purpose of this exercise is to determine if, in your attitude, communications, or actions with these people, you were cruel, hurtful, or destructive toward either them or yourself. It is only identifying the beliefs behind these behaviors that gives the Rider the knowledge, power, and freedom to make new choices in the future.

As in many other areas, one of the best ways to learn about yourself is to ask questions. You can get a better understanding of how competitive you are toward those around you by asking yourself questions like these:

- Have I put myself down by comparing myself to someone else I consider to be successful?

- Have I purposefully hurt a sibling, friend, relative, spouse, or coworker by sabotaging their success in order to make myself feel better?
- Have I lost sight of my real goal because I've chosen to make it my goal to ensure that someone else loses?
- Have I felt guilty about how my competitive choices have affected others?
- Have I slandered or discredited others to further my own ends?
- Have I felt competitive at work toward team members who I know are supposed to be on my side?
- Have I taken credit at work for others' ideas or put them down behind their back to raise my own importance?

If you answered "yes" to one or more of these questions you are clearly being unnecessarily competitive and need to adjust your attitude. And it can definitely be done. Many of my coaching clients have not only gained insight by answering questions like these but have also been able to change their perspective about the nature of competition and, therefore, the choices they make. Perhaps the most dramatic change I've seen—and I've seen it often—is that they begin to help others achieve their goals. The great motivational speaker and writer Zig Ziglar said it best: "You can get everything in life you want if you will just help enough other people get what they want."

LETTING GO OF ATTACHMENTS

Many people have a tendency to look outside themselves for happiness and joy. But real happiness is not dependent on external things, and for those who seek it outside themselves, that happiness is always fleeting, always just over the horizon. When something does temporarily fill the void, that something is considered the source of happiness—until it isn't. And then, disappointed, the happiness seeker must continue the relentless and ultimately fruitless search for the "something" that will make him or her feel complete. These "somethings" are what I think of as negative attachments, and in order to free up space in your mental hard drive, rewire your brain, and transform fear into love, it is essential that you acknowledge and examine these attachments. Only then can you decide whether they add to or take away from the quality of your life, and then make a decision to let go or not.

 LIFE THOUGHT: HAPPINESS LIES ONLY WITHIN YOU, NOT IN OUTSIDE CIRCUMSTANCES, THINGS, OR PEOPLE.

What exactly are attachments? In *Love Is the Answer: Creating Positive Relationships*, Gerald G. Jampolsky and Diane Cirincione define an attachment as " . . . a certain way that we use people, situations, and things to actually create barriers against love and our own inner peace." At their most basic, attachments are the emotional dependence we put on things and people. And these attachments come in an extraordinarily wide range of shapes and sizes, including, for example, food, people, relationships, sex, risk taking, television watching, cars, drugs, being right, pain, illness, depression, guilt, anger, clothing, jewelry, popularity, a public image, having the ideal body, getting attention, blaming, independence, dependence, controlling, being controlled, and many other forms.

They are the kinds of things that the ego leads us to constantly and aggressively search out, acquire, and then subconsciously use to reflect back on ourselves to define our self-worth. These include, for example, large sums of money, numerous sexual conquests, and particularly attractive partners, as well as luxury items such as big houses, the most stylish clothing, or the trendiest, most expensive automobiles. Unfortunately, though, these types of attachments often make false promises that can never be fulfilled. And because the temporary shot of dopamine—the feel-good chemical they provide—fades, the euphoria they generate doesn't last. They do provide the Elephant with instant, short-term gratification, but they can also cause a great deal of disappointment, dissatisfaction, and even pain. Once the initial rush of getting something new goes away, because your sense of self-worth was based on the attachment itself, all you are left with is a feeling of emptiness.

YOUR TURN

This exercise is designed to help you recognize those things in your life—relationships, material possessions, thinking, and behaviors—that are negative attachments. Before you start, though, it is important for you to understand that sometimes these attachments have become so much a part of you that they are essentially invisible. For that reason, it's essential that you examine all aspects of your life closely. The steps outlined below deal with your relationships and material possessions, but you can use the same process to explore your thinking and discover your attachment to worry, guilt, or a specific behavior. Bear in mind that this exercise is not about judging your attachments. It's simply about becoming aware of what you are attached to, and as such represents the process through which, by asking yourself questions, you prepare yourself to let go.

1 Think again about the relationships you listed in the last exercise, and focus on the three most important ones. Then ask yourself, "Do they support, energize, and nurture me, or do they sap my energy?" Examining relationships can trigger strong emotions, but unless you do you won't be able to determine to what extent they, too, may be attachments.

2 Look in your closets, drawers, cabinets, garage, and storage areas, and list all the material "stuff" you have not used in the last year or more. Then ask yourself, "Why am I hanging on to these things? What is the payoff for keeping the clutter?"

3 Go through your lists—one relationship and one item at a time. Vividly imagine yourself without each one. If it helps, imagine that the relationship ended for some reason, or that the item was suddenly lost, stolen, or destroyed. While you are doing this, be aware of your feelings. Breathe deeply. Pay attention to your body. Use your Tool for Truth. If, as a result of imagining these things being lost, taken away,

or destroyed, you feel empty, scared, anxious, poor, alone, diminished, or angry, the chances are that they are attachments.

4 Finally, looking at those things you have identified as attachments, ask yourself, "Which, if any, might I be willing to let go of right now?"

It's important to remember that letting go itself is not actually a step, but rather the result of going through this process. That's because, in fact, the problem isn't really about letting go but about holding on to a thing, person, memory, or situation. It's the grasping that is exhausting, burdensome, and sometimes self-destructive. And that, of course, is because the Elephant needs to keep things the way they are. That's why examining our attachments and asking ourselves questions paves the way to letting go. It lessens the need to hold on until we can safely release our grip. That is, even though the Elephant fears loss, the Rider knows that losing thoughts, habits, fears, and worries that are causing emotional pain is like pulling up the anchor of a ship and sailing away free. Perhaps the best part is that letting go of attachments creates the mental and physical space to let something new, bright, exciting, intriguing, and joyful fill the space you have chosen to create.

LETTING GO OF CONTROLLING OTHERS

"Consider how hard it is to change yourself and you'll understand what little chance you have in trying to change others."
—JACOB M. BRAUDE

We are all familiar with the idea of a "control freak," the kind of individual who feels he or she must be in control in essentially every situation. As you have probably experienced, such people often make life very difficult not only for themselves but also for those around them as well. The fact is, though, that there are times when all of us try to exercise control over others, more often than not without our even realizing it. Here's how it happens.

As we discussed earlier, visualizing is the Rider's unique ability to create mental movies. And although we are not necessarily aware of it, we visualize all the time. We do it naturally and usually without forethought. Stop and think about it for a moment. We get up in the morning and ponder our day. We see ourselves dealing with the children, the electrician, our spouse, friends, business associates, potential clients, and others. If you look carefully, though, you often discover that the scripts of our mental movies include not only our own dialogue and actions but also those of other people as well. That is, in order to mold the outcomes we want, we unconsciously visualize others saying and doing what we would like them to say and do. In fact, it is our mental movies that provide a framework for how we live now and how we want to live in the future.

LIFE THOUGHT: WE WILL OFTEN ATTEMPT TO MANIPU-LATE, CONTROL, OR CHANGE PEOPLE TO CONFORM TO OUR SCRIPTS

There is nothing inherently wrong with projecting your scripts on others. It's natural. In fact, top salespeople do it all the time, usually with great success for both parties. However, when someone writes a script for the way another person "should" act, the outcome is likely to be disappointing or frustrating if the other individual does not want the same thing, is not extremely flexible, or is not working for a win-win outcome. The bottom line is that when our expectations are based solely on how others "should" act, and they don't act that way, we almost certainly—consciously or unconsciously—attempt to manipulate and control. And if we don't get what we want or encounter extreme resistance, we may push harder, display anger, become verbally demanding, or walk away. If, however, we want to live exceptional lives, it is imperative that we become aware/mindful of any attempts we make to exercise control over others, hit our mental pause button, and let go. While it is often challenging to recognize when and if we are trying to exercise such control, especially when we are anxious or fearful, it is not impossible and, with practice, can be learned.

YOUR TURN

Controlling behavior is just another attachment that has originated out of past observation and learned behavior. It is based in fear—fear that we are not in control, that we are not enough, or that others will not meet our expectations. Like letting go of any attachment, the process of letting go of controlling behavior begins with awareness, acknowledgement, and acceptance. When you are able to quiet your mind, turn inward, observe, investigate, and question, you will be able to separate yourself from the fear, examine it, and by doing so loosen its hold and let it go. The first part of this exercise accordingly presents questions that will help you identify and examine your past controlling behavior.

PART ONE

I want you to journey back in your past and recall a specific incident in which you projected your script onto someone with the intention of exercising control, and the effort not only led to a negative result—such as frustration, anger, and hopelessness—but also made you regret your actions, even if you felt perfectly justified at the time. If you have more than one such experience in your memory bank, choose the one that is most emotionally powerful. Once you have captured this memory, write it down, then answer the following questions and determine which, if any, resonate with you.

- What did I actually want to happen in this situation?
- What did I really fear might happen if I lost control?
- Did I enter into the situation with a competitive mindset?
- Did I take the time to envision a win/win outcome?
- Was I afraid that the other person or persons had more power than me?
- Did I feel that if I didn't get what I wanted I would be somehow diminished?
- Was I afraid of appearing foolish?
- If I could redo the situation, would I act differently, and, if so, how?

It is possible—even probable—that you experienced some resistance in answering these questions, or felt embarrassed when you remembered your behavior. If you did, you needn't worry about it—it's quite normal. As we've noted before, not only does self-examination make the Elephant uncomfortable, but you were also reliving a painful past as if it was happening in the present. Remember, though, that you're doing this for a good purpose—to learn and grow.

PART TWO

This second part of the exercise, which consists of five steps, is designed to enable you, over a period of twenty-four hours, to recognize—in the moment—when you are trying to exercise inappropriate control and help you stop yourself from doing it.

1 **Observe Yourself.** As always, the first step in changing any behavior is recognizing when you are doing it. Because doing so with controlling behavior is particularly challenging, it's going to require your total commitment to see it through. For that reason I suggest that you begin your day with whatever short relaxation exercise works for you, and then say to yourself, "Today I am going to be mindful of my interactions with others, catch myself when I am feeling anxious or fearful, and be on the alert for any controlling behavior I exhibit." Making this statement of commitment will prepare your mind to notice what you need to in order to carry out the process. Then, as the day progresses, every time you find yourself micromanaging a situation, worrying, or being overly critical, protective, or aggressively manipulative, write down as clearly as possible in your journal or on your computer exactly what you did.

2 **Identify Your Emotion.** After you have written down the controlling behavior you've exhibited, it's essential that you also write down the particular emotion you felt at the time. Recording both your actions and your feelings immediately is extremely important for a very practical reason. Because once some time has passed, we love to rewrite our history to justify our action; therefore it is quite impossible to realistically look back and objectively reflect on exactly what took

place. Identifying your emotion should be fairly simple, because at the most basic level, the emotion driving any behavior must be either love or fear. However, if you're having difficulty distinguishing between them, remember that joy, high spirits, and happiness are indications of love, while anger, jealousy, and sadness are a result of fear.

3 **Identify Your Thoughts.** At the end of the day, before you go to sleep, review the notes you made about your controlling behavior and the emotions you felt at the time, and try to identify the specific thought that sparked the emotion behind the behavior. Identifying those thoughts is an important part of the process for two reasons. First, doing so actually deflates the hold of the behavior, and second, it paves a way toward changing behavior and letting go of controlling behavior in the future. How you think and relate to events around you forms the wiring in your brain, so if you can change your thinking, you can change your brain.

4 **Visualize and Reframe Your Mental Movie.** By now you are thoroughly familiar with visualization and know that by repeatedly visualizing an event you can actually rewire your brain and, in the process, create change. What I want you to do, then, is visualize the situation in which you exhibited controlling behavior, but this time imagine doing things differently than you did in reality. That is, make up a script using the starting point of the real event, but as you do so ask yourself the following questions:

- "Do I really have any control over the situation or the person?"
- "What does this person actually need and want?"
- "What can I learn from this situation or person?"
- "How can I help this person meet his or her needs?"
- "If needed, what would be a fair compromise?"
- "What do I need to forgive within myself or the other person in order to make this interaction meaningful?"

Reframing can be particularly challenging when it comes to dealing with controlling behavior, but if you give yourself some time and, if need be, visualize the situation several times, you will eventually become comfortable with the result. And once you become comfortable, you'll have developed a fair understanding of the specific triggers that lead you to exhibit controlling behavior, and you'll then be able to start applying your newfound awareness to your future encounters.

5 **Take Action.** Beginning the next day, then, having developed a new awareness of your behavior, you can intentionally let go of controlling your interactions with others. There are, however, a couple of points you should continue to bear in mind. First, cut yourself some slack. You may feel awkward developing new behaviors, and might stumble now and then; but every time you act out of love instead of fear, you rewire your brain or reinforce your present wiring. Second, while you are trying to change your way of dealing with people you may find yourself sometimes being pulled back toward your old behavior. This is because the Elephant will be digging in, wanting to hang on to behavior that has seemed to work in the past. If you find that happening, that is, if you feel the stress, fear, or pull of old controlling behaviors, take a deep breath and remember that what you are experiencing is all part of the letting-go process; in the end you will have taken another step closer to having an exceptional life. In fact, when you let go of controlling others, whether they are your spouse, partner, siblings, children, friends, or business associates, your relationships will be transformed.

LETTING GO OF JUDGING

"Judgements prevent us from seeing the good that lies beyond appearances."
—DR. WAYNE DYER

Can we really let go of judging? To be honest, I am playing with your mind a little bit here. The reality is that we can't let go of judging. In fact, we are judging machines. That's one of the Rider's jobs. We judge the way others vote, dress, and act, what they enjoy as entertainment, what they eat, and if and how they worship. Social media shouts out for us to judge.

We are asked to "like" someone's Facebook page and to judge the quality of a restaurant or business at Yelp.com. We're asked to judge an Uber driver at the same time that the driver is asked to judge us. And the list goes on. So if we can't let go of judgments, what can we do?

Let's begin with a few facts. First, the Elephant is hard-wired for survival. Judging is instinctive. If the Elephant feels threatened in any way—including being judged to be "wrong," "different," "stupid," or "selfish"—it inevitably chooses either fight or flight. Second, when we go into a defensive mode we blind ourselves to the multitude of reasons possible behind someone's behavior, including our own. Third, more often than not, the judgments we make about others stem from our own judgments about ourselves, because they are based on our experience and personal beliefs, that is, our paradigms for the way the world should work. Finally, consistently making negative judgments can make you bitter. Now, bearing these facts in mind, before you do the next exercise, I want you to ask yourself the following questions:

- When was the last time I passed judgment on someone?
- Did my judgment change anything or help in a positive and loving way?
- How did I feel the last time someone judged me?

YOUR TURN

Again, mindfulness is essential if we are to discern when to let go of harmful judgments. For that reason, from the time you get up tomorrow morning until you go to sleep tomorrow night, I want you to do the following:

- Think about your thinking and monitor your judgmental self-talk, looking out in particular for any negative judgments about yourself or others.
- When you catch yourself judging, pay attention to it and ask yourself, "What have I contributed to the other person or myself by my judgment?"

- When you catch yourself judging yourself in an overly critical way, stop, observe, and say, "Isn't that interesting." Then ask yourself, "Is my judging myself helping in any positive way, or is it making me feel helpless, sad, or stressed?"

The fact is that, more often than not, people are just doing the best they can at the moment and working out whatever they have to work out. So you should try to look for the basic goodness in others and remember that when someone disagrees with you or criticizes you, what you are most often hearing is their own pain. Even if you do this for only one day you will become much more aware of when you judge negatively, and, as a result, discover yourself lightening up and letting go of life-diminishing judgments.

LETTING GO OF BLAMING OTHERS AND BEING A VICTIM

"If it's never our fault, we can't take responsibility for it. If we can't take responsibility for it, we'll always be its victim."
—RICHARD BACH

If you look outside yourself for the cause of your problems, anxieties, or worries in general, the chances are you won't have much trouble finding it. That's because you can always find something or someone else to blame. It could be fate, the misalignment of the stars, your boss, the government, a neighbor, a lover, a spouse, a sibling, or a parent. It's easy to slip under the shroud of victimization when you feel things are not going your way, someone has taken advantage of you, or someone hasn't kept his or her promises. In fact, in situations like these victimhood even seems to have advantages. Blaming and finger-pointing allow you to temporarily justify life's unfairness, and provide you with an excuse for not taking charge of your own life.

However, seeing yourself as a victim can, like any paradigm, become a habit, a way of living that reinforces your sense of being powerless. Some people take on the role of being a victim as a result of repeated abuse or because they have let failure break their spirit. Taking on the role of a victim, however, is always a choice on some level. And once the choice is made, we relinquish our power. When we blame we become blind to positive choices. We become bitter and angry. Love recedes.

Here is an example of what I'm talking about. John was downsized over three years ago. Even though he was one of hundreds in his company to be forced out of work, he saw the downsizing as a direct attack on him. He blamed his former boss, hating him for it, and his anger affected not only his marriage but his other personal relationships as well. In the beginning people were sympathetic, but after almost three years of listening to John complain they begin to distance themselves. At that point he not only began blaming his friends and family for what he saw as their lack of loyalty, but he also continued to righteously hold on to his anger, becoming bitter and resentful of other people's success.

Here, however, is how someone in an almost identical situation dealt with it. Rob had also been downsized and was of course upset, but he was also in touch with reality. After realizing that he was one of thousands who were in the same boat, he focused on what he could control. Within six months Rob and his wife decided to sell their house and move into a condominium. They reinvented their lifestyle to match their resources. It wasn't easy for either one of them. Rob took a job at a much lower salary than he'd been receiving, but in a very short time he was promoted to a managerial position. He now finds his job both challenging and absorbing.

The difference between John and Rob is that John chose to be reactive, to blame, and to hold on to what he felt was his righteous anger. Rob chose to be proactive and find the solution within himself. John created his own prison. Rob was free. How often do you find yourself rerunning your grievance scripts or living in a revenge mindset? How many times have you chosen to take on the role of a victim rather than taking responsibility for your feelings and your life? You have by now learned what it means to accept that responsibility, that you are at choice, and that people treat you the way they do because you have taught them to do so. You have also developed the presence of mind and courage to say "no" to others when necessary. So if you have seen yourself as a victim, the time has come for you to stop being a victim and to stop blaming others. It isn't easy. It takes courage, time, work, and persistence, but you can do it.

YOUR TURN

There are numerous things you can do to help yourself stop being a victim and blaming others. Those listed below are among the most effective.

- Be mindful of the Rider's critical inner self-talk that focuses on biases, injustices, and unfairness, and supports your thinking of yourself as a victim. Lines such as "I deserve better than this," "I have no right to be successful," "Life is not fair," and "I never have any luck" keep people trapped in victimization, ignite resentment and anger, and open the path to revenge thinking. By monitoring your thinking and your language you can catch yourself when ideas like these occur to you, and instead say, "Isn't that interesting" and reframe your thinking.

- Notice and mentally reject the same kind of victimization dialogue you hear from people who consider themselves victims, such as bad-mouthing and blaming others for their life circumstances. We are easily influenced, so it's best whenever possible to surround yourself with life enhancers.

- Pay attention to the words you use when making excuses or blaming. The words "should," "would," and "could" often imply obligation or trigger guilt, as in "You should love me more" or "If you really loved me you would . . ." Similarly, the words "always" and "never" can form a self-created trap, as in "He is always wrong" or "Life never gives me a break." If you make it your mission to become mindful of the words you use that support being a victim, you will be able to question and challenge your own thinking.

- Notice when you are complaining and ask yourself, "What is it that I really want? Am I expressing this just to get sympathy?" If the answer is "yes," just stop it! Any attempt to draw sympathy only reinforces victimization thinking, and that's not what you want to do.

- Forgive yourself if, on occasion, you slip back into feeling fear, resentment, or anger as you give up being a victim. Just move back onto your path to living an exceptional life.

Letting go of being a victim can be unsettling because it also means you have to stop dumping responsibility on others, stop complaining and blaming others, and start taking responsibility for yourself—your thoughts, your words, and your actions. And it can be difficult. If it helps, talk to a good friend about your new way of thinking or seek out support from other trusted sources. Remember you are rewiring your brain to form new thinking and new behavior.

LETTING GO OF DENIAL

"What I'm doing, really, is to look at things as they are. It's what you must do. Forget your ideals, your theories, your notions as to what people OUGHT to do. Consider what they ARE doing. Once a person is oriented to face facts rather than delusions, problems tend to disappear. At the very least, they fall into their true perspective and become soluble."

—ISAAC ASIMOV, "BELIEF"

If you are human you are in denial about something—your behavior, your relationships, your family, your beliefs, your finances, your career, or your health. Denial is one of the top self-sabotaging strategies people employ to cope. It's our nature to want everything to be comfortable within our own private sphere, but it isn't always so, so we use denial to cushion us from the perceived pain of truth. That doesn't mean that denial is necessarily an act of deliberate willful deception. Rather, it is an automatic psychological process by which we avoid and protect ourselves from things that threaten us, a coping mechanism that gives us the time we need to adjust to reality. Like a hypnotic suggestion, this mechanism distorts reality and keeps us from feeling the pain and discomfort of things we do not want to face until we can get back on track. In other words, when in denial we see what we want to see instead of what actually is, and that's not necessarily always a bad thing.

The downside of denial, however, is that it keeps us stuck in the illusion that everything is all right even when it is not, and makes it difficult if not impossible for us to take positive action. Of course, there are some individuals who are so self-aware and tuned into their consciousness that they can recognize when they are leaning toward denial. Others, however, are not. As a result, they may not realize the consequences of their actions or see the necessity of making any significant changes in their behavior. Perhaps the greatest downside of being in denial is that most people don't recognize it until it is too late. Unfortunately, denial is not always easy to break through. It takes commitment and desire to identify whether or not denial is limiting you. You have to commit to be willing to see the world as it is, know that you can handle whatever life throws your way, and move forward from there. It is only when you expose your self-defeating beliefs and behavior that you can "own" them, become your true authentic self, and transform future behavior. It *is* possible.

YOUR TURN

Denial is a particularly difficult habit to break because the perceived—if unconscious—benefits of doing it are so attractive. But letting go of denial is just as important, if not more so, than any of the other efforts you have made up to this point. The following steps are designed to help you break that habit.

1 Put yourself in a relaxed state through whatever method works best for you.

2 Challenge yourself to identify an area in which you feel stuck—mentally, physically, spiritually, emotionally, or socially—by looking for recurring negative themes in your life.

3 Recognize and analyze the fear that's keeping you stuck. As you do so, understand that, in this case, fear is a good thing because it provides you with a signpost that enables you to bring to light, examine, and

challenge the Elephant's outdated programming—that is, the hidden biases, beliefs, motives, ideologies, or unresolved issues that are clouding the Rider's perception of life.

4 Challenge both your thinking and your fear with solid logic by asking yourself questions like: "How likely it is that what I fear is really going to happen?" "How often has it happened before?" "Realistically, what is the worst that can happen?"

5 Identify why what you are denying is so difficult to face. Do you feel embarrassed, ashamed, afraid, angry, or out of control? Pay attention to your body and use your Tool for Truth.

Again, I don't want to sugarcoat the difficulty of letting go of destructive denial. It is challenging, but you already have all the tools you need in your mental tool kit to do it. What's most important is that once you've identified negative patterns of behavior and the fear behind the behavior, you can make friends with reality, rewrite your own script, and imprint a new and different positive behavior.

LETTING GO AND LEARNING TO LIVE IN THE MOMENT

"Flow with whatever may happen and let your mind be free. Stay centered by accepting whatever you are doing. This is the ultimate."

—ZHUANGZI, *NAN-HUA-CH'EN-CHING, OR THE TREATISE OF THE TRANSCENDENT MASTER FROM NAN-HUA*

Living in the present, or being mindful, simply means accepting the way things are, what is happening now, and being aware and honest about your feelings and emotions. In other words, it means making friends with reality and dealing immediately with whatever life presents. When you live in the present, you catch yourself when you rationalize, justify, or blame; you say to yourself, "Isn't that interesting," and you reframe your thinking to make new, more empowering choices. Here's an example of what I'm talking about.

My clients—I'll call them Bonnie and Kevin— vacation in Florida once a year to renew themselves. When they arrive there they are usually exhausted and burnt out from their fast-paced lives, and they look forward to basking in the sun, reading, and relaxing. On a recent trip they had a bad patch of weather that lasted for a number of days. They might have allowed their expectations to ruin their vacation and resisted the reality of what was happening, railing against the weather and complaining about how they felt cheated. They might have gotten caught up in the vicious loop of griping, and filled their days with sadness, self-pity, or anger about the way things should have been, and missed the present moment.

Were they disappointed by the poor weather? Yes. Would they have liked circumstances to be other than they were? Yes. That being acknowledged, they asked themselves, "Given the reality of our circumstances what can we do that would be enjoyable?" So they sat on the balcony playing cards, talking, and enjoying each other's company. They took naps, read, wrote, made love, and watched DVDs. They cooked. They went out to dinner. By accepting what was and acknowledging how they felt about it, numerous possibilities opened up. By living in the present, they transformed their survival selves into their loving selves. They had a wonderful vacation.

Despite its benefits, though, spending more time in the present presents a whole new set of challenges. In order to live in the present, we have to confront all those things that many of us find uncomfortable or prefer to ignore—human frailty, change, aging, failure, loss, death, loneliness, rejection, and survival in general. But when we confront the uncomfortable head-on, the payoff is enormous. Life takes on a much deeper and richer meaning and we are able to focus on controlling what can be controlled and let go of the rest. So how do you become mindful and experience the full bounty of the present? You train your brain to pause, slow down, and expand your awareness by either learning and practicing one of dozens of meditation techniques available, or by practicing a relaxation exercise like the following.

Link Alert: Enter the URL **https://vimeo.com/mapes/11-relaxation** in your web browser and then the password **"relaxation"** and I will guide you through this relaxation exercise. Or you can simply follow the instructions below.

BASIC RELAXATION EXERCISE

It's best to do this exercise at least once a day, starting in the morning, for five to ten minutes. Practice is the key. If you do so the relaxation process will become the foundation for the tools for forgiveness you will learn about in the next chapter. You should note, however, that some elements of the relaxation exercise may resonate more strongly than others. You will discover which steps work best for you only after you practice. If your mind wanders during the exercise, breathe and bring your attention back, refocus, and then proceed. You will be amazed at how this positively affects your experience as you go through the day—like wearing an invisible shield to ward off being stressed.

1 Make sure you are not disturbed; turn off your cell phone or Blackberry, and sit or lie down in a comfortable position.

2 Close your eyes.

3 Tense your entire body, starting by clenching your hands, then your face, buttocks, stomach, and everything else. Hold to the count of five and then relax.

4 Take three very slow deep breaths to the slow count of four, inhaling through your nose. On the inhale fill up your lungs completely and hold your breath for a beat before exhaling, then exhale through your mouth, again to the count of four.

5 Scan your body for tension from the top of your head to the tip of your toes. Take your time. Be aware of how you feel physically. If you discover tension, breathe into it and let it go.

6 Relax your body point-by-point, beginning with your face, moving to your neck, upper back, chest, stomach, upper arms, lower arms, hands, upper and lower legs, and ending with your feet.

7 Imagine (see and feel) a relaxing, healing, colored light flowing through your body from your head to your toes as you slowly count down from ten to one.

8 Recall the most relaxing and peaceful place you have ever been—in vivid detail. What do you see, smell, and hear? What's the air temperature? Are you alone or with others? Make it real. Vividly see it in your mind's eye.

9 Switch your mental movie—your visualization. Recall an individual or pet who makes you feel loved or whom you love. Vividly picture that person or pet.

10 Holding that emotion, open your eyes and go about your day.

Although the practice of being mindful and living in the present is centuries old, it is perhaps even more important in today's world than it was in the past. The key to doing so is letting go of your inner mind chatter, including worrying, planning, judging, holding grudges, and regretting, among others. It's important to remember, though, that the past is dead and the future unborn. All you have is "now"; and when we learn to let go and live in the moment, your life becomes truly exceptional.

• • •

"The Mind Is Like A Wild Elephant"

The Seeker and Shaman Woman were reviewing the events of the day. "Worrying makes my life hell, Shaman Woman," said the Seeker. "Why can't I control my mind?"

"Your mind is like a wild elephant that you must master," said the Shaman as she handed the Seeker his tea. "When you tether the elephant, it flaps its ears, slaps its tail, and tries to run away."

"That's just what my mind does. It runs wild whenever I try to control it," the Seeker said excitedly. "What should I do when it runs away, Shaman Woman?"

"Don't scold the elephant for running," answered the Shaman. "Simply grab the chain and pull the elephant back. Again and again the elephant will run away and again and again you must pull it back. Eventually, the elephant will be tamed when it learns that you are the master."

"Then will my wild mind obey me?" the Seeker asked.

"Then you will have great power," the Shaman replied, "because once tamed, both elephants and minds will work for you."

—DR. BEVERLY POTTER, *THE WORRYWART'S COMPANION*

This book is about growing at your own pace. So if there is something you can't let go of right now, it's enough for the moment to simply explore the beliefs, judgments, feelings, and fears that surround it. If you are persistent, you will be able to let go when you least expect it. And then, when you are ready, you can proceed to the final chapter where you will discover the ultimate let go—forgiveness. Imagine that!

THINKPOINTS

- Your ego is ultimately the cause of fear and, therefore, of unhappiness.
- Letting go means taming the ego.
- You don't need to compete to win.
- Attachments are the things we think we need to be happy.
- Trying to control those around us is often due to fear and almost always creates separation between others and ourselves.
- We judge others based on our values. Learn to turn judgment into curiosity.

- By blaming others and taking on the role of victim we avoid taking responsibility for our own lives.
- Denial distorts reality, blinds us to destructive life choices, and often leads to self-sabotaging behavior.
- Letting go means learning to live in the present.
- Letting go is always a choice.

12

PRACTICE FORGIVENESS—
THE ULTIMATE "LET GO"

"A wise man will make haste to forgive, because he knows the true value of time, and will not suffer it to pass away in unnecessary pain."
—SAMUEL JOHNSON, THE RAMBLER, NO. 185

In "How to Seek Forgiveness," Deepak Chopra retells a fable told by the great Vedic scholar Eknath Easwaran:

> At the end of a lifetime, a person's soul goes to a plane of existence where each life is reviewed. The soul enters a theater in which a movie of the recent life is playing. The soul begins watching the movie but often has to turn away because of terribly uncomfortable scenes. Sins of omission and sins of commission cramp the heart, and the scene becomes too painful to watch. As a result of not being able to watch the complete movie, important lessons are missed, and the soul must reincarnate to learn them in the next lifetime.

According to this story, the primary cause for not being able to watch the painful scenes of life is a lack of forgiveness—for others and for oneself. Forgiveness is the essence of letting go. It means relinquishing attachments to the past and clearing encumbrances that constrict the heart.

In other words, forgiveness opens up a direct pathway to pure love, and creates harmony. Most important, it is a conscious choice made by the Rider. Here's an example of why learning to let go is so important.

My personal assistant is a very precise woman, which is one of the reasons she is so superior at doing her job. She is organized, neat, and often one step ahead of me in the business of running my life. Linda does, however, have a nemesis, and it's the computer. She just wants it to work, to do the job that it is supposed to do; but she often finds herself at odds with it. I was acutely reminded of this a number of years ago when, early one morning, I received a phone call from her. Linda's voice communicated a frustration so great that I thought for a moment that her stress level had tilted into the danger zone. There was a serious problem with our old office computer. Every time she attempted to download critical information, the machine displayed a warning that the hard drive was full. She was frantic. I suggested she delete some old files that she no longer needed. Her immediate response was, "What if we do need them?" She was afraid to let go of the old stuff. Nevertheless, in a frantic attempt to make space, she deleted some outdated and useless information. But two days later the problem recurred. More deletions, a few new downloads, and the hard drive was full again. After a great deal of anguish, she did what had to be done. She deleted a large portion of the past to make room for the present.

This same concept holds true for your mind. If you live your life day in and day out filled with grievance scripts and thoughts of revenge, there will be little if any space for love and peace. What if, however, there was a program that would help the Rider make space in your mental hard drive by eliminating useless data? And what if, further, it could provide you with an antidote to the mental viruses of worry, guilt, and fear? Well, there's good news—there is such a program. And all that is required is for you to embrace it, learn it, and use it. The program that enables you to let go is forgiveness—the single most powerful tool in the Rider's mental tool kit.

• • •

One spring day some years ago I was taking a walk on the beach with an acquaintance of mine named Jack. As I was giving a great deal of thought to forgiveness at the time, I steered the conversation in that direction. Out of nowhere he said rather defensively, "I won't forgive my brother for the pain he's caused me and my family. He should suffer." I was totally taken aback by his outburst. He went on to explain what a selfish, unfeeling human being his brother had been. He laid out his grievance script in a very logical, convincing manner. The longer he spoke, the angrier he got. I was tempted to ask him how often he had repeated this story but, wisely, I kept silent.

When we moved on to other subjects, he calmed down and became as friendly, even jovial, as he usually was. But when I broached the idea of letting go of his anger, he reverted to his survival self, defending his position. Without realizing it, I had pushed his fear button and he was ready to do battle! As our conversation progressed, it became clear that his Elephant desperately wanted to hold on to its grievances. In spite of being spiritual and believing in the concept of forgiveness, he would not consider forgiving his sibling. By holding on to his anger, he felt that he was punishing his brother. "He doesn't deserve to be let off the hook!" he exclaimed.

This incident raised several good questions in my mind: Why shouldn't we hold on to anger and thoughts of revenge? Doesn't it give us a kind of special satisfaction to imagine getting even with the people who have wronged us or hurt someone we love? Isn't it justified? After all, don't these people deserve to be punished? On reflection, however, I realized that the answer to all these questions is "No." And the reason that's the answer is that harboring these kinds of toxic feelings of revenge has little or no effect on those with whom we are angry. All we're really doing, then, is hurting ourselves.

Let's be logical. How can you ingest poison and expect someone else to die? That is faulty thinking. Learning to forgive is the secret to muting the Elephant's fear and creating harmony. The challenge is that forgiveness sometimes requires a major shift in thinking as well as patience and practice. Consider this possibility: What if forgiveness has to do more with you than it does with anyone else? What if forgiveness actually has nothing to do with others? And, as a matter of fact, it's true. Forgiveness *is* about you.

LIFE THOUGHT: BY FOCUSING ON YOUR PAST HURTS, WOUNDS, AND LOSSES, YOU REINFORCE YOUR FEAR AND PAIN.

Where you focus and what you focus on creates your experience. Old wounds and hurts are exactly like hypnotic suggestions that color your perceptual lens. They originated when something happened that you did not want to happen. Perhaps it was being ignored by your parents or passed over for a promotion, losing a job, or being rejected by a lover. Maybe your best friend or spouse betrayed you, your parents favored your sibling over you, or someone died and you felt abandoned. As you have learned, when you vividly recall a negative event from your past, you reexperience the memory "as if" it was taking place *in the present*! If you have revenge thoughts associated with the past, you will blame yourself or others in the present. Of course your blame seems logical and justified. Focus does equal reality, and the reality is that the resentments we hold on to become toxic to both ourselves and others. Once blame is assigned, we give color, shape, and clarity to our victim and grievance scripts. As both writer and performer, we give these revenge scripts life, rehearsing and refining them until they become absolutely, totally real. When the world of "unforgiving" becomes reality, our rationalizations for refusing to forgive sound very reasonable. The world becomes hostile because we believe it is hostile, and the world becomes unforgiving because we are unforgiving.

What Are Beliefs?

A "belief" is a programmed suggestion. During presentations I often demonstrate this by hypnotizing people and having them say or do something that totally goes against what they consider to be their "real" belief systems. For example, working with a group of volunteers, I might discover one individual who is a staunch Democrat and another who is a diehard Republican. Through deep hypnosis, I suggest that the Democrat is now a Republican and the Republican is now a Democrat. After temporarily "reprograming" or "switching" their beliefs, I set up a debate. The result is truly mind-boggling. Each individual absolutely believes his or her role and debates brilliantly, both passionately supporting beliefs that only a few moments before they would have shunned. Of course, these individuals possess these beliefs only because I temporarily programmed them to do so. And they will retain those beliefs only as long as I am there to reinforce the suggestion or some other reinforcement mechanism is put in place. If I were to physically remove myself from the auditorium, their reinforcement system would be taken away and both subjects would revert to their original and ingrained belief systems.

The same holds true for all our beliefs. Reinforcement is the key to imprinting the suggestion or making a suggestion "stick" in the Elephant. The more any belief is reinforced, the stronger it becomes until it is reality. The less reinforcement, the weaker a new belief becomes until it is muted. It takes patience, consistent practice, and the right tools to make a new, positive belief stick. But it can be done. Developing a new belief and making it stick requires that it be constantly reinforced through the imagination with visualization, self-talk, affirmations, action, and support. Look at the process of developing a belief as a form of self-hypnosis. Through reinforcement, a new belief builds on itself and takes on a life of its own.

Although this is beneficial when the belief is positive and empowering, the sword can cut two ways. When you relive grievance scripts in your imagination or verbally complain about how you have been hurt in the past, you reinforce your belief and reignite the original emotional distress. By the Rider's telling and retelling its story you essentially become your own hypnotist, keeping the Elephant's emotional pain and fear alive and well. By living and reliving grievance scripts the Rider unintentionally triggers the Elephant's survival self, which further gives strength to the ego. When you allow yourself to get trapped into this negative loop of your own making, you don't have the space to notice and be grateful for the gifts you do have.

Everyone has been emotionally hurt. You have. I have. Sometimes we let go. Often, we don't. What is curious is that a small number of people seem to be able to let go of their grievances quickly, like water rolling off a duck's back. Perhaps these individuals have better coping skills than others, or perhaps they have learned how to forgive quickly and consistently. They have most certainly developed the power of being "at choice" in shaping their lives. So clearly you can change a negative belief, but only if your desire for inner peace is greater than your desire to hold on to the negative belief. In order to free yourself of emotional pain, you must choose to let go of the investment you have in holding on to grudges, resentments, guilt, fear, and anger.

In order to see things differently, however, you must first be willing to acknowledge your emotional pain. Once you recognize and accept the long-term value of forgiveness, I am convinced you will choose forgiveness as the ultimate "let go." Why wouldn't you? If you suddenly stumbled on a trunk full of valuable treasures, would you choose to ignore it? Learning to forgive is more valuable than any material treasure you could find because forgiveness can heal. I am not suggesting that you ignore your problems, hurts, losses, and betrayals. They are an integral part of your memory. Neither do I advocate that learning to forgive will stop bad things from happening in your life. Stuff happens. But these negative events do not have to take up permanent residence in the Elephant. What I am suggesting is that you learn how to let go by shifting your thinking, redirecting your focus, and letting your imagination be your friend. That is, let go of the past and make room in your hard drive for the present.

Link Alert: Enter the URL **https://vimeo.com/mapes/12** in your web browser and then the password **"forgiveness"** to see and hear me discussing forgiveness. Or you can simply read the following.

What Is Forgiveness?

"This all sounds good," you may think, "but what is forgiveness really?" That's an excellent question. But how does one characterize something so elusive and subjective that even researchers have trouble defining it? One way to do it may be to first look at the effects of forgiveness and then work our way back to what it actually is.

Medical research has shown that forgiving is good for both the mind and the body. For example, Tom Farrow, a clinical psychologist from the University of Sheffield in England, studied the effects of forgiveness on the brain. Using high-definition MRIs to scan the brain, he and his colleagues found that when a person is forgiving, there is increased activity in the frontal lobe of the brain, the zone also responsible for problem-solving and complex thought—that is, the higher functions of reasoning and thinking. Other studies of forgiveness have found it is good for your heart. One study reported in the *Journal of Behavioral Medicine* associated forgiveness with lower heart rates, lower blood pressure, and stress relief. Another from the University of Tennessee and the University of Wisconsin suggested that patients who were able to forgive had fewer medically diagnosed chronic conditions and fewer physical symptoms from illness. Perhaps most important of all, a 2008 study by Cosgrove and Konstam in the *Journal of Mental Health Counseling*, titled "Forgiveness and Forgetting: Clinical Implications for Mental Health Counselors," states that "the willingness to forgive and be forgiven was identified as one of the ten most important characteristics of long-term healthy relationships."

If forgiveness can be credited with these kinds of results, it is not a huge leap to acknowledge that holding on to grudges is bad for the body, mind, and spirit. Living and reliving your grievances—revenge, anger, and bitterness— affect you physically because it creates negative stress. When you run your grievance script, your heart rate goes up, your blood pressure rises, and you perspire more profusely. Does any of that sound familiar? If it does, it's because the same physiological reaction takes place when you slip into the survival mentality of illusory fear. When you forgive, however, old programmed feelings of anger, resentment, or bitterness are replaced with new chemical reactions in the body. According to Everett Worthington, the chairman of the psychology department at Virginia Commonwealth University, "It's about letting go of the bitterness eating at us. By giving an unwarranted gift to someone who doesn't deserve it, we find paradoxically that it is we, ourselves, who are free from that bondage." In other words, unforgiveness keeps you in the struggle; forgiveness allows you to let go of the rope. Ultimately, though, forgiveness is about creating harmony with the Elephant. It is only when the Rider chooses to forgive that the Elephant can let go of its toxic programming.

· · ·

Ten years after being imprisoned, beaten, and tortured, two monks encounter each other. They sit in silence for some time before one monk asks the other, "Have you forgiven them yet?" The second monk exclaims, "I shall never, ever forgive them!" After a pause the first monk responds, "Well then, I guess you are still imprisoned by your captors."

This simple Tibetan Buddhist story illustrates what happens when the space in your mental hard drive is filled with bitterness, rage, anger, or revenge thoughts. When you forgive you create space for love; you liberate yourself from a prison of your own making. It's important to remember, though, that in order to make sense of the world and keep our equilibrium, sometimes forgiveness must be a gradual process—like decompressing after a deep and lengthy underwater dive. For those who are ready to let go, transformation can happen with lightning speed. For others it takes tremendous patience and practice. You won't know how quickly you can forgive until you do it. When it comes to forgiveness, everyone's challenge is a little different; but the end result is the same.

LIFE THOUGHT: THE KEY TO BECOMING A FORGIVING PERSON IS TO PRACTICE BY FORGIVING SMALLER GRIEVANCES.

What is a small grievance? You don't have to look hard to find one. It could be your child breaking a rule or your partner barking at you for no obvious reason. It might be the person who almost hits your car while talking on a cell phone or someone who pushes ahead of you in a checkout line. Perhaps it is a boss who gets cranky, an employee who says something disrespectful, a friend who forgets your birthday, or someone who neglects to thank you for a favor. The list is endless, but the opportunities to forgive on a daily or even hourly basis are abundant. And that's where you have to start. "Learning to let go of minor offenses can make you better at dealing with more serious transgressions," says Fred Luskin, PhD, cofounder and director of the Stanford University Forgiveness Project, in "The Healing Power of Forgiveness" on redbookmag.com. "Forgiveness is like a muscle: When you practice on smaller things, you gain the skill to deal with bigger ones," Luskin explains. "Learning to practice it today can make you more resilient against future hurts."

When I began studying martial arts, I had to learn the basic combinations and *Katas*, that is, movements designed for defending oneself against several attackers. Through constant practice and repetition, I built a solid foundation that enabled me to integrate the basic karate moves into a complex whole that I could use without conscious thought—automatically and instinctively—in the process building confidence. Like a martial artist who consistently rehearses basic moves in order to grow his skill, practicing forgiving small grievances imprints the skill of forgiveness so it becomes your natural, instinctive response to anger and hurt. It becomes your default setting. By forgiving small grievances, you build confidence in your ability to forgive, and arm yourself with the tools to handle the heavy stuff when it comes your way. You become an Artist of Choice.

The Six Steps to Forgiveness

"Happiness is when what you think, what you say,
and what you do are in harmony."
—MAHATMA GANDHI

This final chapter is about learning one of the most challenging skills—creating harmony between the Elephant and the Rider through forgiveness—and it is fitting for us to end our journey, and for you to begin yours, by having you experience this process. Becoming a forgiving person ultimately requires you to go through the Six Steps to Forgiveness—(1) Acknowledge, (2) Accept, (3) Create Insight, (4) Relax, (5) Visualize, and (6) Let Go. Although these steps are based on my working with thousands of individuals with both minor and major forgiveness issues, it is always a challenge to try to devise a foolproof system for success, especially when it concerns the mind and spirit. That's because your relationships, dreams, challenges, goals, and needs are yours, and they are unlike those of anyone else walking this planet. The Six Steps to Forgiveness do, however, encompass your uniqueness, and become a strategy you will want to have as part of your mental tool kit.

FORGIVENESS STEP ONE: ACKNOWLEDGE

What doesn't get acknowledged doesn't get changed. Many people carry around their grievances, suppressing the truth of what they feel. And when they do, hurts turn to bitterness, and relationships suffer because grievances have not been confronted and healed. It is only by looking inside yourself that you can discover who it is you need to forgive to achieve peace. And the way to do that is by clearly stating to yourself both your grievances and your intention to forgive. However, while doing so may seem like the logical choice, the Elephant resists turning inward, reflecting, and uncovering grievances. As you now understand, it prefers to keep ambling along the same safe, well-worn path. But we do have the analytical abilities, awareness, and consciousness of the Rider to help bring to light and examine anger memories and revenge thoughts, and choose to let them go. It is the Rider who can break the cycle of the self-destructive replaying of grievance scripts by choosing to acknowledge them. Doing so doesn't change the situation, but it opens the door to moving on toward forgiveness and healing.

YOUR TURN

In this exercise you are going to shine a light on the Elephant's hidden grievances. By acknowledging without judging, you can open up the path to forgiveness. You start by writing the following question in your journal or on your computer: *Whom, from my past, do I feel resentment and anger toward in the present?*

After you have written down the question, read it over three times, then sit back, take three deep breaths, and allow yourself five to ten minutes to scan your life. Begin with your earliest memories and work up to the present. I guarantee there will be at least one name that jumps out of all those stored memories. Who is it? Write down the name and specifically what the individual (or individuals) did or said that created the grievance. Remain aware of your emotions.

Now, next to the name and grievance, write the approximate date that this betrayal, slight, or wrong was committed. How old were you? Next to your age, write the length of time that has passed since the grievance was committed. (Don't worry if you can't remember the exact dates or details—they are not as important as acknowledging the grievance itself.) Once you have the name, grievance, approximate date, and how much time has passed since the grievance occurred, you have completed your work for this exercise. You have acknowledged, and set the forgiveness process in motion.

FORGIVENESS STEP TWO: ACCEPTANCE

When I discovered I had an aortic aneurism, I had three choices. First, I could allow my fear to rule me, ignore it, and die. Second, I could rant, rave, whine, and blame the universe for my fate. And third, I could make friends with reality. It was only by accepting my situation that I could focus on creating a positive outcome and do what needed to be done. Only then was I able to reach down inside to summon my courage, seek support, gain insight, let go, and trust. And accepting what I choose to accept in my physical experience is no different from accepting the hurts and resentment we often hold toward others or ourselves.

But exactly what is acceptance? It is most easily defined by saying what it is not. It's not sticking your head in the sand and ignoring the resentments and hurts you feel or the revenge thoughts you hold. It is not giving up, or giving in. Nor it is forgetting, settling, compromising, or resigning yourself to anything. It is about living in the present. It is about what is happening now, the quality of life now, your joy now. Therefore, it means taking whatever is causing you dis-ease, emotional pain, or suffering, and refusing to resist it by accepting it.

It's also important to remember that acceptance is not about sitting and thinking endlessly about something. It is more like choosing to throw a switch or push a button and in the process creating instant change. To be honest, sometimes acceptance is tough going, although sometimes it's smooth as glass. Sometimes it's frightening and sometimes it's glorious. Regardless, however, you can do it if you try hard enough. The following exercise will help you throw your mental switch and clear the path for you to forgive. Before you start, though, it wouldn't be a bad idea for you to close your eyes and take a few deep breaths.

YOUR TURN

1 Identify what you can't change. Worrying or trying to change the unchangeable is pointless and exhausting. The reality is that regardless of how tough or unfair your issue may be, you must choose to let go of the false hope that it will change on its own.

2 Identify what you can change. What is within your control now? Perhaps it is distancing yourself from someone who continues to be negative and drains your energy, forming a new relationship that will support you in your personal growth, or looking at a situation in a different way. For example, if you are dealing with the death of a loved one, you can acknowledge that you cannot do anything to bring the person back, but you can change how you view the situation. Of course, you probably won't be able to change your attitude in a split second, but you can change it over time. Simply realizing that it is possible to change your perspective is the first step in creating change.

3 Focus on what you can gain by forgiving. As challenging as this step may be, there is *always* something to be gained by choosing to forgive, the least of which is letting go of the weight of unforgiveness. If nothing else, being accepting will enable you to become a stronger person.

4 Seek support if necessary. Remember that people, even those closest to you, are not mind readers. Seek out those you trust to lend emotional support or a psychologist versed in forgiveness. Realize that you will hit tough patches in this process, and that it's all right to get help to keep you on the path to forgiveness.

FORGIVENESS STEP THREE: CREATE INSIGHT

The *American Heritage Dictionary* defines insight as "1. The capacity to discern the true nature of a situation; penetration. 2. The act or outcome of grasping the inward or hidden nature of things or of perceiving in an intuitive manner." Insight is the "Ah Ha!" of life. It is through insight that we gain self-knowledge and self-awareness. You have gained insight throughout this book by identifying what is most important to you, what values drive you, and what fears manipulate you—all of which will help you work your way through the forgiveness process.

There are many ways to gain insight. Some people choose to go off and meditate in a cave for years; others go into therapy. You can achieve insight at any given moment, often when it's least expected. Sometimes it is triggered by a conversation, reading a book or article, watching a movie, walking on the beach, or spending time with others who are also on the path of spiritual growth, awareness, and love. There is, however, nothing quite as powerful as asking yourself specific questions to reveal where you stand on your journey toward forgiveness.

THE FORGIVENESS QUIZ

Answering the questions in the following two groups, and reflecting on the answers, will enable you to gain insight into how far you have progressed. Before you start, however, recall the individual—the friend, spouse, family member, or coworker—you identified as having hurt you in Step One. Then, with that person in mind, respond as honestly as you can.

Question Group One

- When I think about this person, do I get upset and feel angry?
- Am I constantly telling my grievance story to others?
- Do I find myself caught in an endless loop, playing and replaying the hurt in my mind?
- Do I intend to get even?
- When I think about him or her, do I feel like a wall has been built between us?
- Do I keep as much distance as possible between this person and me, and live as if he or she had never been born?
- Do I still feel hostility and resentment toward this person?

Question Group Two

- Do I understand and respect his or her point of view?
- Have I forgiven both the little and the big grievances?

- Do I choose the process of forgiveness on a consistent basis with people?
- Have I actively pursued forgiveness by doing a forgiveness visualization, writing a letter, or having a personal conversation?
- When I think about the person who hurt me, do I feel only peace?

If you answered "yes" to most or all of the questions in Group One, it should be clear to you that you need to develop your forgiveness skills further. If, however, you answered "yes" to most or all of the questions in Group Two, you are well on your way to being able to forgive. In either case, if you would like to explore your ability to forgive in greater depth, I suggest you take the forgiveness quiz developed by research pioneer Michael McCullough and his colleagues that can be found online at: http://greatergood.berkeley.edu/quizzes/take_quiz/2.

FORGIVENESS STEP FOUR: RELAX

There are numerous benefits of learning to reduce stress and relax, but perhaps most important is that it gives you an edge in life, centers you, and opens up your ability to be creative. Living from a relaxed and peaceful center enables you to ward off negativity and stress. Doing a daily relaxation exercise helps keep your thinking clear and enhances your ability to visualize. Ultimately, reducing the Rider's stress and endless mind chatter allows you to tap into the Elephant's beliefs, emotions, and intuition. You can achieve this kind of relaxation by using a stress reduction exercise like the one under "Letting Go and Learning to Live in the Moment" in Chapter Eleven, or a simple deep breathing exercise like the one that follows. In any case, it is essential that you go through some kind of relaxation exercise before you go on to the next step.

YOUR TURN

Deep breathing is an excellent way to relax. It helps because when we feel overwhelmed, stressed-out, or fearful, our breathing becomes shallow, cutting off much-needed oxygen to the brain, and the Elephant becomes automatically more inclined toward either fight or flight. If, however, you get more oxygen to your brain by consciously taking a few deep breaths, the Elephant calms down and clarity of thinking returns.

So, after you finish reading this paragraph I want you to close your eyes and become aware of your breathing for about fifteen seconds. Then inhale through your nose deeply and slowly, approximately to the count of four, filling up your diaphragm. Hold that breath for about a second, and then exhale through your mouth deeply and slowly again to the count of four. Repeat this approximately twenty times, resume normal breathing, and open your eyes. After you do this, I guarantee you will feel much calmer. In fact, whenever you feel stressed you can relax yourself by taking two or three slow deep breaths.

FORGIVENESS STEP FIVE: VISUALIZE

Visualization—the art of creating your own mental movies—is at the core of the forgiveness process. When you visualize, you can direct the enormous power of your imagination to create the outcome you desire. Whether you realize it or not, you visualize all the time. However, to achieve specific positive goals and forgive, you must choose to harness and direct your imagination purposefully, that is, to use what is called "Applied Imagination." In this respect, visualization is similar to hypnosis. By relaxing the judgmental, conscious mind, the Rider—that is, the hypnotist—is able to communicate and give suggestions to the Elephant, the subconscious mind. The imagination then grabs hold of the suggestion, accepts it as fact, and creates powerful images. Visualization, then, is like a mild form of self-hypnosis.

This all happens because of the way the imagination works. As you have already seen, when you vividly recall something sad, negative, or fearful from your past, such as losing someone you love, being rejected, or failing to achieve a goal, you feel the pain in the present and trigger the Elephant into fight or flight. At the same time, when you mentally relive an event from your past that was joyful, pleasurable, or exciting, your emotions reflect that, and you feel good. The point is that you do it to yourself!

And the beauty of learning to manage these moments is that when you become aware of disempowering, debilitating, negative visualization you can stop, let go, reframe, and rescript your mental movies to powerful, empowering, motivating, or peaceful images.

Visualization also gives you the opportunity to create something you want to happen. You do that by visualizing your goals "as if" they were already complete, and then "living in the result" by reinforcing those goals with self-talk, affirmations, and support. Of course, visualizing your goals doesn't always mean that you will accomplish them. But it does increase your odds because when you visualize something realistic and possible, you are preparing your mind for success. You are in fact rehearsing success. You set up a positive expectation. Like my wife's ability to find a parking space, visualization prepares your mind to notice clues you might have otherwise missed. Imagine, for example, staring at a photograph of a group of men and women with blond hair, and then going out to take a walk on a crowded street. Where would you most likely focus your attention? What would you notice? Of course, you would notice those individuals with blond hair because that would be your mindset. Now imagine what you might notice or be attracted to if you visualized specific elements that, for you, represent a loving, creative, inspired life.

FORGIVENESS STEP SIX: LET GO

Letting go is the final step and ultimate goal of the forgiveness process. When you forgive, you let go of resentment, guilt, anger, hate, vindictiveness, and fear. Letting go is a process of releasing the grip of attachments, including thoughts of pain and revenge. You can let go of people who have a negative impact on your life. You can let go of material clutter. You can let go of habits that are destructive, and you can let go of your grievances by forgiving yourself and others. Letting go frees the space in your mental hard drive for love.

Although we have examined letting go in many areas, if you want to live an exceptional life it is particularly important that you learn how to let go of anger and resentment. The following exercise is one of the most successful means I know of for accomplishing that goal. It's especially useful not only because you can adjust it to your own ability to relax, visualize, and reframe, but also because you can use it to forgive everyone for both small or large grievances. It will become a favorite tool in your personal tool kit, so I would advise you to practice, practice, and then practice some more.

> **Link Alert:** Enter the URL **https://vimeo.com/mapes/12-forgiveness** in your web browser and then the password "**lettinggo**" to hear me speak about forgiveness. Or you can simply follow the instructions below.

YOUR TURN

1 Do your favorite relaxation exercise.

2 Imagine the individual, living or deceased, whom you need to forgive sitting in a chair opposite you. You are both silently looking into each other's eyes.

3 Surround yourself and the other person with a healing white light.

4 As you observe the person observing you, define your feelings and emotions. Pay attention to your body.

5 Ask yourself, "What have I not said or not been able to express to that person that I would now say if I had the chance?" Don't censor yourself. Say what you need to say now, whether positive or negative. Observe the reaction of the other person.

6 Imagine the person responding to you. What does he or she say? If the person does not verbally respond, does he or she change his or her body language?

7 Regardless of how, or if, the person responds, tell the truth about what you feel. Keep talking until you express whatever needs to be said.

8 Once you have expressed everything you want to say, ask yourself, "Am I now willing to forgive him or her?"

9 When you are able to, say, "I forgive you."

10 Surround the person in a healing white light, and imagine him or her drifting away—becoming smaller and smaller—until he or she disappears.

Because forgiveness is the ultimate let go, it's important that you take your time with this exercise. It's equally important to remember that if, after completing it, you still feel you are holding on to negative feelings, doing it again will lighten your spirits. Also, while this exercise is presented as a means of forgiving others, you can use it to forgive yourself as well. You simply need to imagine sitting in a chair opposite yourself and going through the same process. That is, having the same kind of conversation with yourself, and then, yes, forgiving yourself.

There is another exercise you can do to help you forgive and let go—one that entails writing what I refer to as forgiveness letters—first from you to someone against whom you have grievances, and a second one from that individual responding to your letter. As simple as it may seem, this is a particularly powerful exercise that has helped a multitude of people let go and forgive. It can be used either in combination with the exercise above or on its own.

Link Alert: Enter the URL **https://vimeo.com/mapes/12-letterwriting** in your web browser and then the password "**letter**" and I will guide you through the forgiveness letter writing exercise. Or you can simply follow the instructions below.

YOUR TURN AGAIN

In writing the first of the two forgiveness letters, there are three things you should bear in mind. First, this letter may be written to an individual, either living or deceased, against whom you hold grievances. Second, if the individual is living, you should not deliver your completed letter unless and until you have given it serious consideration. And, third, if you choose not to deliver your letter, you should destroy it within forty-eight hours. That's right. I want you to burn it or rip it up and throw it in the trash. It is the writing of the letter that will accomplish the purpose of this exercise, not delivering it to the individual to whom it's addressed.

1   Begin your letter by listing all the things this person has done that are positive. Look closely. There is a very good possibility that in spite of not wanting to find something good, you will.

2   After you have written down all the positive things the person has done, write down all the ways he or she has harmed you and, importantly, how it has made you feel. Do not blame! Instead of writing, "You were a jerk and ignored me," write something like, "When you ignored me it made me feel invisible and worthless." There is a big difference between blaming, which does not help you let go and heal old wounds, and stating how it made you feel.

3   Once you have finished writing the letter—and it can take you anywhere from fifteen minutes to two hours to write it—imagine forgiving that person.

4   After you have imagined forgiving the person, write a second letter from his or her point of view. If you can suspend your judgment, become an actor, and pretend to walk in that person's shoes, you will be able to better understand why they did what they did, which in turn will help enable you to forgive him or her.

As with the previous exercise, you can also use this one to forgive yourself for some past wrongdoing, in this case by writing a letter to yourself. You should, however, write the letter as if you were a different person—that person being the individual you were when you made the transgression. Remember that, in terms of your emotional growth, you are not the same individual now as you were then, and that your grievance is with that you in the past. Then, in order to forgive yourself, you may need to ask yourself the following questions: "What would I have to believe to forgive myself?" "What stops me from believing that now?" "What is the payoff for not forgiving?" "What do I need to let go of in order to forgive myself?" "Am I willing to change my belief in order to achieve harmony?"

Practicing Forgiveness

When I was young, I didn't know the value of practice. I wanted to be instantly perfect at whatever I was doing. Eventually I discovered—the hard way—that practice and persistence are absolutely necessary to develop a new skill. Sometimes practice is boring and sometimes it is invigorating, but one thing is certain—it always pays off. Like every other skill, forgiveness requires practice. It is through practice that forgiveness and peace will become a way of life. It is through practice that you will become a forgiving person. It is by becoming a forgiving person that you will feel connected to others, and will make a positive difference for your family, your friends, your community, and your world.

The most important thing to remember is that forgiveness is about you. It's not about condoning or tolerating bad behavior, nor is it about forgetting, nor does it require you to keep people in your life who are energy drainers, complainers, or victims. Forgiveness doesn't require you to remain silent and hold back from speaking your truth. It's about letting go and getting rid of toxic thoughts and energy on a moment-to-moment basis, and that happens only with practice, the same kind of practice necessary to develop any new habit.

• • •

There is no end point to emotional and spiritual growth. You don't suddenly get there and then stop. A journey is an ongoing process of discovering and rediscovering. With each discovery you make, you will uncover new and interesting challenges. The game of possibility may be unsettling, scary, exciting, or fun, but it's never boring. There will be times when you will hit a plateau and think you are stuck. Don't worry. This is part of the growth process. This is how we grow—by sudden leaps. We seem to be standing still, but we are actually learning, practicing, processing, and resting, letting life catch up with us until we take another leap. Remember that if you keep playing the game—if you develop your awareness, break through fear, turn judgment into curiosity, let go, and forgive on a continuous basis—you will always be able to take that Quantum Leap. Imagine that!

THINKPOINTS

- Letting go makes space for something new and unexpected to happen.
- Forgiveness is the ultimate let go.
- Forgiveness only has to do with you.
- Learning to forgive is the secret to getting out of emotional pain.
- Focusing on your past hurts, wounds, and losses reinforces your fear and pain.
- Blaming others and holding on to your grievances is toxic to you and to your relationships.
- Forgiveness means making peace your number one priority.
- The key to becoming a forgiving person is to practice forgiveness.

A FINAL NOTE FROM THE AUTHOR

Link Alert: Enter the URL **https://vimeo.com/mapes /conclusion** in your web browser and then the password "**conclusion**" to see and hear my final thoughts.

This book has been many years in the making—more, even, than I'd like to remember—but now both you and I have come to the end. And yet, it isn't actually over. It's really only the beginning of your never-ending journey toward an exceptional life. I'm not going to tell you that it's an easy life to attain—as you've already seen, it takes effort, sometimes serious effort. But think of what you've already learned!

You've learned the traits you need to develop if you want to live an exceptional life. You know that in order to do so, you have to be curious, say "yes" to opportunities, commit to lifelong learning, focus on what you can control, and let go of what you can't. You also have to be a partner in your own wellness, be willing to make short-term sacrifices for long-term payoffs, commit to self-knowledge, take personal responsibility, and then acknowledge grievances, let them go, and forgive. Finally, and most importantly, you have to apply your imagination and influence your subconscious mind.

In addition, following the steps you've learned in this book, you've discovered how your mind works, and how to manage your thinking, shatter limiting myths, and become an Artist of Possibility. You have also learned how to meet your needs, create a stretch goal, set the stage for loving communication, and begin communicating as you never have before. In addition, you've discovered how to transform fear into love, what makes you feel loved, and, most important, how to let go of the rope and forgive. In other words, you have now created a mental tool kit filled with strategies designed to help you apply your imagination to create positive and productive outcomes and attain an exceptional life. My deepest desire is to have you share that life and what you have learned with those around you. You have the power to make living an exceptional life go viral.

RESOURCES

Allman, John M. *Evolving Brains*. New York: W. H. Freeman, 1999.

Baumeister, Roy E., Ellen Bratslavsky, Mark Muraven, and Dianne M. Tice. "Ego Depletion: Is the Active Self a Limited Resource?" *Journal of Personality and Social Psychology*, 74 (1998): 1252–1265.

Begley, Sharon. *Train Your Mind, Change Your Brain*. New York: Ballantine Books, 2007.

Borchard, Therese J. "The Power of Forgiveness." *Psych Central*. May 21, 2010. http://psychcentral.com/blog/archives/2010/05/21/the-power-of-forgiveness.

Bretherton, Inge. "The Origins of Attachment Theory: John Bowlby and Mary Ainsworth." *Developmental Psychology* 28, no. 5 (1992): 759–775. doi: 10.1037/0012-1649.28.5.759.

Buckingham, Marcus, and Donald O. Clifton. *Now, Discover Your Strengths*. New York: Free Press, 2001.

Buscaglia, Leo. *Loving Each Other: The Challenge of Human Relationships*. New York: Ballantine Books, 1986.

Carey, Benedict. "Who's Minding the Mind?" *New York Times*, July 31, 2007.

Chopra, Deepak. "How to Seek Forgiveness." *Care2*, September 1, 2010. www.care2.com/greenliving/how-to-seek- forgiveness.html.

Chopra, Deepak, and David Simon. *Grow Younger, Live Longer*. New York: Harmony, 2001.

Clarey, Christopher. "Their Minds Have Seen the Glory." *New York Times*, February 22, 2014.

Cosgrove, L., and V. Konstam. "Forgiveness and Forgetting: Clinical Implications for Mental Health Counselors." *Journal of Mental Health Counseling* 30, no. 1 (2008): 1–13. doi: 10.17744/mehc .30.1.r1h1250015728274.

Davidmann, Manfred. *The Human Mind and How It Works*. London: Social Organisation Ltd., 2011.

de Bono, Edward. *Lateral Thinking: Creativity Step by Step*. New York: Harper & Row, 1973.

————. *Six Thinking Hats: An Essential Approach to Business Management*. Boston: Little, Brown & Company, 1985.

Domino, Connie. *The Law of Forgiveness: Tap in to the Positive Power of Forgiveness—and Attract Good Things to Your Life*. New York: Penguin, 2009.

"Forgive Their Trespasses." *WebMD*. June 18, 2001. http://www.webmd .com/balance/features/forgive-their-trespasses.

Foster, Glenn, and Mary Marshall. *How Can I Get Through to You? The Tried-And-True Method for Achieving Breakthrough Communication in Personal Relationships*. New York: MJF Books, 2001.

Frankl, Victor. *Man's Search for Meaning*. 2nd ed. New York: Pocket Books, 1997.

Fredrickson, Barbara L. "What Good Are Positive Emotions?" *Review of General Psychology* 2, no. 3 (1998): 300–319.

Glasser, William. *Choice Theory: A New Psychology for Personal Freedom*. New York: Harper Perennial, 1998.

Gregory, Richard, and Patrick Cavanagh. "The Blind Spot." *Scholarpedia*, 6, no. 10: 9618. doi: 10.4249/scholarpedia.9618.

Haidt, Jonathan. *The Happiness Hypothesis: Finding Modern Truth in Ancient Wisdom*. New York: Basic Books, 2006.

Farquhar, Amelia. "Healing Power of Forgiveness." *Redbook*. November 17, 2008. http://www.redbookmag.com/health-wellness/advice/emotional-healing-forgiveness.

Heath, Chip, and Dan Heath. *Switch*. New York: Broadway Books, 2010.

Herrmann, Dorothy. *Helen Keller: A Life*. New York: Alfred A. Knopf, 1998.

Hill, Napoleon. *Think and Grow Rich*. Revised edition. New York: Jeremy P. Tarcher, 2005.

Jampolsky, Gerald, and Diane V. Cirincione. *Love Is the Answer: Creating Positive Relationships*. New York: Bantam Books, 1990.

Jeffers, Susan. *End the Struggle and Dance with Life*. New York: St. Martin's Press, 1996.

Kohn, Alfie. "The Case Against Competition." *Alfie Kohn*. Accessed August 27, 2011. http://www.alfiekohn.org/article/case-competition.

_____. *No Contest*. New York: Houghton Mifflin Company, 1992.

Korb, Alex. "The Grateful Brain: The Neuroscience of Giving Thanks." *Psychology Today*. November 20, 2012. https://www.psychologytoday.com/blog/pefrontal-nudity/201211/the-grateful-brain.

Laut, Phil. *Money Is My Friend*. Second edition. New York: Ballantine Books, 1999.

Levi-Strauss, Claude. *The Raw and the Cooked: Mythologiques, Volume 1*. Chicago: University of Chicago Press, 1983.

Lipton, Bruce H. "Are You Programmed at Birth?" *You Can Heal Your Life*. August 17, 2010. http://www.healyourlife.com/are-you-programmed -at-birth.

Lynch, Gary, and Richard Granger. *Big Brain: The Origins and Future of Human Intelligence*. New York: Palgrave Macmillan Press, 2008.

MacLean, Paul D. *The Triune Brain in Evolution: Role in Paleocerebral Functions*. New York: Springer, 1990.

May, Rollo. *Love and Will*. New York: W. W. Norton, 1969.

_____. *Man's Search for Himself*. New York: W. W. Norton, 1953.

Mayo Clinic Staff. "Positive Thinking: Reduce Negative Self-Talk to Reduce Stress." Rochester, MN: Mayo Clinic, 2014. http://www .mayoclinic.com/health/positive-thinking/SR00009.

McGraw, Phillip C. *Relationship Rescue: A Seven-Step Strategy for Recon- necting with Your Partner*. New York: Hachette Books, 2001.

Mitchell, Stephen, ed. *The Enlightened Heart: An Anthology of Sacred Poetry*. New York: HarperPerennial, 1989.

Muraven, Mark, Dianne M. Tice, and Roy Baumeister. "Self-Control as Limited Resource: Regulatory Depletion Patterns." *Journal of Person- ality and Social Psychology* 74, no. 3 (1998): 774-789. doi: 10.1037/ 0022-3514.74.3.774.

Nazario, Brunilda. "Boost Your Health with a Dose of Gratitude." *Medi- cineNet.com*. Last modified January 31, 2005. http://www.medicinenet .com/script/main/art.asp?articlekey=50414.

"News and Events: Lifestyle Choices Can Change Your Genes." *UW Health*. October 10, 2010. http://www.uwhealth.org/news/lifestyle -choices-can-change-your-genes/13915.

Norem, Julie K. *The Positive Power of Negative Thinking: Using "Defensive Pessimism" to Harness Anxiety and Perform at Your Peak*. New York: Basic Books, 2001.

Null, Gary. *Choosing Joy: Change Your Life for the Better*. New York: Carroll & Graf Publishers, 1998.

"Peak Performance." *Dr. Hallowell*. http://www.drhallowell.com/crazy -busy/peak-performance/.

Plato, *Phaedrus*. Translated by Christopher Rowe. New York: Penguin Classics, 2005.

Potter, Beverly. *The Worrywart's Companion: Twenty-one Ways to Soothe Yourself and Worry Smart*. Oakland: Ronin Publishing, 2014. http:// www.docpotter.com/ww_self-talk.html.

Rakel, David. "Lifestyle Choices Can Change Your Genes." *UW Health Newsroom*. October 10, 2011. http://www.uwhealth.org/news /lifestyle-choices-can-change-your-genes/13915.

Ranganathan, Vinoth K., Vlodek Siemionow, Jing Z. Liu, Vinod Sahgal, and Guang H. Yue. "From Mental Power to Muscle Power— Gaining Strength by Using the Mind." *Neuropsychologia* 42, no. 7 (2004): 944–956.

Read, Hadley. *Communication: Methods for All Media*. Urbana: University of Illinois Press, 1972.

"Reticular Activating System: Your Automatic Goal Seeking Mechanism." *Personal Goals*. http://www.make-your-goals-happen.com/reticular -activating-system.html.

Reynolds, David K. *Handbook for Constructive Living*. New York: William Morrow & Company, 1995.

Rinpoche, Sogyal. *The Tibetan Book of Living and Dying*. Revised Edition. San Francisco: HarperSanFrancisco, 2012.

Robinson, Ken, and Lou Aronica. *Creative Schools*. New York: Viking/Penguin, 2015. Available at: http://ww2.kqed.org/mindshift/2015/04/22 /sir-ken-robinson-creativity-is-in-everything-especially-teaching.

Samuelson, Paul A. and William D. Nordhaus. *Economics: An Introductory Analysis.* New York: McGraw-Hill, 1985.

Scott, Elizabeth. "The Benefits of Forgiveness." *About Health.* Last modified June 30, 2015, accessed October 29, 2011. http://stress.about.com /od/relationships/a/forgiveness.htm.

Schucman, Helen A. *Course in Miracles.* Roscoe, NY: Foundation for Inner Peace, 2007.

Simon, Stephen. *The Force Is with You.* Charlottesville, VA: Hampton Roads Publishing, Inc., 2002.

Strong, Michael. *Be the Solution: How Entrepreneurs and Conscious Capitalists Can Solve All the World's Problems.* New York: John Wiley & Sons, 2009.

Tice, Lou. *Personal Coaching for Results.* Nashville, TN: Thomas Nelson Publishers, 1997.

Tracy, Brian. *Goals! How to Get Everything You Want—Faster Than You Ever Thought Possible.* Second Edition. San Francisco: Berrett-Koehler Publishers, 2010.

Waldroop, James, and Timothy Butler. *Maximum Success: Changing the 12 Behavior Patterns that Keep You from Getting Ahead.* New York: Currency Books, 2000.

Williamson, Marianne. *A Return to Love: Reflections on the Principles of "A Course in Miracles."* New York: HarperOne, 1996.

Zhuangzi. *Nan-Hua-Ch'en-Ching, or The Treatise of the Transcendent Master from Nan-Hua.* Somerset, England: Llanerch Press, 1995.

ENDNOTES

Introduction

1 James Thurber, *Further Fables for Our Time: The Shore and the Sea* (London: Hamish Hamilton Ltd, 1956).

2 Ken Robinson and Lou Aronica, *Creative Schools: The Grassroots Revolution That's Transforming Education* (New York: Viking (division of Penguin Random House), 2015).

3 Gianni Sarcone, "Circus in the Clown," Based on Illustration of Larry Kettelkamp. giannisarcone.com.

Chapter 1

1 Benedict Carey, "Who's Minding the Mind?," *The New York Times*, July 31, 2007, http://www.nytimes.com/2007/07/31/health/psychology/31subl.html?_r=0.

2 Gary Lynch, *Big Brain: The Origins and Future of Human Intelligence* (New York: St. Martin's Press, 2008).

3 John Haidt, *The Happiness Hypothesis: Finding Modern Truth in Ancient Wisdom* (New York: Basic Books, 2006).

4 Ibid.

5 Sharon Begley, *Train Your Mind, Change Your Brain* (New York: Ballantine Books (Imprint of The Random House Publishing group), 2007).

6 John Haidt, *The Happiness Hypothesis: Finding Modern Truth in Ancient Wisdom* (New York: Basic Books, 2006).

Chapter 2

1 VK Ranganathan, V Siemionow, JZ Liu, V Sahgal, GH Yue, "From Mental Power to Muscle Power—Gaining Strength by Using the Mind," *Neuropsychologia* 42, no. 7 (2004): 944-56.

2 Christopher Clarey, "Olympians Use Imagery as Mental Training," *The New York Times*, February 22, 2014, http://www.nytimes.com/2014/02/23/sports/olympics/olympians-use-imagery-as-mental-training.html?_r=0.

3 Mayo Clinic, "Positive Thinking: Stop Negative Self-Talk to Reduce Stress," last modified March 4, 2014, http://www.mayoclinic.org/healthy-lifestyle/stress-management/in-depth/positive-thinking/art-20043950.

4 Maddy Malhotra, *How to Build Self-Esteem and Be Confident: Overcome Fears, Break Habits, Be Successful and Happy* (United Kingdom: For Betterment Publications, 2013).

5 William Glasser, *Choice Theory* (New York: HarperCollins Publishers, 1998).

Chapter 3

1 Claude Lévi-Strauss, *The Raw and the Cooked: Mythologiques, Volume 1* (Chicago: The University of Chicago Press, 1983).

2 Julie Norem, *The Positive Power of Negative Thinking: Using Defensive Pessimism to Harness Anxiety and Perform at Your Peak* (Cambridge: Basic Books, 2002).

3 Rollo May, *Love & Will* (New York: W. W. Norton & Company, Inc., 1969).

4 Sogya Rinpoche, *Tibetan Book of Living and Dying* (New York: HarperCollins, 2002).

5 David Reynolds, *A Handbook for Constructive Living* (New York: University of Hawai'i Press, 2002).

6 Rollo May, *Man's Search for Himself* (New York: W. W. Norton & Company, Inc., 1953).

7 Gary Null, *Choosing Joy: Change your Life for the Better* (New York: Carroll & Graff, 1998).

Chapter 4

1 Alan Alda, "62nd Commencement Address" (Commencement Speech, Connecticut College, New London, CT, June 1, 1980) http://www.graduationwisdom.com/speeches/0020-alda1.htm.

2 Lou Tice, *Personal Coaching for Results* (Seattle: Pacific Institute Publishing, 1997).

3 David Rakel, "Lifestyle Choices Can Change Your Genes," University of Wisconsin School of Medicine and Public Health, last modified October 10, 2011, http://www.uwhealth.org/news/lifestyle-choices-can-change-your-genes/13915.

4 Ibid.

5 Ibid.

6 Viktor Frankl, *Man's Search for Meaning* (New York: Washington Square Press: 1985).

7 Stephen King, *Under the Dome* (New York: Pocket Books, 2009).

8 Stephen Simon, *The Force Is with You: Mystical Movie Messages That Inspire Our Lives* (Charlottesville: Hampton Roads Publishing Company, Inc., 2002).

9 Stephen Mitchell, ed., *The Enlightened Heart: An Anthology of Sacred Poetry* (New York: Harper and Row, Publishers, 1989).

Chapter 7

1 Norwood Russell Hanson, *Patterns of Discovery: An Inquiry into the Conceptual Foundations of Science* (Cambridge: Cambridge University Press, 1958).

Chapter 8

1 James Waldroop and Timothy Butler, *Maximum Success: Changing the 12 Behavior Patterns That Keep You from Getting Ahead* (New York: Doubleday Business, 2000).

2 Alex Korb, "The Grateful Brain: The Neuroscience of Giving Thanks," *Prefrontal Nudity* (blog), Psychology Today, November 20, 2012, https://www.psychologytoday.com/blog/prefrontal-nudity/201211/the-grateful-brain.

Chapter 10

1 Bruce Lipton, "Are You Programmed at Birth?," You Can Heal Your Life, last modified August 17, 2010, http://www.healyourlife.com/are-you-programmed-at-birth.

2 Leo Buscaglia, *Loving Each Other* (New York: The Random House Publishing Group, 1984).

3 Hadley Read, *Communication: Methods for All Media* (Champaign: University of Illinois Press, 1972).

Chapter 11

1 Tom Wilson, *Ziggy*, 2000. Universal Uclick.

INDEX

survival instinct
    developing personal strategies for,
      25–30, 32
    ego as driver of, 72–73
    Elephant's mechanisms for, 59
    fear and, 87, 199, 234
    fight-or-flight, 15, 118, 203, 276
    going into, 119
    judging as part of, 249
    mechanisms for, 21, 23, 24
    unconscious programming for,
      109–110
survival self, 30–31
Switch (Heath and Heath), 19

T

teaching others how to treat you, 193
technical communication, 160–161,
  169–170
temper, losing your, 87
thanking others, 186–187, 194
"thank you" list exercise, 192–193
thinking
    abundance, 209
    effects of self-talk on, 42–44
    faulty, 48, 183
    fear-based, 59, 65–66
    identifying your thoughts, 247
    listening to your thoughts, 92
    love-based, 202
    managing your (*See* reframing your
      thinking)
    negative (*See* negativity)
    positive, 44, 63–68, 155–156
    seeing what you think, 117, 122
thinking (Blue Hat), 147
Thinking Hats system, 146–149
thirty-day gratefulness exercise, 192
threats, perceived, 48–50. *See also*
  survival instinct
three brains, 32
    mammalian brain (Brain Two),
      23–24
    neocortex (Brain Three), 24–25, 190

reptilian brain (Brain One), 23
Tibetan Buddhist story (forgiveness),
  267–268
Tice, Lou, 96
timing of communication, 229
Tool for Truth, 88–89, 91–92, 210–211
toolkit for the mind, 283, 284
    coping tools, 59
    coping tools/skills, 59, 253, 266
    developing awareness, 50
    foundation of, 15
    imagination as tool, 70
    meditation, 85–86
    Tool for Truth, 88–89, 91–92
touch/touching. *See* kinesthetic (touch/
  touching) input
toxic programming, 268
Tracy, Brian, 152
trances, 104. *See also* hypnosis
transforming fear into love. *See* fear; love
treatment by/of others, 172–173
Trickster
    about the, 62, 72
    awareness of the, 215–216
    ego as, 72, 233–234
    fear of failure, 203–204
    influence of the, 119, 203
    silencing the, 210
triggers, emotional, 118, 199, 203,
  221–228. *See also* Love Triggers
truth(s), 76, 88–89, 91–92, 173
two minds concept, 15–16, 18

U

uncertainty, effect on conscious mind
  of, 20
unconscious body functions, 23–24
unconscious mind. *See* subconscious
  mind
unconscious recognition system, 218
unknown, fear of, 202
unloving state, 81
Urban Dictionary, 72

ABOUT THE AUTHOR

The founder of Quantum Leap Thinking™, creator of The Transformational Coach™, and an expert on the psychology of "applied imagination," James Mapes is a highly acclaimed business speaker and personal excellence coach. For more than thirty years, he has dedicated himself to helping individuals, teams, and organizations break through barriers to reach their goals and achieve success. His clients include Fortune 500 companies and major nonprofit organizations in the areas of finance, technology, healthcare, academia, and the military, including IBM, U.S. Coast Guard, Lockheed Martin, and the Princeton Center for Leadership Training.

Mapes' success as a speaker and highly regarded authority on the imagination, creative thinking, managing change, and leadership is due in part to his early training as an actor and his experience as a theatrical producer. Working in repertory theater, off-Broadway, television, and movies, he developed a unique stage presence with a special talent for connecting with his audience. He also staged his own one-man show, *Journey into the Imagination*, on Broadway, as well as at performing arts centers and universities, and presented *A Whirlwind Tour of the Mind* at Lincoln Center in New York City. His work in creativity and clinical hypnosis has earned him appearances on CNN, *The Today Show*, *Good Morning America*, and the Fox Family Channel, among other media outlets.

Mapes is the author of *Quantum Leap Thinking: An Owner's Guide to the Mind* (2003), which has been translated into seven languages, and *The Workbook: The Magic of Quantum Leap Thinking* (2000). He also created a DVD, *Breakthrough Thinking: Practical Insights for Influencing Your Mind and Your Results*; an ongoing series of CDs, "Toolkit for the Mind™"; a two-CD set, "Patient Pre-Op/Post-Op Healing Therapy ™"; and an on-line coaching program, "Mental Hacks to Achieve Your Goal." In addition, he writes a syndicated column, "Strategies for Living an Exceptional Life."

When not touring, Mapes and his wife divide their time between residences in Westport, Connecticut, and St. Thomas in the U.S. Virgin Islands.

For booking information, please contact James at james@jamesmapes .com or visit www.jamesmapes.com.